Veiled and Silenced

Veiled

How

and Silenced Culture Shaped Sexist Theology

Alvin John Schmidt

ISBN 0-86554-327-5

Library of Congress Cataloging-in-Publication Data
Schmidt, Alvin J.
   Veiled and silenced : how culture shaped sexist theology / Alvin John
Schmidt
      238 pages   15 x 23 cm.   6 x 9"
Includes index
   ISBN 0-86554-329-1 (alk. paper).—ISBN 0-86554-327-5 (pbk. : alk.
paper)
   1. Woman (Christian theology)—History of doctrines.   2. Women in
Christianity—History.   3. Sexism—Religious aspects—Christianity—
History of doctrines.   I. Title.
BT704.S36881989   89-30453
261.8'344—dc20   CIP

CONTENTS

FOREWORD

Relentless. Yes, that is the adjective one needs. The argument of this book is relentless, as the author pursues evidence—as if anyone needed it—that the Christian Church through the ages has worked to "veil" women. Veiling means that males in the church have, at worst, endeavored to demean, limit, inhibit, and degrade them, and, at best, failed to help them realize their potential.

My phrase "as if anyone needed it" may throw some people off. If no one needs it, then why this book? I made that comment because it is easy to picture a radical feminist, Christian or not, picking up these chapters and saying, "So what else is new?" or "We've been saying that all along," or "Why belabor the obvious?" In some respects, what they would say is true. They may find some of this material to be a late entry into the debate.

It happens, however, that the kind of advocate who sees no need for this layering of evidence is likely to have reached the limits of influence in many parts of the churches and the culture. Advocates continue in their mission, but the various camps are polarized. Sign up with the Gloria Steinems or the Rosemary Ruethers, in world and church, and you go the radical route—and who wants that? Sign up with the George Gilders and the Beverly LaHayes or Phyllis Schlaflys in the same world and churches, and you thicken the veil over women—and who needs that?

It is on that littered field that Alvin Schmidt's discourse finds its place. His pursuit of documentation has been relentlessly thorough, and he holds little of it back. This work can become as much a reference book or an anthology as it is an argument. He combines the rigor of the sociologist, the patience of the historian, the passion of someone engaged with his culture, and the concern of a church person as he finds and sets forth the evidence for his case.

If that case looks obvious, stating it is not beside the point. When I questioned whether anyone needed a book like this, I slighted the vast majority of Christians who are caught between the Steinems and the Gilders, the Ruethers and the Schlaflys. It is not as if the only thing to say is "a plague on both your houses"; more important is the thought, "They did not convince me, but I am open to the evidence." If that thought is spoken by anyone in the majority, this book will serve its purpose.

If the argument I read against a more fulfilling and responsible role for women in the church (and also beyond it) is representative, then clearly most of the arguers have not yet caught the Schmidt message. They do find it hard to see how much of the Christian witness has been compromised by norms of culture that have little to do with focal and central Christian witness—to Jesus, most of all. Here his case is devastating, and to picture someone reading it and not assenting is to believe that there can be intellectual hardness of heart.

Is Schmidt, then, an enemy of the tradition? As a sociologist, he is allowed to be that; much modern social science has been of a debunking sort. As a free citizen, he has a right to be what he wants to be. But as one reads on, it is clear that the author is involved in a constructive process. To that great moderate, evangelical, conservative, and traditional—as opposed to fundamentalist or modernist—membership of the church, he is stripping veils away in order that something can take their place. That something is someone: the Christian woman, as Jesus saw her. Such a woman is free, fulfilling, rich in promise for roles long denied her.

As I read the book, coming from the same communion as the author, I suddenly picked up a clue to its structure. He may not even have been aware of it, so internalized do the norms of this communion become to those who have heard good sermons or read well. By this I mean that laypeople and clergy like Schmidt and myself are trained to speak and hear both "Law" and "Gospel." The Law refers to the accusing, devastating, annihilating word of God that reaches the ignorant and errant, stabbing them and, yes, "killing" them.

Then comes Gospel, good news, the re-creative activity of God, which out of the dead remains of the old makes something new: the new person in Christ. To come to Gospel without preaching the Law is to offer cheap grace, to remove all motive for repentance, renewal, and change. To leave people with Law is to cheat them out of the promises of God.

Alvin Schmidt is not preaching a sermon here, but making a case to the Christians and, indirectly, to the culture shaped by the Christian tradition. Chapter after chapter devastates; the accumulation of evidence leaves little escape. Then one comes to the figure of Jesus (and, to a lesser and more con-

troversial extent, Paul) and finds them unveiling a new aeon, new ways of
being, new persons, new women, new men who can understand and cope with,
who can enjoy and work with, women as Jesus Christ wanted.

Hardness of heart there is, and it may be that entrenched readers will
fail to follow the logic of the Gospel as Schmidt sees it in the record. And
even where there is not hardness of heart, sharpness of eye and mind will
give critics license to counterattack, to find flaws. So there are legitimate
reasons for moderate liberals to find Schmidt too conservative, for example in his reference to "the apostle John" as the author of all the Jo-
hannine literature, or to Paul as the author of some controverted letters.
And moderate conservatives may think that he goes too easy on Paul, that
there are harder sayings in the writings of the apostle than Schmidt grants.

A rereading of the book, however, convinces me that for all the possibil-
ities of finding something to fault—a nuance here, a detail there, a turn of
phrase here and there—the cumulative evidence is convincing. Is he too harsh?
Historians teach students to judge people of the past in terms of the possibil-
ities then open to them. Don't expect Augustine to sound like a free person
in an urban and technological society—a society that many of us think veils
women in new ways, more than Schmidt has time to enumerate while making
his case. See Augustine for what he was, when and where he was.

Well and good. And, of course, one cannot repent for the sins of great-
grandparents. But one can open the record, see what went wrong and why,
and set out with new resolve to correct things in one's own generation.

"As if anyone needed it." The Christian minority that has begun to
enjoy unveiling came to it only in the past decades. If Schmidt had dropped
this book in mainstream Protestant or even liberal Catholic circles three
decades ago, he would have found that its time had not come as yet. Offer
this book to the majority of the Christian world—Roman Catholic and Orthodox, many kinds of Anglican and Lutheran, evangelical and fundamentalist (though not always Pentecostal)—and it will become clear that
its argument is still not entirely accepted.

That vision of the odds may seem daunting to many. It must not have
dispirited Schmidt, who passes this work on, as I now do by joining him
in this foreword, with some faith in the power of the record to inform, convince, and perhaps open the way for changes of mind and attitude.

Martin E. Marty
The University of Chicago

PREFACE

When one is finished writing a book, there are a few things one wants to say to the readers at the very beginning. With regard to this book, I wish to note that fifteen years ago I would never have dreamed that I—who then was ignorant of the magnitude of sexism—would write a book revealing the prejudicial views and practices that existed for centuries with regard to women in church and society. My interest in how religious leaders and religious organizations defined the role of women in church and society began in 1973, when I was appointed to a mainline denomination's task force for women. Serving on this group for four years resulted in extensive and intensive reading and studying about the role of woman in ancient, medieval, and modern societies. I first believed that the traditional, especially the religious, views of subordinating women would be easily defended from the biblical perspective. To my surprise, the evidence overwhelmingly showed that it was the forces of an agrarian-patriarchal culture—really a pagan culture—that often had shaped the theological opinions regarding women.

Most authors undoubtedly write books so that good things might result from people's reading them. One good result intended by this book is that women will someday be able to realize genuine freedom and equality, especially in churches that still cling to sexist formulations and practices. If this book will help some theologians and clergy recognize the power and hiddenness of culture, which for centuries has largely shaped theological views (frequently seen as biblical or God-pleasing) concerning women, it will have produced a good result.

Although the book does not discuss female equality with regard to family life, advocating the removal of sexism does not mean that wives must forsake family duties and obligations. Rather, men need to become equal participants with women in the daily affairs of family living, no longer expecting that child rearing and domestic chores are to be borne by women alone, as they once were in agrarian cultures. Men and women need to recognize that the urban-technological culture (discussed in chap. 12), which has slowly given women more freedom and equality, requires creative and wholesome changes—not negative reactions—in order to achieve greater family stability. If this book were to make some small contribution toward that end, it will have served still another good purpose.

I wish to thank a number of libraries for their help as I did the research for this book. The Allen County Library, Fort Wayne, Indiana, which has an unusually good and varied selection of holdings, provided many worthwhile sources relative to how culture defined women in different societies. Also very helpful were the libraries of Northwestern University, Evanston, Illinois, and the University of Chicago. The fine holdings of these libraries greatly facilitated my research. In working with ancient sources, one is indebted to many dedicated scholars and translators, living and deceased, too numerous to mention here. Their contributions, I am sure, have influenced many of my expressions and insights.

The Bible text on pages 120-21 is from the Revised Standard Version Bible, copyright 1946, 1952, 1971 by the Division of Christian Education of the National Council of the Churches of Christ in the USA, and is used by permission.

I am also indebted to Martin E. Marty for taking time to read the manuscript and for writing the book's foreword. I am grateful, too, for the time and effort of David Moberg, Catherine Clark Kroeger, Gretchen Gaebelein Hull, David Clowney, and Daniel Bruch in reading and commenting on the manuscript. Last, but not least, I want to thank my wife, Carol, and my sons, Tim and Mark—for their patience while I wrote this book.

INTRODUCTION

Most men have at one time or another heard, and perhaps even believed, that women are "inferior" and "unequal" to men. But the fact that women have also been portrayed as "evil" and "unclean" apparently is not so well known to men, at least not today. Yet, the latter two perceptions of women are as widespread in the literature, especially in the writings of the past, as are the former two perceptions. These sexist beliefs about women, my research discovered, were integrally tied to ancient patriarchal values and practices that had their origin in agrarian culture(s). Women often were considered to be no better or wiser than slaves or children. Moreover, these negative perceptions of women were also common in theological writings. Why?

The answer to this question appears to be that men, in religion and politics, throughout most of Judeo-Christian history, unknowingly reflected the values of their culture—specifically, an agrarian-patriarchal culture—that since ancient times portrayed women in a negative light. Given this observation, I contend that culture shaped the many sexist beliefs and practices in the church. The awareness of culture and its accompanying effects, however, have not been (and still are not) readily recognized; and when they are, they are not remembered for very long. Thus the first chapter focuses on how culture is, to the majority of us, most of the time, a hidden dimension.

The second chapter tries to show how culture—unbeknownst to the theologians—shaped the church's theology relative to war, usury, slavery, and beliefs regarding birth control. The following chapter demonstrates how culture also shaped the definitions and treatment of women as "evil." This chapter, among other accents, tells how woman for centuries was seen as having brought evil into the world, and how she was defined and treated as a witch.

The fourth chapter discusses how the agrarian culture, which defined woman as "inferior," also influenced theologians to adopt this view. Here one prominent example was her supposed intellectual inferiority. The fifth chapter focuses on how woman had been defined as "unclean," given the long-standing superstitions regarding menstruation and childbirth. In the sixth chapter I illustrate how cultural definitions of woman being "unequal" influenced theologians to see her in that negative light, whether it was accepting the double standard of adultery laws or seeing her as property of the man.

Other writers have in the past sometimes cited a reference or two relative to how woman had been pictured as "evil," "inferior," "unclean," and "unequal," but I know of no publication that has dealt with any of these negative definitions in an extensive manner. Moreover, I know of none that has tried to show that these cultural definitions, which often were widespread and institutionalized, influenced theological formulations. Thus I devote a separate chapter to each of these sexist definitions.

Chapter 7 gives insight into the practice of veiling woman, a practice that was thought to mitigate the effects of woman's "evil" and "unclean" nature. The eighth chapter focuses on how culture shaped the theology that silenced women. Both these chapters, in conformity with the book's title, stress that in ancient times woman only became veiled and silent after she was *veiled* and *silenced*. In short, she did not choose these confining roles. Rather, they were forced upon her by men who had internalized the patriarchal values of an agrarian cultural milieu.

Chapter 9 shows how Jesus broke with the agrarian-patriarchal view of woman. His interactions with women frequently violated established cultural and theological beliefs and practices. The tenth chapter delineates how the church of the apostolic period followed Jesus by giving women equality. The efforts of Jesus and the apostles, however, were not heeded for very long. Thus chapter 11 discusses why and how the church and its leaders reverted to the sexist definitions of the agrarian-patriarchal culture. Finally, in the twelfth chapter, I attempt to show how modern culture with its urban-technological bases has become woman's ally, enabling her slowly to attain the rights and privileges she had been denied for centuries.

In writing this book, I took great care to have the quotations truly reflect their original contexts. Some of these citations, those from the church fathers, for example, may surprise many uninformed Christians, especially those who have had a high regard for the church's early leaders. Many of the church fathers' strong, often negative words are cited not to shock but to help the readers understand how powerful the forces of culture really were in shaping sexist opinions and statements. That such negative words were uttered by church men does not make them less sexist or less degrading to women than similar words spoken by the pagan philosophers or poets of Greece or Rome, who, by preceding the church fathers, often directly or indirectly influenced their theology.

Citations from the Talmudic literature, from the Greco-Roman poets and philosophers, as well as those from the church fathers, are documented by noting the respective work(s) immediately following the quotation rather than creating the usual footnote reference. The other, more recent references are noted at the end of each chapter. The reader may find the cited work(s) of the ancient Greek and Roman writers by referring to the appropriate work in the multivolume set known as the *Loeb Classical Library,* published by Harvard University Press. Many of the quotations from the church fathers are cited from the English translations of the *Ante-Nicene Fathers,* edited by Alexander Roberts and James Donaldson, and from the *Nicene and Post-Nicene Fathers,* edited by Philip Schaff. A few references are from *The Fathers of the Church,* published by the University of America Press. Some of the church fathers' citations are also taken from Migne's multivolume sets, *Patria Graeco-Latina* and *Patrologia Latina.* Where given translations from the latter works were available, I often used them with only slight changes in some instances. Leonard Swidler's *Biblical Affirmations of Woman* (1979) was also helpful. Some other ancient quotations in English are my translations.

This book has two basic objectives. One, being very appreciative of the liberty I have as an American, I wrote this book with the hope of contributing to the growing liberty and equality of women, especially in the church, which so long has defended ancient sexist practices rather than emulate Christ, who found no pleasure in seeing woman veiled and silenced. Two, it was my goal as a professional sociologist to help theologians and clergy become more aware of the presence and power of culture and how it, for centuries, shaped and molded sexist opinions and practices in the church and society. I hope that a greater awareness concerning the role of culture in theological formulations—whether with regard to women or some other concern—will make theologians and clergy in the future less likely to surprise God when they so quickly and often say: "Thus says the

Lord." Often it was culture, as in the case of woman's role, and not God, that shaped the theology.

The book's frequent reference to agrarian culture, along with its accompanying values and practices, is used in a relatively broad sense, including what anthropologists commonly call herding and horticultural societies. Basically, I use the term *agrarian* with reference to a cultural milieu that dominated most societies prior to the mid-1800s, when urban-technological culture was largely nonexistent.

When one discusses phenomena in terms of a dichotomy, as this book does in terms of agrarian-patriarchal versus urban-technological culture, many facts and details, which sometimes are exceptions to one's hypothesis, had to be overlooked. Thus in writing this book, I was very much aware that certain exceptions and anomalies (often minor ones) had to be omitted, although chapters 9 and 10 are devoted primarily to the exceptional acts of liberation and involvement that Jesus and the apostolic church accorded women. Moreover, the few exceptions, where women had more freedom and equality than they commonly had, did not become institutionalized and thus they never became a part of any society's cultural fabric. It is not that exceptions are unimportant, but rather that exceptions primarily support, not nullify, the book's basic hypothesis, namely: agrarian-patriarchal culture shaped sexist theology.

The book's final chapter argues that whereas the old or agrarian culture hampered woman's humanity, freedom, and equality, the new culture, which is referred to as urban-technological, has become her friend and ally. This is not to say that the urban-technological culture is improving the social conditions of woman in an uninterrupted, unilinear process and thereby ushering in a female utopia. To be sure, technology has in some instances been detrimental to woman's pursuit of freedom and equality, as Corlann Gee Bush, for instance, has shown.[1] Nor do I wish to overlook the many problems that have been spawned by technology, such as the various pollution problems that confront many societies today. Yet, on the whole, when technology is linked to urban life, the potential and probabilities for freedom increase. As a German expression says, *"Die Stadtluft macht frei"* (the city liberates). Thus, one is compelled to ask: when have women in

---

[1]Corlann Gee Bush, "Women and the Assessment of Technology: To Think, to Unthink, to Free," in Joan Rothschild, ed., *Machina Ex Dea: Feminist Perspectives on Technology* (New York: Pergamon Press, 1983) 151-70.

so many societies ever had the opportunities for freedom and equality—
and in many instances even realized some of them—that they now have in
the urban-technological context?

Although the book cites numerous historical incidents, it primarily accents a sociological perspective. Historical examples are used to support a
sociological hypothesis. Finally, the reader needs to know what I mean by
sexism. My definition of sexism has been influenced by the way many social scientists in recent years have defined racism. That definition says that
racism is an attitude, belief, or practice that subordinates an individual or
group on the basis of race. Thus I define sexism as an attitude, belief, or
practice that subordinates an individual or group on the basis of sex.

CHAPTER 1

CULTURE:
THE HIDDEN DIMENSION

If fish could think, the last thing they would likely discover is water. Moving from fish to people, who can think but frequently do not, the last thing they discover is culture. Fish are immersed in water. People are immersed in culture. Yet neither is conscious of how their environment influences and affects them. Culture is to most people a hidden dimension.

Given the hypothesis of the present book, which says sexist theology (in and outside the institutional church) has been shaped by culture, the reader will want to know what I mean by culture. The phenomenon of culture is as old as humankind, but the existence of the concept of culture is relatively recent in human history. It was Edward Burnett Tylor, an early anthropologist, who first defined the concept in his groundbreaking work of 1871, *Primitive Culture*. The role and function of what social scientists today call "culture" was essentially unknown to the philosophers, poets, historians, and theologians.

Lacking the concept of culture, the ancients were unable to perceive or understand the effects of the phenomena to which the concept of culture refers. It could hardly be otherwise. When people lack the appropriate concept to point to a given referent, they are usually unable to perceive the existence of that referent, much less notice its effects. Thus the ancients were unaware that it was culture, for example, that shaped their religious or theological views of women. Similarly, many individuals who know about the concept of culture do not believe that culture has shaped centuries of sexist theology that is imbedded in their minds and in the social fabric of their society (for example, in religious and educational institutions).

Culture Defined

The Greek thinkers during the so-called Golden Age of Greece were loquacious about the nature of human life, but they had no word for culture. When Herodotus (fifth century B.C.) described the customs, manners, and mores of some non-Greek societies, he sometimes used the Greek word *nomos* (law), a concept that many Greek thinkers linked to what has been called "natural law" in Western thought. In ancient Greek thought the law (*nomos*) was derived from God through nature. This thinking, with only minor variations, was pervasive in Western societies for centuries. In some quarters this type of thinking still prevails.

Although Aristotle distinguished between *physis* (natural laws) and *nomos* (conventional laws) in his *Nicomachean Ethics*—thereby giving the impression that the former was derived from nature and the latter devised by humans—in his *Politics* he pictured *nomos* as that which expressed the divine will. Here Aristotle sounds like Plato in his *Menexenus*. Thus, although Herodotus and Aristotle sometimes used *nomos* to refer to varying laws and customs of different societies—which we today would see as part of culture—there is no convincing or consistent evidence suggesting that they, or others, really saw these phenomena as the products of mere human development. The ancient belief in natural law was too dominant for this to happen. Moreover, one can—as Herodotus did—speak of manners and customs being different from one society to the next without really seeing such practices as the products of human creativity.

The ancient and medieval understanding of laws, customs, and mores as a reflection of natural law logically left no room for seeing human societies develop different systems of values, beliefs, and practices, at least not "correct" systems. Given that there was only one world of nature, there could be only one set of laws and mores. If a society had different laws and customs, it was seen as deviant and given ethnocentric labels. Thus the Greeks called the non-Greeks "barbarians." The Hebrews called other societies "uncircumcised" or "unclean."

Prior to Tylor's defining culture as "that complex whole which includes knowledge, belief, art, morals, law, custom, and any other capabilities and habits acquired by man as a member of society," the word first meant social refinement. This meaning was derived from the Latin word *colere,* meaning to cultivate. Even Francis Bacon, who some have said was the first to adopt the word from its Latin base, in his *Advancement of*

Learning (1605, book 2) used the term *culture* in the sense of advanced or refined learning. It is the Baconian understanding that is still commonly expressed by individuals who, for instance, see someone's love for the fine arts as "cultured."

Another popular conception depicts culture as antithetical to nature in that culture mars or spoils nature, especially human nature. This belief goes back at least to Jean Jacques Rousseau. Modern advocates of "back to nature" often fall prey to this understanding of culture. They fail to see that culture in many ways is often complementary, not contrary, to human nature. This is particularly so if we remember what the ancient Greeks understood by *physis*. To them *physis* commonly meant the way something, including the human being, grew and developed. Thus as human beings grow and develop, which includes acquiring culture, they are not having their human nature spoiled or diminished, but rather enhanced and developed. If one has any doubts, one needs only to recall the studies that have reported the unfortunate effects on individuals who, in social isolation, were deprived of culture.

Translators selected the Latin term *natura* to convey the Greek meaning of *physis*. As Robert Nisbet has shown, this translation has had many unfortunate results.[1] The Latin word *natura,* from which the English "nature" is derived, does not convey the meaning of growth and development. It refers to the physical, often static, characteristics of various entities in the universe. Thus to see culture as contrary to nature is just another of the unfortunate understandings that have resulted from equating *physis* with *natura.*

There are, of course, important distinctions between the concepts of nature and culture. But one cannot say that cultural practices are contrary or antithetical to nature, nor is culture unnatural. For one, is it not the nature of human beings to have culture? Moreover, people universally consider it "natural" to regulate, say, given sexual or biological activities, even though such regulations are culturally derived and differ from society to society.

Although Tylor's definition above does not explicitly say so, it does imply that culture is a unique possession of human beings. It is unique to humans because they alone are capable of symboling, that is, assigning

---

[1] Robert Nisbet, *Social Change and History* (Oxford: Oxford University Press, 1969) 22.

meaning to objects and activities that have no inherent or innate meaning. In the words of Leslie A. White: "Culture consists of all the ways of life of each people which are dependent upon symboling and which are considered in an extrasomatic context."[2]

When speaking about culture it is also appropriate to define the concept of society, a term often used loosely as synonymous with culture. "Culture," said Herskovits, "is the way of life of a people; while society is an organized interacting aggregate of individuals who follow a given way of life."[3]

In the present book I define culture as society's institutionalized (established) values, beliefs, norms, knowledge, and practices that are learned through human interaction.

Pervasiveness of Culture

A student of culture soon recognizes that culture permeates every aspect of human life. Even anthropologists and sociologists often forget how the culture in which they live influences them. In fact, forgetting the role and function of culture is in itself an effect of culture. If one is to live effectively in society, even as a social scientist, one can hardly be continually conscious of culture. Such consciousness would either lead to social ostracization or make it extremely difficult to get along with people, even with one's close associates, who for the most part are quite oblivious to culture and its effects.

While sociologists and anthropologists frequently are very much aware of the pervasiveness of culture, the average citizen (in any society) rarely, if ever, is conscious of it. "Culture hides much more than it reveals, and strangely enough what it hides, it hides most effectively from its own participants."[4] Nor does seeing foreign cultural practices necessarily mean that people really notice them.[5]

How many people recognize the pervasiveness and the effects of culture in such daily activities as greeting friends in a given way, wearing cer-

---

[2]Leslie A. White, "The Concept of Culture," *American Anthropology* 61 (April 1959): 227-51.

[3]Melville J. Herskovits, *Cultural Anthropology* (New York: Alfred A. Knopf, 1963) 316.

[4]Edward T. Hall, *The Silent Language* (New York: Doubleday & Company, 1959) 30.

[5]Zygmunt Bauman, *Culture as Praxis* (London: Routledge and Kegan Paul, 1973) 18.

tain styles of clothes, making facial expressions, how and what one eats, how and what one believes religiously, and how and where one makes love? People no more see their daily activities pervaded and influenced by culture than fish see the pervasiveness of water.

How many individuals—even in a society where much time is spent in educational institutions—are aware of the fact that culture pervades their thinking and speaking? In the words of Benjamin Lee Whorf: "We cut nature up, organize it into concepts, and ascribe significance as we do, largely because we [as members of a society] are parties to an agreement to organize it in this way."[6] Or as Walter Lippmann once observed: People do not respond to stimuli (objects and activities); they respond instead to how their culture has *defined* the stimuli.[7] To speak of the pervasiveness of culture is to say that culture intervenes between the human organism and his/ her physical environment.

The pervasiveness of culture is present in every society's basic social institutions: the family, government, economics, education, and religion. It is no accident that large, extended families are found in agrarian societies and that small, nuclear families predominate in highly urbanized societies. In agrarian societies a large family is an economic asset; children help make an agrarian economy more productive. They are needed to till the soil, to tend the herds, to harvest crops, and to help provide family staples. In an urban society children are an economic liability; they have no significant opportunities to help in the urban economy. In fact, large families require large expenditures for larger living quarters, formal education, and other necessities.

Nor does religious life escape the pervasive effects of culture. One need only note that American denominations—whether Episcopalian, Lutheran, or Roman Catholic—strongly favor the separation of church and state, whereas their European counterparts are quite comfortable with the state-church system. Obviously, American culture has been absorbed and internalized by these mainline denominations in the United States. In fact, most denominations have theologians who even find biblical support for this cultural practice. On the other hand, their denominational kin overseas

---

[6]Benjamin Lee Whorf, "Science and Linguistics," *Technology Review* 44 (1940): 229-31, 247, 248.

[7]Walter Lippmann, *Public Opinion* (New York: Macmillan Co., 1932).

are very satisfied, and see it as equally biblical and God-pleasing, to have the state support the church with public tax monies.

Will Herberg contended in his *Protestant, Catholic and Jew* (1955) that the American cultural value of democracy was not only institutionalized in the three major religious groupings, but it was also that which all had in common. Doctrinal differences, often touted by some clergy, are not seen to be very significant by the person on the street or in the pew, regardless of denominational affiliation.

Coerciveness of Culture

Culture not only is pervasive; it is also coercive. Culture is what the French sociologist Emile Durkheim called a social fact, a phenomenon that is external and coercive to every human being or group of humans. None of us has had any part in creating the culture into which we were born. "An Eskimo, Bantu, Tibetan, Swede, or American is what he is, thinks, feels, and acts, as he does, because his culture influences, stimulates, him in such a way as to evoke these responses."[8]

Where is the brave soul who will deliberately ignore society's mores? For instance, who will go bathing in the nude at a public beach, while others are clad in swimming garb, even where there is no law prohibiting such behavior? What adult would dare spurn the sex-distinguishing labels, appropriate to his or her sex, on public lavatories in the United States or Canada? We all know what happens to individuals who disagree with some law or *mos* and then proceed to violate it. Written laws, similar to the unwritten mores, are very much a part of society's coercive culture. The individual's tastes and preferences must give way to cultural norms (mores or laws).

The coercive character of one's culture, although to a lesser degree, is also evident in society's folkways. Our customs of a woman's wearing lipstick and men shaving are folkways. Violating or ignoring either one is not seen as disruptive to a society's social or moral well-being, and yet very few will choose not to conform to these folkways when they are in an environment where these behaviors are expected. To reject the folkway is to experience too many social discomforts, even though they are minor. The

---

[8]Leslie A. White, *The Science of Culture* (New York: Farrar, Straus and Giroux, Inc., 1949) 340.

coercive nature of culture is everywhere. In the words of Edward Hall, "There is not one aspect of human life that is not touched by culture."[9]

Culture Shapes Personality

Many Americans raised in a relatively individualistically oriented society, upon hearing that one's personality is shaped by culture, react in disbelief: "By no means! I am an individual; my society's culture definitely did not shape my personality." Such a remark not only is common but also ironic in that it supports the very assertion that is being rejected. From where did the person who thinks that he or she is so individualistic receive that strong belief? From that person's American culture, of course. This is one way of showing how culture remains hidden to most people, even though its effects are operative in shaping and molding people's thoughts and actions.

That culture shapes the personalities of a society's people has been empirically and scientifically corroborated by anthropologists for more than a half century. In the 1920s Ruth Benedict studied the Zuni Indians of the Southwestern United States. She found them to be a placid people whose children were reared in an atmosphere of warmth, love, and tenderness. Physical punishment was never exercised, and yet the children became well-behaved adults, among whom conflict and alcoholism were almost non-existent. They craved no individual power or leadership roles. Cooperation was a deeply internalized characteristic of every Zuni member. Zuni ceremonies were calm, not frenetic as in some other societies. Suicide was unknown to them; it was an act too violent for them to contemplate. Divorce was rare, and when it did occur, it was simple and without conflict. The wife would simply place her husband's possessions outside the home (pueblo), whereupon he would take his goods and go home to his mother.[10]

In her book *Patterns of Culture* (1934), Benedict shows how the personality of one society differs dramatically from that of another. Such differences are produced by culture. For example, a child of the Dobuans in Melanesia, unlike the Zuni offspring, enters a world where the father resents his or her birth, because he now must abstain from sexual intercourse

[9]Edward Hall, *Beyond Culture* (New York: Anchor Press, 1976) 16.

[10]Ruth Benedict, *Patterns of Culture* (Boston: Houghton-Mifflin, 1934) 74.

with his wife until the child is weaned.[11] The child therefore receives no care or love from its father but instead from its mother's brothers. Frequently the mother offers very little nurturance as well. Early in life the child is exposed to sorcery and witchcraft, which is taken with the utmost seriousness. Everything to the Dobuans is the result of sorcery. Everyday associates are seen as sorcerers who threaten one's daily life and affairs. Yam crops only grow if one had successfully stolen them from one's neighbors by means of magic and witchcraft. Benedict says: "A good crop is a confession of theft."[12] Thus gardens are physically guarded. Trust among the Dobuans is a rare commodity; they see suspicion and deception as virtues. It is taken for granted that every good man has stolen, killed children, and deceived others. Theft and adultery are "valued charms of the valued men of the community."[13] Every day the Dobuan lives in fear of being poisoned. Even husbands and wives distrust each other.

Dobuan life is virtually void of humor or mirth, even though there is little verbal conflict. Arguing is seen as heightening the possibility of being poisoned. The avoidance of conflict, however, is no assurance that one is safe. Friends may be polite and calm in order to prepare themselves for some harmful act, such as stealing or poisoning one's food. The Dobuan is not born distrustful, hostile, deceitful, jealous, and suspicious. These paranoidlike qualities of the Dobuan personality are clearly and distinctly inculcated by the Dobuan culture.[14]

For centuries it has been erroneously taught as fact that temperamental differences between men and women are a constant, universal phenomenon. Males are naturally aggressive, active, and dominant, whereas women are said to be nonaggressive, passive, and submissive. In 1935 Margaret Mead published *Sex and Temperament in Three Primitive Societies* as a result of her fieldwork among the Arapesh, Mundugumor, and the Tschambuli, three different societies in New Guinea. She provided em-

---

[11]Benedict's knowledge about the Dobuans was largely derived from R. F. Fortune's *The Sorcerers of Dobu* (New York: E. P. Dutton & Company, 1932).

[12]Benedict, *Patterns of Culture,* 148.

[13]Ibid., 169.

[14]I use the term *paranoidlike* rather than *paranoid* because, as Horton and Hunt say, the Dobuans really are not paranoid. "[T]heir fears are justified and not irrational; the dangers they face are genuine, not imaginary." See Paul B. Horton and Chester L. Hunt, *Sociology* (New York: McGraw-Hill, 1972) 72.

pirical evidence that the traditional (Western) understanding of male and female differences is not invariable or universally true.

The Tschambuli, for instance, did indeed have sharply different sex roles, accompanied by differing temperamental behavior. But their roles were reversed from those commonly found in Western societies. The Tschambuli men, unlike their Western counterparts, were concerned with their appearances and how their jewelry appealed to the women. They entertained and catered to the social tastes of the women. The men gossiped, were very nurturant toward the children, and devoted themselves to the finer tasks of life. In Western societies women derive their emotional and psychic income by revolving their lives around men and their values, but among the Tschambuli this process was reversed: the men's emotional and psychic lives revolved around the women. The Tschambuli women, on the other hand, assumed the roles that men commonly exercise in Western societies. The women were practical, uninterested in jewelry or fashionable clothes. In courtship and marriage the sexually aggressive role was exercised by the female. And the women were also the primary economic providers in terms of family support.

The Arapesh culture, Mead found, taught both men and women to emulate and attain what Western men still characterize as the ideal female temperament. The man was expected to display a gentle, unaggressive, and maternal disposition, similar to that of the female in his society. The Mundugumor tribe, on the other hand, socialized both males and females to assume a cold, tough, and unremitting temperament.

Another striking example of culture shaping the personality has been found among the Alorese, inhabitants of Indonesia. The painstaking research of Cora du Bois revealed that the culture of the Alorese had mothers of neonates feed them irregularly and inconsistently. Crying is sometimes heeded and sometimes totally ignored. After age one the child is responsible for his or her own feeding, which forces the young toddler to beg from other children. Mothers commonly try to arouse jealousy among their children. By brandishing knives the mother will, on other occasions, threaten to slice off her children's ears or hands. Between the ages of two and five, the average child engages in frequent and violent temper tantrums. Says du Bois: "Rages are so consistent, so widespread, and of such long duration among young children that they were one of my first and most striking observations.''[15] The rages, like the early feeding practices, received unpredictable and inconsistent responses. One time they are completely ignored; the next time the mother will physically punish the child; and still another time she will trick the child and desert it for a period of time. By adulthood the typical Alorese had developed a personality that is suspicious, given to lying, deception, and insecurity. These qualities are also reflected in the Alorese religious beliefs. For instance, religious spirits have no idealized form or definition and there is no concept of propitiation for the many plights in life, here or hereafter.

These brief accounts of several different cultures illustrate that the human being's personality is not biologically inherited but largely shaped by the culture in which the individual is socialized. The influence of culture is so hidden that when it is revealed, many seek to reject the evidence. It is difficult for many to accept that human behavior, to a large degree, can be explained and predicted in terms of culture, rather than explaining culture in terms of human behavior. Why? The difficulty lies in that for thousands of years humans have, in the words of Leslie White, ''cherished the illusion of omnipotence.''[16] Thus to speak of culture shaping people's thoughts and minds appears almost frightening, especially when one recalls the ancient Greek saying: ''Man is the measure of all things.''

Utterances such as this Greek proverb have prevented people from seeing the presence and the force of culture, which shapes not just the human personality but also shapes human philosophy, art, leisure, work, play, and religion. To assert that culture has always played a powerful role in shaping the lives and activities of people in every society will sooner or later, as any social scientist knows, bring forth the remark (almost a fearful one): ''You are promoting cultural determinism. You are saying that the human being is irrelevant to the cultural process.'' Not at all! No one has ever argued that culture can exist without people. While it is indeed true that one cannot have a culture without people, it also needs to be said that one cannot find people without culture either. As Leslie White once put it: ''What the culturologist contends is that in this system [the human-and-culture] the human organism is not the determinant; that the behavior of the culture process cannot be explained in terms of this organism but only

---

[15]Cora du Bois, *The People of Alor: A Social-Psychological Study of an East Indian Island* (Minneapolis: University of Minnesota Press, 1944) 51.

[16]White, *Science of Culture,* 341.

in [terms] of culture itself."[17] For instance, some societies have a low suicide rate; others have a relatively high rate. Are we to say that suicide determinants are more abundant in the chromosomes where the suicide rate is high and vice versa? No, the only plausible or scientific way of explaining the differing suicide rates is to recognize that cultural determinants vary from one society to the next.

Nor is this reifying culture as though it were "a self-contained 'superorganic' reality with forces and purposes of its own."[18] While culture indeed is powerful, often coercive, it is not a superorganic entity. Here we need to remember that culture is often affected and changed by noncultural factors or by exceptional human beings, as I will discuss later in this chapter. To accent the pervasive and powerful influence of culture, so often a hidden dimension, is not the same as reifying it.

Culture and Human Nature

If one has trouble accepting the powerful role of culture, it is not because there is a lack of strong empirical data, but because for most of human history the role of culture was largely unknown and unrecognized. What was commonly described or explained as "human nature," seen to be true of all human beings, was not really human at all, but rather the reflection of particular cultural values and norms. While it is a requirement of nature for human beings to eat, there is no natural force that tells people how *many times* per day they should eat. Nor does nature have much influence in terms of *what* people eat, *where,* and with *whom.* The latter are dictated by culture, not by nature.

Even the so-called universals, as anthropologists refer to them, are affected by culture. The universal existence of marriage rites, education, family life, age-grading, gift giving, government, religious rites, music, leisure, and so forth take on different cultural forms in different societies. In some societies marriage, for instance, is polygamous and in others it is monogamous; in some areas spouses are chosen by parents and in others individuals select their own mates. Government (to cite another cultural universal) may be exercised by a group of elders; it may be democratic, socialistic, communistic, or fascistic.

---

[17]Ibid., 350-51.

[18]Clifford Geertz, *The Interpretation of Cultures* (New York: Basic Books, 1973) 11.

Some people believe that certain aspects of human nature are phyloge-netically determined and therefore culturally invariant. Freud, for example, theorized that the Oedipus complex was a universal product of human nature. Research by Bronislaw Malinowski and Margaret Mead has shown Freud to be wrong.[19] The Oedipus complex is not a universal phenomenon.

Even if one defines human nature in the context of biological needs (momentarily setting aside the biological needs of nonhumans), one soon realizes that culture channels and meets those needs in different ways from one society to another. As mentioned above, the basic biological need to eat is met by humans in a cultural context. The need to sleep, to love and be loved, and to defecate are exercised according to cultural prescriptions.

To contend that even the basic biological needs of humans are cultur-ally channeled is not to deny the existence of human nature, but rather to suggest that it be seen as a phenomenon with a limited set of properties. A broad, or rather loose, understanding of human nature does not stand the test of empirical scrutiny. All too often what is called "human nature" turns out, upon close examination, to be nothing more than the effects or results of culture.

What then are some of the common properties of human nature, dis-tinct from the nature of nonhumans? One quality is the exclusively human ability to symbol, to assign value(s) and meaning(s) to phenomena that have no inherent or innate value or meaning. No object or phenomenon posses-ses innate value or meaning. Only humans provide that quality. It is the ability to symbol that prompts most humans to recoil and declare the in-carceration and killing of millions of people by Hitler and Stalin, for ex-ample, as "inhuman." Another distinctively human quality is possessing the consciousness that someday one will die. Still another property of hu-man nature is planning and foresight. And still another attribute unique to human beings is that they alone are able to blush, and—as Mark Twain so aptly noted—only they have reason to blush.

If biological needs alone cannot be considered valid indicators of hu-man nature, then might not symboling, planning, foresight, awareness of death, shame, and creating values also be seen as poor reflectors of human nature because they too are tempered by culture? The answer is no. The

---

[19]Bronislaw Malinowski, *Sex and Repressions in a Savage Society* (New York: Har-court, Brace, 1927); Margaret Mead, *Coming of Age in Samoa* (New York: Morrow, 1928); Margaret Mead, *Growing Up in New Guinea* (New York: Morrow, 1930); Margaret Mead, *Sex and Temperament in Three Primitive Societies* (New York: Morrow, 1935).

biological needs of humans are not unique or even significantly different from those of nonhumans; but the processes of symboling, planning and foresight, blushing, and consciousness of birth and death, while tempered by culture, are unique to human beings. In fact, it seems that the properties of human nature give impetus to culture itself, even though culture and human nature are mutually reinforcing entities.

Culture as a Predictor

Given that culture shapes personalities differently from one society to another, and given that the vast majority of individuals conform to their culture's norms, sociologists and anthropologists contend that culture is a better predictor of human behavior than knowing people's skin color, for instance. One does not need to know whether people are black, red, white, or yellow in order to predict whether they will eat dog meat or beef steak, whether they will circumcise their offspring (male or female) at infancy or at puberty, whether they sleep on beds elevated above the floor or on some material lying directly on the floor. To predict these and other behavioral activities, one only needs to know the society's culture. Upon knowing where a given person is from—say, England—we can predict with a high degree of accuracy whether he/she will drive an automobile on the left side of the road, drink tea, spell words like ''color'' or ''honor'' differently than people in the United States. The concept of human nature is completely irrelevant in predicting such behavior. Knowing that the Americans, British, or Chinese possess ''human nature'' helps little or nothing in predicting their behavior. Only by knowing a society's culture can one predict the regular social behavior of its citizens. Thus the predictability of a society's members' social and personal behavior on the basis of culture is another hidden dimension not commonly recognized.

Cultural Change and Growth

While culture does shape and coerce a society's population, it is necessary to note that human beings are not totally passive vis-à-vis their culture. They are not mere robots who have no effect upon their culture. Indeed there have been—and always will be—individuals who are agents or instruments of cultural change in any cultural system.

Cultural change is produced in several ways; in each, the individual plays a prominent role. Considerable cultural change has occurred as a result of individuals who consciously and deliberately question specific cultural values, beliefs, or practices with the intent of removing or replacing them. Such individuals are social deviants, swimming against their culture, often at very high costs. They are always few in number, appearing only now and then. They differ from the vast majority in any society who accept whatever their particular culture hands them. They are unlike their fellow citizens who love their native culture and are comfortable with it. They find it difficult to display a strong sense of ethnocentrism. They are not happy living within the cage of culture, "confined by bars of tradition and custom that restrict actions as strongly, if not as obviously, as the bars of the zoo."[20]

A partial list of individuals who knowingly challenged given aspects of their culture would include persons such as Jesus Christ, Joan of Arc, Martin Luther, Copernicus, Vesalius, Galileo, Rene Descartes, Isaac Newton, Florence Nightingale, Louis Pasteur, Mary Wollstonecraft, Abraham Lincoln, Karl Marx, Charles Darwin, Jane Addams, Margaret Sanger, Martin Luther King, Jr. All of these people, to varying degrees, have changed their respective culture and that of others. They demonstrated the reciprocity—the interplay—that exists between culture and human beings. Such individuals reveal that "society is in man" and "man in society," as Peter L. Berger expresses it. Or, in the words of Morris Opler: "The impress of each [culture and the individual] is on the other. They are not found in isolation from each other, and they are so interdependent that it is doubtful that they can be entirely extricated from each other for research purposes or in the process of living."[21]

The role of the individual must, however, not be oversimplified so that the interplay between culture and the individual is ignored. The change-promoting person is never the sole, autonomous determiner of cultural change. Ideas, whether change-directed or otherwise, do not have an autonomy of their own. They all arise in sociocultural settings. "It is not the consciousness of men that determines their existence, but on the contrary, their social existence determines their consciousness," said Karl Marx.[22]

---

[20]Morston Bates, *Gluttons and Libertines: Human Problems of Being Natural* (New York: Vintage Books, 1967).

[21]Morris E. Opler, "The Human Being in Culture Theory," *American Anthropologist* 66 (June 1964): 507-28.

[22]Karl Marx, *A Contribution to the Critique of Political-Economy* (New York: International Publishers, [1859], 1970) 21.

So too with cultural change. Individuals promoting change are sensitized by some of the prominent incongruities, inadequacies, conflicts, and contradictions within their culture.

The second method of cultural change effected by the individual(s) is less dramatic than that prompted by the person who publicly challenges traditional beliefs or practices. I refer to the inventor or innovator of some new material item of culture. The inventor is primarily intent on exercising his/her talent or genius in seeing the invention function mechanically. While conveniences may be the intended goal, cultural change is not. The person who invented the automobile had no intentions or awareness of how profoundly the new vehicle would alter culture in terms of travel, transportation, jobs (e.g., manufacturers, assembly persons, traffic persons), courting habits, land use for roads, urban sprawls, architectural design of housing, energy consumption, traffic jams, frayed nerves, parking regulations, independence of family members, and life-styles. Similarly, unforeseen results arose with the advent of television, the telephone, mechanical farm equipment, the airplane, household appliances, and last but not least, the influential computer.

A third manner by which individuals produce change is to participate in minor or even petty social grievances, on the formal and informal level. Those making the grievances and complaints often have no specific change or alternative in mind. They just do not like the way things are presently done. Or they make given suggestions for change, knowing that no change will soon occur, if ever, because their grievances are seen as not serious enough, too limited in scope, or too temporal. Yet, even these minor voices of discontent have at times gained broader and more concentrated attention that eventually produced some change in a society's culture. Change resulting from this and similar types of social interaction in part depends on the availability of mass communication instruments.

New ideas and practices introduced by an individual(s) and accepted within the boundaries of a society's culture are the result of cultural-change agents. Yet not all sociocultural change occurs in this manner. Cultural change more commonly is the result of diffusion, borrowing cultural elements from other societies.

Perhaps most of the cultural changes that have taken place in human history were brought about by diffusion. Yet this process has not been widely recognized by the general populace. Why not? Apparently the role and significance of the individual, especially in Western society, has been so highly emphasized that the role of diffusion has been all but overlooked. The individual's control over culture has quite rightly been called "an anthropological illusion," to cite Leslie A. White.[23]

Ralph Linton, the anthropologist, has shown how a wide variety of foreign cultural items have been diffused into the life-style of millions of Americans. Says Linton:

> Our solid American citizen awakens in a bed built on a pattern which originated in the Near East but which was modified in northern Europe before it was transmitted to America. He throws back the covers made from cotton, domesticated in India, or linen, domesticated in the Near East, or wool from sheep, also domesticated in the Near East, or silk, the use of which was discovered in China. All of these materials have been spun and woven by processes invented in the Near East. He slips into his moccasins, invented by the Indians of the Eastern woodlands, and goes to the bathroom, whose fixtures are a mixture of European and American inventions in India, and washes with soap invented by the ancient Gauls. He then shaves, a masochistic rite which seems to have been derived from either Sumer or ancient Egypt.

> Returning to the bedroom, he removes his clothes from a chair of southern European type and proceeds to dress. He puts on garments whose form originally derived from the skin clothing of the nomads of the Asiatic steppes, puts on shoes made from skins tanned by a process invented in ancient Egypt and cut to a pattern derived from the classical civilizations of the Mediterranean, and ties around his neck a strip of bright-colored cloth which is a vestigial survival of the shoulder shawls worn by the seventeenth-century Croatians. Before going out for breakfast he glances through the window, made of glass invented in Egypt, and if it is raining, he puts on overshoes made of rubber discovered by the Central American Indians and takes an umbrella, invented in Southeastern Asia. Upon his head he puts a hat made of felt, a material invented in the Asiatic steppes.

> On his way to breakfast he stops to buy a paper, paying for it with coins, an ancient Lydian invention. At the restaurant a whole new series of borrowed elements confronts him. His plate is made of a form of pottery invented in China. His knife is of steel, an alloy first made in southern India, its form an Italian invention, and his spoon a derivative of a Roman original. He begins breakfast with an orange, from the eastern Mediterranean, a cantaloupe from Persia, or perhaps a piece of African watermelon. With

---

[23]White, *Science of Culture*, 330.

this he has coffee, an Abyssinian plant, with cream and sugar. Both the domestication of cows and the idea of milking them originated in the Near East, while sugar was first made in India. After his fruit and first coffee he goes on to waffles, cakes made by a Scandinavian technique from wheat domesticated in Asia Minor. Over these he pours maple syrup, invented by Indians of the Eastern woodlands. As a side dish he may have the eggs of a species of bird domesticated in Indo-China, or thin strips of flesh of an animal domesticated in Eastern Asia which have been salted and smoked by a process developed in northern Europe.

When our friend has finished eating, he settles back to smoke, an American Indian habit, consuming a plant domesticated in Brazil in either a pipe derived from the Indians of Virginia, or a cigarette, derived from Mexico. If he is hardy enough he may even attempt a cigar, transmitted to us from the Antilles by way of Spain. While smoking he reads the news of the day, imprinted in characters invented in Germany. As he absorbs the accounts of foreign troubles he will, if he is a good conservative citizen, thank a Hebrew deity in an Indo-European language that is 100 per cent American.[24]

Cultural change and growth, similar to culture in general, is rarely perceived by people. Is this not why Linton's above illustration is so interesting? Baseball undisputedly is an American game. It was invented by Abner Doubleday in 1839 in Cooperstown, New York. Yet many items and features of this game are borrowed from other cultures. Most other social practices and customs, if closely analyzed, would reveal considerable cultural borrowing.

Borrowing cultural elements from other societies receives varying degrees of acceptability, ranging from outright rejection to eager acceptance. A number of factors account for this phenomenon. I shall mention only two.

The compatibility of a foreign cultural element with that of present culture is a common variable that either prompts an entire culture or subculture to accept or reject the foreign element. For example, the American aborigines, especially on the Great Plains, accepted the horse from the Spanish settlers because the horse facilitated the task of hunting, a vitally important function in their culture.

Another factor related to the rejection-acceptance continuum seems to be the degree of social security that is present. A society, or a subcultural group, that is still striving for security will more likely reject the importation of an outside cultural trait than one that already has achieved social

---

[24]Ralph Lintron, *The Study of Man: An Introduction* (New York: Appleton-Century, 1936) 326-27. Reprinted by permission of Prentice-Hall, Inc., Englewood Cliffs NJ.

security. For instance, during the first 300 years the early Christians, who lacked considerable social security, avoided the use of candles in their worship activities. Gordon Laing says candlelights reminded the early Christians of pagan rituals. Similarly, the use of incense, then widely used by the Greco-Roman cults, was spurned.[25] However, after Christianity was legalized by Emperor Constantine in A.D. 313, the Christians began using some of the once-spurned "pagan" rituals in formal worship. Evidently, with the legalization of Christianity, the Christians felt relatively secure in a society that once persecuted them, and so practices that once were defined as "pagan" now had become acceptable.

---

[25]Gordon Laing, "Roman Religious Survivals in Christianity," in John Thomas McNeil, Matthew Spinka, and Harold R. Willoughby, eds., *Environmental Factors in Christian History* (Port Washington NY: Kennikat Press, 1970) 72-90.

CHAPTER 2

CULTURE:
THE SHAPER OF THEOLOGY

The Polish astronomer Copernicus some 450 years ago showed that our planet Earth was not the center of the universe, around which the sun and other celestial bodies revolved. Since Copernicus, we have learned that the Earth is *not even* the largest of the nine planets. Moreover, it is but one of millions of heavenly bodies in space. Yet people, for the most part, live as though the Copernican revolution had never happened.

The pre-Copernican understanding of the Earth as the center of the universe or solar system led to a variety of beliefs and actions. One such belief said *"homo sapiens ueber alles,"* meaning that mankind, being on the universe-centered planet, was therefore also "the measure of all things," as Protagoras put it. With the Copernican revolution many were asking whether this age-old assumption still could be maintained. Following Copernicus, other revolutionary concepts and models came on the scene of human knowledge. Let us recall the theories of John Locke. Only fifty years after Copernicus died, Locke (in the 1690s) seemed to have caught the significance of the Copernican spirit by creating yet another revolution in human thought. Locke held that the human being at birth essentially was a tabula rasa, although he never used that particular term. Locke's theory said that ideas were not innate, as Plato and other ancients believed; ideas were the result of environmental experiences. If Copernicus stood Ptolemy, the ancient astronomer, on his head (to use a metaphor of Marx), Locke stood Plato on his head.

The full impact of Locke's theory did not make itself felt until the latter two-thirds of the nineteenth century, when sociology and anthropology—

two closely related disciplines—made their appearance. Both disciplines discovered that the behavior of human beings could no longer be explained in the light of metaphysical perspectives. There were, as Durkheim said, social facts (e.g., cultural norms, beliefs, practices) that had to be treated as "things" and explained in terms of other social facts.[1] No longer could social phenomena be explained by reductionist methods, whether biological or psychological. Social facts, moreover, were external and coercive to human beings. They not only influenced what humans did, but also developed uniformities in human behavior even though they varied from one society to another.

If cultural norms, beliefs, and practices shaped human personalities (briefly shown in the previous chapter), then it is also necessary to see how culture shapes theology. This pursuit is significant and relevant, for theology—like other traditional attempts to explain human behavior—has all too long been perceived and taught as though it were a subject unaffected by sociocultural forces.

Theology Is Part of Culture

Although in recent years there have been many theologians who have recognized that theological formulations and practices reflect culture, there still are some, especially those unfamiliar with the social sciences, who seem to be oblivious to the fact that culture shapes and has shaped theology. They often strain out an exegetical or grammatical gnat, but swallow a cultural camel. This latter posture appears to be particularly true of those who call themselves "conservative." There are very few "conservative" theologians who, like James I. Packer, will say: "We may be sure, therefore, before we ever sit down to look, that any version of Christianity produced anywhere at any time will bear marks of one-sidedness or myopia, not only because of imperfect exegesis and theologizing but also for reasons of cultural limitation."[2]

Theology is part of a society's culture not only in that its content is significantly shaped by culture, but also because its meaning cannot be con-

---

[1]Emile Durkheim, *The Rules of Sociological Method,* trans. Sarah A. Solovay and John H. Mueller (New York: Free Press, 1938).

[2]James I. Packer, "The Gospel—Its Content and Communication: A Theological Perspective," in John Stott and Robert T. Coote, eds., *Gospel and Culture* (Pasadena: William Carey Library, 1979) 140.

veyed apart from specific cultural forms. When Jesus, for instance, said "I am the good shepherd," he used a common cultural expression—a cultural form—from his society to convey a specific theological meaning to his audience.

The theological enterprise has no choice but to use cultural forms to express its various teachings. No teachings, meanings, or messages can be communicated to human beings apart from given cultural forms and expressions. The problem, however, is that the common person, including many theologians, tend to be unaware of this phenomenon. One reason for this unawareness stems from the hiddenness of culture. Another reason is that specific cultural forms that convey a given meaning are frequently equated or identified with the meaning itself.

There seem to be at least two reasons why cultural forms are commonly equated with specific teachings or meanings. One, people are commonly ignorant of the fact that different cultural forms can be used to convey the same or similar meaning. Two, people fear relativity. If one can transmit a given meaning by another and different cultural form, then the cultural form is seen as relative. This conclusion, of course, does not necessarily follow, but it appears to be one that is widely held. Nevertheless, theology is not only part of culture in that its meanings cannot be imparted without particular cultural forms, but also because people usually identify the meaning with the cultural vehicle that transmits it.

Culture Shapes Theology

A wide variety of examples can be cited to show the powerful influence culture has on religion or theology. I shall mention only a few.

Christians and War. There are probably few, if any, historical accounts that show more clearly the influence of culture on Christian theology than what it has said about war. The early Christians not only were opposed to war, but they also refused to serve in the military, even for police purposes. In the words of Roland Bainton: "From the end of the New Testament period to the decade of A.D. 170–180 there is no evidence whatever of Christians being in the army."[3] Even in the third century, when Christians were slowly accommodating themselves to the Roman ("pagan") culture, one finds an inflexible resistance to warfare and military

---

[3]Roland H. Bainton, *Christian Attitudes toward War and Peace* (New York: Abingdon Press, 1960) 67-68.

life by prominent church fathers. Tertullian, Origen, Athenagoras, Minucius Felix, Justin Martyr, Hippolytus, Cyprian, and others unmistakably denounced war and Christian participation in it.

In A.D. 211 Tertullian, the influential Latin church father, argued that "when a man has become a believer, and faith has been sealed, there must be either an immediate abandonment of it [the army], which has been the case with many" (*De Corona* 11). In another of his works he wrote: "The Lord . . . in disarming Peter ungirt every soldier" (*On Idolatry* 19). To Tertullian, military service was a clear-cut example of serving two masters (*De Corona* 1), something that Christ had said could not be done. Again, he asserted: "Shall it be lawful to make an occupation of the sword, when the Lord proclaims that he who uses the sword shall perish by the sword?" (*De Corona* 11).

Origen (A.D. 185–254), the Eastern church father, in the year 240 conceded to Celsus (the first literary opponent of Christianity), saying: "We do not indeed fight under him [the emperor], although he requires it; but we fight on his behalf, forming a special army—an army of piety—offering our prayers to God" (*Contra Celsum* 8.73). Christians were only *miles Christi* (soldiers of Christ), said Origen in his *De Principiis* 3. This early celibate also said, "He [Christ] nowhere teaches that it is right for his disciples to offer violence to any one, however wicked. For he did not deem it in keeping with such laws as his, which were derived from a divine source, to allow the killing of any person whatever" (*Contra Celsum* 3.6).

Irenaeus (A.D. 115?–202), a contemporary of Tertullian and Origen and an eminent teacher of theology, attested to the pacifist behavior of Christians by saying they beat swords into plowshares. They did not fight, but turned their other cheek (*Against Heresies* 4). Similarly, Justin Martyr (A.D. 100–116) proclaimed: "We who were filled with war and mutual slaughter and every wickedness have each through the world changed our warlike weapons,—our swords into ploughshares, and our spears into implements of tillage" (*Dialogue with Trypho* 110). Cyprian (A.D. 200–258), bishop of Carthage, said that God did not give mankind iron for killing but for tilling (*De Habitus Virginum* 11).

The sixteenth canon of *The Apostolic Tradition* (early third century) did not permit a soldier to kill or to take a military oath. This canon indicates that when military service was permitted at all, it had to be in the role of police work only. It asserted: "If a catechumen or a baptized Christian wishes to become a soldier, let him be cast out. For he has despised God."[4]

Lactantius (A.D. 240–320)—a church father who has often been referred to as the "Christian Cicero"—in the year A.D. 305 declared: "So neither will it be permitted a just man, whose service is justice herself, to enter military service, . . . since killing is prohibited." He further stated: "It is always wrong to kill a man" (*Divine Institutes* 4.20).

The early Christians rejected war for more than one reason. In their opinion, it was unthinkable to participate in war because it would have given aid and comfort to their enemy, the Romans. In addition, and perhaps most important of all, they took a pacifist stand because war was contrary to the teachings of Christ. Jean-Michel Hornus thinks that the early Christians primarily refused to participate in war service because they were opposed to violence, not because they rejected idolatry, as some have contended.[5] This is why there were soldier martyrs among the early Christians, says Hornus. The position of Hornus is given credence by Minucius Felix (third century), the Roman lawyer who defended the Christians. He maintained that Christians could not stand to hear or see a person killed (*Octavius* ch. 30). Similarly, Martin of Tours remained in the Roman army for two years after becoming a Christian. But when "an actual battle was imminent," he declined to serve.[6] His rejection of military life occurred in A.D. 336. Maximilian, a pacifist martyr, when summoned before the Proconsul to serve in the army, said: "I cannot serve as a soldier; I cannot do evil. I am a Christian." He was therefore executed in A.D. 295 at the early age of twenty-one.[7]

The Christian refusal to participate in military conflict was seen by the Romans as nationally disruptive. As T. G. Tucker has observed: "He [the Christian] weakened the martial spirit of the soldier."[8] Christian pacifism contributed in part to their being persecuted by the Romans.

---

[4]Gregory Dix, ed., *The Treatise on the Apostolic Tradition of St. Hippolytus of Rome* (London: SPCK, 1968) 26-27.

[5]Jean-Michel Hornus, *It Is Not Lawful for Me to Fight,* trans. Alan Kreider and Oliver Colwin (Scottsdale: Herald Press, 1980) 256.

[6]Bainton, *Christian Attitudes,* 81.

[7]Albert Marrin, *War and the Christian Conscience: From Augustine to Martin Luther King, Jr.* (Chicago: Regnery Co., 1971) 41-43.

[8]T. G. Tucker, *Life in the Roman World of Nero and St. Paul* (New York: Macmillan, 1910) 386.

The Christian accommodation to the culture of war and military life became a growing reality by the early fourth century. The Council or Synod of Arles in A.D. 314, although it spoke only about soldiers refusing to serve in time of peace, nevertheless made a complete about-face from the positions of Tertullian, Irenaeus, Origen, Justin Martyr, Cyprian, Lactantius, Minucius Felix, and other early Christian theologians. In its third canon the Synod of Arles barred pacifists from receiving the Lord's Supper. Hornus thinks that Arles made this declaration as a result of a compromise, "a bargain which the Church struck with the emperor in exchange for his protection."[9] Sociologically speaking, the third canon not only shows the cultural accommodation made by the church, but it also portrays social reciprocity. For it was only one year earlier (A.D. 313) that the Roman emperor Constantine issued the Edict of Milan, legalizing the Christian religion. In return the church legitimated military life, even though it first did so only in time of peace for police purposes.

By the latter part of the fourth century, and especially by the fifth, the church's theologians had completely woven the secular society's culture of war into their theology. Athanasius, writing to Amun (a monk) in the fourth century, said: "It is not lawful to kill. But to destroy adversaries in war is legal and worthy of praise" (*Letters of Amun* 48). By the fifth century, Augustine (A.D. 354–430), one of Christendom's foremost fashioners of doctrine, saddled the church with his "just war" concept, an expression that goes back at least to Aristotle some 300 years before the birth of Christ (see Aristotle's *Politics* 1). Aristotle used the just war concept to justify war that enslaved individuals who, he believed, were by nature created for servitude. Slavery was the result of what he called the "natural law." Among the Romans, especially for Cicero, the idea of a just war meant only the state, not groups or individuals, could wage war. Augustine refashioned the concept and gave it to the Christian church. He characterized war as just if it avenged injuries (vindicated justice), was authorized by the ruler, and did not engage in atrocities, vengeance, reprisals, looting, or profaning temples.[10]

The war-shunning posture of the church's first 300 years, which began to erode by the early fourth century, was completely overturned by Augustine in the fifth century. In fact, by the year 416 one had to be Christian

---

[9]Hornus, *Not Lawful*, 177.

[10]Bainton, *Christian Attitudes*, 96-97.

to enter the Roman army.[11] As time progressed, the once-despised culture of war became more and more a part of the church's theology. Thus by 1095 Pope Urban II launched the infamous, bloody crusade with his speech at Clermont. Now Christians no longer had any misgivings about war. Theirs was not only a just war but also a holy one. "Even monastic pacifism collapsed and there came to be military orders, the Templars, the Hospitalers, and the Knights of St. John."[12] Need one doubt that the church fathers of the first three centuries would have stood in holy horror!

In the sixteenth century Martin Luther, the one-time Augustinian monk, slightly reworked Augustine's just war concept, but rejected the crusades because they were instigated by the papacy, according to Bainton.[13] The echo of Augustine's just war idea is clearly evident in the sixteenth article of the Lutheran Church's Augsburg Confession. That article asserts that it is "right" for Christians to "engage in just wars, to serve as soldiers." Luther and his followers accepted the just war concept because they apparently thought its objective was peace. Whether or not he or his followers were aware of it, such reasoning is a good example of the end justifying the means, an ethic that had traditionally been rejected by the Christian church.

The thirty-seventh of the Church of England's Thirty Nine Articles reads: "It is lawful for Christian men, at the commandment of the magistrate, to weare weapons and serve in the warres." Similarly, the Calvinists approved of just wars. The Westminster Confession in its twenty-fifth article declares: "It is lawful for Christians to . . . wage war upon just and necessary occasions."

The one-time pagan or secular ethics of war practiced by the ancient Hebrews, Greeks, Romans, and other cultures now had become a part of Christian theology. Today in the twentieth century, every mainline denomination in America and Western Europe has incorporated into its theology the permissibility of Christians' participating in the horrors of war. Most denominations have legitimated war for Christians in still another way, namely by sending chaplains into the military where they pray and give moral support to missions and expeditions. The military establish-

[11]Ibid., 88.

[12]Ibid., 114.

[13]Ibid., 136-37.

ment, of course, is pleased with the presence of chaplains. They give social and moral stability to military life. Their presence helps soldiers see their fighting and killing as God-pleasing activities. It lessens the probability of conscience pangs. In fact, one study shows that seventy-nine percent of the military chaplains interviewed felt that "a man with good religious training would make a better soldier than one who lacked such training." This same study also found that "45 percent of the respondents [chaplains and ex-chaplains] believed that the killing of an enemy soldier was a righteous act and the remainder called it a justifiable act." [14]

Candles and White Robes. For 300 years the Christian church resisted the use of candles in its services. Lights reminded the members of pagan rituals. [15] But eventually candles became an integral part of the church's worship life. Today what Roman Catholic, Lutheran, or Episcopalian church, as well as some others, would feel its worship ritual is complete without candles? A once-despised cultural practice, seen as pagan, was adopted and adorned with theological meaning. It is now part of the liturgical churches' formal worship. Again, culture shaped theology and its practice.

As Gordon Laing has shown, monasticism—so pervasive and encompassing in the church's life during the Middle Ages—first entered Christendom by way of the Egyptian cults of Serapis and Isis. St. Anthony (A.D. 251–356), the "father" of Christian monasticism, was once an Egyptian hermit. By the fourth century, when the cults of Serapis and Isis began to decline, many of their followers found a new home in Christian monasticism. Here many of the Egyptian recluses could, apparently in a somewhat modified manner, still practice their hermitlike beliefs. [16]

Other ritualistic elements—for example, the use of incense, the monk's tonsure, and the use of white robes—adopted by Christians in the fourth and fifth centuries were borrowed and integrated into the church's worship life from surrounding cultural and subcultural milieus. A number of other

---

[14]Waldo Burchard, "Role Conflicts of Military Chaplains," *American Sociological Review* 19 (October 1954): 533, 534.

[15]Gordon Laing, "Roman Religious Survivals in Christianity," in John T. McNeil, Matthew Spinka, and Harold R. Willoughby, eds., *Environmental Factors in Christian History* (Port Washington: Kennikat Press, 1970) 89.

[16]Ibid., 87.

ritualistic practices in the church have likewise been the result of cultural accommodations.

The "Sin" of Usury. The Jews, before the Christians, definitely outlawed usury—the simple process of making money by lending money.[17] There are a number of passages in the Old Testament that clearly reject usury: Exodus 22:25; Leviticus 25:35-37; Deuteronomy 23:19; Psalm 15:5; Ezekiel 18:8, 17; Jeremiah 15:10.

The early Christian church in its twentieth canon at the Council of Elvira (A.D. 305 or 306) declared its first formal prohibition concerning usury. At the Council of Arles (A.D. 314) the twelfth canon forbade clergy, under the pain of being deposed, to take interest on money lent to someone. The Council of Nicaea in A.D. 325 was the third church council to take a stand against usury. It too barred clergy from deriving any income by lending money.[18]

Ecclesiastical opposition to usury persisted. Numerous church fathers preached and wrote against it: Tertullian, Cyprian, Lactantius, Chrysostom, Jerome, Ambrose, and Augustine. Later men like Thomas Aquinas and Luther also condemned usury. Although usury was unequivocally prohibited, ironically the monasteries were allowed to practice the despised economic art, apparently because they were defined as corporations.[19] In addition, the papacy also engaged in the practice.

During the Reformation era Martin Luther continued to echo the previous utterances of the church councils and the church fathers with respect to the "sin" of usury. Sometimes he would even cite Cato or Seneca to argue against it.[20] Luther saw usury in the same light as the sins of adul-

---

[17]Contrary to what one sometimes hears, usury did not mean charging exorbitant rates of interest. See James Parkes, *The Jew in the Medieval Community* (New York: Hermon Press, 1976) 279. Note Martin Luther saying: "When man lends money and then receives more than he lent, that is usury, and under all circumstances condemned." See his "An die Pfarrherrn, Wieder den Wucher zu Predigen," *Saemmtliche Werke,* vol. 23 (Erlangen, 1826) 283.

[18]Carl Joseph von Hefele, *A History of the Councils of the Christian Church,* trans. William R. Clark, vol. 3 (Edinburgh: T & T Clark, 1883) 145, 190, 424.

[19]James Thompson, *An Economic and Social History of the Middle Ages* (New York: Century Co., 1928) 638.

[20]Luther, "Wieder den Wucher," 283.

tery, robbery, and murder.[21] Lending money to make money was contrary to the "natural law," as he called it.[22] Three years before he died he said that the "usurer is an arch thief and a robber who should rightly be hanged on gallows seven times higher than other thieves."[23] Thus Luther's outspoken opposition to usury did not change from youth to old age. He preached against it in 1519 and as late as 1543.

James Parkes believes the early church opposed usury for three reasons: (1) it was following Jewish (Old Testament) practices; (2) it had a great concern with helping the poor and needy by providing them with money and goods as a work of love; (3) it saw no need or value in a laissez-faire policy.[24] Parkes's reasons, however, are only plausible if usury had been confined to the Hebrews and the pre-Renaissance period of the church. But it was not! In the ancient world there was a widespread culture of opposition to usury that was not confined to the Hebrews. Plato, the Greek philosopher, condemned usury in his *Republic* and also in the *Laws*. Aristotle denounced it in his *Rhetoric,* in his *Nicomachean Ethics,* and in his *Politics.* The Roman writer, Cicero, warned his son about money lending in *De Officus* 1. Cato saw money lending as dishonorable in his work *On Agriculture* 1.

The "evils" of lending money to make money even preoccupied a small number of American Lutherans, namely the conservative Lutheran Church–Missouri Synod. In the 1860s its president, C. F. W. Walther, simply regurgitated what Luther said some 300 years earlier. The taking of interest money, said Walther, was contrary to the nature of Christianity, and banking institutions were an abomination ["*Greuel*"] to God.[25]

Walther's culturally outdated views—which he erroneously thought were given by God, independent of any cultural *Sitz-im-Leben*—were soon overpowered by the cultural forces of American capitalism. The biblical

---

[21]Martin Luther, "Temporal Authority: To What Extent It Should Be Obeyed," *Luther's Works,* vol. 45, ed. Walther I. Brandt (Philadelphia: Muhlenberg Press, 1962) 115-16.

[22]Martin Luther, "Trade and Usury," *The Christian in Society* 2, *Luther's Works,* vol. 45, ed. Walther I. Brandt (Philadelphia: Muhlenberg Press, 1962) 292.

[23]Martin Luther, "On the Jews and Their Lies," *The Christian in Society* 4, *Luther's Works,* vol. 47, ed. Franklin Sherman (Philadelphia: Fortress Press, 1971) 121.

[24]Parkes, *Jew in the Medieval Community,* 279-80.

[25]C. F. W. Walther, *Die Wucherfrage* (St. Louis, 1864) 56.

references that the church fathers, Aquinas, and Luther cited in opposition to usury today are either not known, overlooked, or reinterpreted. Today most, if not all, mainline denominations—including such conservative groups as the Lutheran Church–Missouri Synod and others—see nothing wrong with usury, now called interest income. In fact, now the Lutheran Church–Missouri Synod pays interest monies to individuals who lend money to its church-building extension fund so that new congregational facilities might be constructed. What better example is there to illustrate that culture shapes theology?

Slavery. Benjamin Rush once said that there was no idea so absurd that it could not be supported by some biblical passage. To illustrate Rush's observation, as well as show how culture shapes theology, one needs only to look at what theologians once taught and preached regarding slavery.

The cultural acceptability of slavery among the ancients already was woven into the theology of the Hebrews. In his discussion of Old Testament ethics, John L. McKenzie says that among the Hebrews "slavery [was accepted] without question or reservation."[26] Says McKenzie again: "In Israelite law the killing of a slave was not murder."[27] In the Christian Era slavery persisted as an acceptable social institution, and only occasionally was a contrary voice raised. One such voice was that of Gregory of Nyssa (fourth century) who said in his *Homily IV on Ecclesiastes* that slavery was evil. But for the most part, however, the church fathers only urged the lords or slave owners to provide better treatment, "but they did not in any way see the human disgrace of slavery as such."[28] Speaking clearly of early Christianity, Stephen Benko and John O'Rourke assert: "It never challenged the institution of slavery as such, nor did it exert any influence on Roman attitudes. . . . I Peter 2:19 even demands obedience to cruel masters on grounds that suffering is pleasing to God."[29] So it is not surprising to read that in 1487 Pope Innocent VIII accepted a gift of slaves from Queen

[26]John L. McKenzie, "The Ethics of the Old Testament," in John Cumming and Paul Burns, eds., *The Bible Now* (New York: Seabury Press, 1981) 81.

[27]Ibid., 90.

[28]Hayes Van der Meer, *Women Priests in the Catholic Church: A Theological Investigation,* trans. Arlene Swidler and Leonard Swidler (Philadelphia: Temple University Press, 1973) 84.

[29]Stephen Benko and John O'Rourke, *The Catacombs and the Colosseum* (Valley Forge: Judson Press, 1971) 110.

Isabella of Spain, or that in 1548 Pope Paul III granted all men and clergy the right to keep slaves.

In the United States, people who questioned slavery were accused by ecclesiastical leaders of rejecting the authority of the Bible.[30] The defenders of "Christian" slavery cited passages such as Leviticus 25:44-46, Matthew 8:9-13, Luke 17:7-10, 1 Corinthians 7:20-24, Ephesians 6:5-8, and 1 Timothy 6:1-2. Alexander McCain (who spoke to the General Conference of the Methodist Protestant Church in 1842) argued in his "Slavery Defended from Scripture: Against Attacks of the Abolitionists" that slavery was designed by God "to be perpetuated through all time . . . and to sustain the great claim of subordination, so essential to the Divine, as well as all human governments."[31] Still others asserted that American slavery "spread the blessings of Christianity" to what was called "a degraded race."[32]

Slavery in the days of the Hebrews, Greeks, and Romans was not racially based.[33] However, racism to some degree might have been present when the Israelites were told to enslave their neighboring nations, as recorded in Leviticus 25:44-46. For the most part, the linkage between slavery and race began in earnest by the mid-fifteenth century, often referred to as the era of modern slavery.[34]

The perpetuation of slavery—culturally practiced for centuries—received renewed support from theologians as they saw direct biblical legitimacy in linking slavery to the black race. The so-called curse of Ham in Genesis 9:20-27 made black slavery "God-pleasing." This section of Genesis—filled with ambiguities and complexities—curses Canaan, the son of Ham, for something his father did to Noah. The curse of Canaan for centuries became known as the curse of Ham in theological circles. Ham's children were cursed to blackness and slavery, a conclusion that can be traced back to the rabbinic

---

[30]H. Shelton Smith, Robert T. Handy, and Lefferts A. Loetscher, *American Christianity,* vol. 2 (New York: Scribner's, 1963) 177.

[31]Cited in James Buswell III, *Slavery, Segregation and Scripture* (Grand Rapids: Eerdmans, 1964) 17-18.

[32]See *The Southern Literary Messenger* (January 1835).

[33]William Linn Westermann, "Slavery and the Elements of Freedom in Ancient Greece," in Moses I. Finley, ed., *Slavery in Classical Antiquity* (New York: Barnes and Noble, 1960) 1-32.

[34]James Pope-Hennessy, *Sins of the Fathers: A Study of the Atlantic Slave Traders, 1441-1807* (New York: Alfred A. Knopf, 1968).

commentary *Bereshith Rabbah,* a work that was begun in the second century and completed by the fifth.[35] By the latter part of the fourth century, Pseudo-Ambrose (Ambrosiaster) used the curse of Ham to explain slavery to some Christians (see his *Epistolam B. Pauli Ad. Colossenses).*

While the curse of Ham provided theological legitimation to enslave the black race, and while it was compatible with the cultural pervasiveness of centuries of slavery, it was by no means compatible with Genesis or the biblical account itself. The biblical record portrays Cush—another of Ham's sons—as the progenitor of the African nations (Ethiopia), not Ham or his cursed son Canaan. The latter was the ancestor of the Canaanites, a white people.

Yet in spite of the fact that there was no biblical basis for linking black people to slavery, a vast array of clergy and professional theologians in all American denominations preached and taught this racist theology. Even after the American Civil War, high-status theologians—prejudiced by the culture of racism—kept telling their "flocks" that the black person was doomed to slavery because of the curse of Ham. It was a matter of "Thus saith the Lord."

The enslavement of American black people, said one Virginian, was "agreeable to the order of Divine providence."[36] Some even resisted the Christianization of the slaves because black people were seen as soulless, and others feared that the gospel would free them.[37]

The culture of slavery that helped give rise to slavery— reputedly derived from the Bible—also led to other inhumane definitions and treatment of black slaves. Some, like Richard Jobson, who refused to buy black slaves, apparently because of the "enormous Size of the virile member of the Negroes," saw such perceptions of the black male, for example, as further evidence that the curse of Ham was real for black people.[38] Others, like Ariel (pseudonym for Buckner B. Payne), said blacks were nonhumans and that the tempter of Adam and Eve was a black talking beast.[39]

---

[35]Gene Rice, "The Curse That Never Was (Genesis 9:18-27)," *Journal of Religious Thought* 29 (1972): 5-27.

[36]Trevor Bowen, *White Right* (New York: Harper, 1934) 110.

[37]Buswell, *Slavery,* 29.

[38]Thomas Browne, "Pseudoxia Epidemica," in Geoffrey Keynes, ed., *The Works of Sir Thomas Browne,* vol. 3 (London, 1928) 232-46.

[39]Ariel, *The Negro: What Is His Ethnological Status?* (Cincinnati, 1867) 45-46.

Still others treated the black slaves inhumanely. The Society for the Propagation of the Gospel in Foreign Parts (founded in England) branded slaves with hot irons for identification purposes.[40] Many black slaves had spurs jammed into their mouths, salt and pepper rubbed into wounds, half a foot chopped off, and some were slowly burned with fire.[41]

Even those who were Christianized were not humanely treated, not even in church services. Not only were black slaves forced to sit in separate sections of the church, but their pews were often inferior in quality and appearance.[42] Such discrimination—as in so many other instances—was not without theological justification. For instance, the Lutheran Synod of Tennessee in 1866 said that "owing to the plainly marked distinctions which God had made between us and them [blacks] . . . there ought to be separate places of worship, and also separate ecclesiastical organizations."[43]

While the curse of Ham biblically legitimated the enslavement and mistreatment of blacks, theologians and clergy—influenced by the cultural acceptability of slavery—also saw yet another "biblical" reason for the legitimacy of slavery. That reason was the doctrine of original sin. Greek (Aristotelian) culture—some 300 years before Christ—said people were slaves "by nature" (see Aristotle's *Politics*). If by nature all people were born sinful, as the doctrine of original sin stated, then it seemed logical for some theologians (e.g., Thomas Aquinas) to argue that some people were destined to be slaves because of original sin. (Conveniently, these theologians failed to ask why not everyone was destined to slavery, if all were born with original sin.) Over decades and centuries, the relationship between slavery and original sin became so firmly established that "one could not," says David Brion Davis, "begin to assert the universal sinfulness of slavery without questioning the doctrine of original sin."[44]

Nevertheless, some protests were raised against the evils of slavery, even concerning the inherent sinfulness of the "peculiar institution." The

---

[40]Pope-Hennessy, *Sins of the Fathers,* 78.

[41]David Brion Davis, *The Problem of Slavery in Western Culture* (Ithaca: Cornell University Press, 1966) 472.

[42]Raymond Bost, "The Reverend John Bachman and the Development of Southern Lutheranism" (Ph.D. thesis, Yale University, 1963) 125.

[43]*Minutes of the Evangelical Lutheran Tennessee Synod* (Statesville NC, 1866) 16-17.

[44]David Brion Davis, *The Problem of Slavery in the Age of Revolution, 1770–1823* (Ithaca: Cornell University Press, 1975) 44.

Wesley brothers in the 1770s advocated freedom for black slaves, saying they feared God would depart from the Methodists if they persisted in upholding slavery.[45] The Reverend Albert Barnes in 1857 argued: "Nowhere in the New Testament is the institution [slavery] referred to as a good one, or a desirable one."[46] In 1864 the United Presbyterian Church published a book, *The Bible against Slavery,* condemning the unjust social and economic aspects of slavery. Here and there other opposing voices were occasionally uttered by individuals and groups. Some also lamented and despised the little freedom the blacks possessed in nineteenth-century America.

For the most part, however, the opponents (abolitionists) were ignored; often they were ridiculed and maligned. C. F. W. Walther, the Missouri Synod Lutheran who had his reservations about usury, approved slavery, saying the abolitionist, who held slavery to be sinful, was a "child of unbelief and its corollaries: rationalism, deistic philanthropism, pantheism, materialism, atheism, and a brother of modern socialism, Jacobinism, and communism."[47] Ten years earlier Josiah Priest used similarly strong words in condemning the abolitionists. According to him, abolitionism was "a withering blighting curse, a pestiferous excrescence upon the body politic, a hideous deformity, begotten by the father of lies, born of the mother of harlots, and nursed by the bloody hand of vile misanthropy; its breath is pestilences and death, its practical operations the destruction of all domestic tranquility and social order, of all peace, friendship, and good will amongst men."[48] The Reverend Edwin T. Winkler, who held an honorary doctor of divinity degree and editorship of the *Alabama Baptist,* decried the decline of slavery by writing: "The Negroes here, as in Africa, are adepts in stealing." He also said: "The [black] children were once controlled by the master through the parents, or were managed directly by him when they became old enough to be employed in the field. Now they are permitted, for the most part, to act as they please. The father cannot govern them; for he is himself but a child."[49]

---

[45]H. Shelton Smith, *In His Image, But . . . Racism in Southern Religion, 1780–1910* (Durham: Duke University Press, 1972) 37.

[46]Albert Barnes, *The Church and Slavery* (Philadelphia: Parry and McMillan, 1857) 42.

[47]Carl F. W. Walther, "Vorwort," *Lehre und Wehre* 9 (February 1863): 34.

[48]Josiah Priest, *Bible Defense of Slavery* (Glasgow KY: W. S. Brown, 1853).

[49]Edwin T. Winkler, "The Negroes in the Gulf States," *International Review* 1 (September 1874): 585.

Today, racist practices, once approved and advocated by the leaders of the churches, are rejected by all reputable theologians and laypeople, especially since the civil rights legislation of 1964. But why? Was it because of urgings from within the church? Hardly! Rather, it was because the culture at large had shifted to an antislavery and antiracist posture. So once again, the evidence looms large that the culture had shaped the theology of the churches.

Onanism and Birth Control. I shall cite one more example of culture shaping theology. For centuries theologians fulminated against the so-called sin of Onanism, derived from the account in Genesis 38:8-10. Onan's married brother died. Thus, according to the Levirate law (then practiced among the Persians, Indians, Babylonians, Hebrews, and other societies), Onan was obligated to marry his brother's widow, in spite of his already being married. Onan was to sire and raise sons for his departed brother. This polygamous custom was a patriarchal device to ensure that the deceased brother's property and lineage would go to male heirs. But Onan for some reason refused to take the ancient Levirate law seriously. Whenever he sexually cohabited with his sister-in-law, he practiced coitus interruptus. For this behavior the Genesis account says, "God slew him."

For centuries Jewish and Christian theologians cited the Onan incident as evidence to condemn contraception, especially coitus interruptus. Rabbi Johanan (third century A.D.) said: "Whoever emits semen in vain is deserving of death; as it is written: '[What Onan did] displeased the Lord, and He slew him' " (*Niddah* 13a). Augustine in the early fifth century saw Onan's act as wrong because it prevented offspring (*Adulterous Marriages* 2.12). Luther, a former Augustinian monk, called Onan's coitus interruptus "a most disgraceful sin . . . far more atrocious than incest or adultery."[50]

Catholic and non-Catholic theologians continued to cite the Onan incident in their oppositions to contraception right into the second half of the twentieth century. Father Joseph S. Duhamel wrote in the early 1960s: "My personal opinion is that the detestable thing for which he [Onan] was slain by God was mainly, if not exclusively, the sin of contraception."[51] In 1930 Pope Pius XI, in his papal bull *Casti Connubii* said that "intercourse even

---

[50]Martin Luther, "Lectures on Genesis," *Luther's Works,* vol. 3, ed. Jaroslav Pelikan and Walter A. Hansen (St. Louis: Concordia Publishing House, 1965) 20.

[51]Joseph Duhamel, *The Catholic Church and Birth Control* (New York: Paulist Press, 1963) 21.

with one's wife is unlawful and wicked when contraception of the off-spring is prevented. Onan, the son of Juda, did this and the Lord killed him for it." A Protestant commentary on Genesis— published as late as 1953— said that Onan's act was "perhaps the very deadliest of all sins as effecting [*sic*] definitely body, mind, and soul.''[52]

For hundreds of years, every society's ethics and morality were influenced by agrarian values. In an agrarian society children were a vital economic asset. They were the instruments of survival, both in terms of labor and in terms of providing for their aged parents. Widespread birth control would have produced economic disaster. Thus the agrarian culture shaped an anti–birth control mindset within the ancient societies, including Judeo-Christian theology. Only in recent years, with the shift from an agrarian economy to one that is highly industrialized, in which children have become an economic liability in urbanized society, has the culture begun to shape a theology that accepts or even approves of birth control. Whereas the Onan reference once was seen as prohibiting birth control, now most theologians no longer see it as applicable to the issue of contraception. The passage never did apply to the issue of birth control, but the agrarian culture influenced theologians to such a degree that they sincerely thought it did.

Cafeteria Theology. Behavioral scientists (for example, Joseph Klapper) have shown that human perception is very selective.[53] Theological interpretation is no exception. Throughout history various theological formulations have demonstrated a considerable amount of selectivity. Much of that selectivity was prompted by cultural or subcultural influences on the religious leaders.

When Luther, for instance, cited biblical references in opposition to earning interest money, he did indeed have some clear references from the Old Testament on his side. For example, Deuteronomy 23:19 reads: "You shall not lend upon interest to your brother, interest on money, interest on victuals, interest on anything that is lent for interest." What he tragically overlooked, however, was the fact that the Old Testament commands against usury reflected an agrarian culture where such prohibitions were needed and made good economic sense. But in Luther's day the agrarian culture had already evolved

---

[52]W. H. Griffith Thomas, *Genesis: A Devotional Commentary* (Grand Rapids: Eerdmans, 1953) 365.

[53]Joseph Klapper, *The Effects of Mass Communication* (New York: Free Press, 1960).

into a more complex economic structure, one in which, increasingly, people no longer lived off the soil, as they once did in the days of Moses and the Old Testament prophets. The new, nonagrarian business ventures required interest money in order to obtain capital for producing goods and services. Without interest money, the new and fledgling capitalist system was doomed. Most borrowers of money were not the poor or ailing, as they were when the Old Testament usury prohibitions were issued. Prompted by ancient values, and a corresponding hermeneutic, Luther selected passages—as if ordering in a cafeteria—to castigate usury. In doing so, he overlooked Jesus' Parable of the Talents in Matthew 25:14-30, which commended individuals for industrious ingenuity.

Luther's attempt to apply ancient usury ethics from the agrarian cultural era to his day is a good illustration of cultural conflict, where a given cultural practice or belief from one time or place conflicts with values of another cultural time or place. It might also be seen as an example of cultural lag, where one or more cultural elements have changed more rapidly in relationship to some related cultural values. Whether Luther's defense of ancient usury prohibitions reflects a cultural lag or not, it does clearly demonstrate that he, like countless other theologians, failed to recognize that his theology and the Bible have a *Sitz-im-Leben*.[54] This realization by biblical interpreters—particularly those who are ultraconservative in their theological opinions—has frequently been lacking.

The cultural influence behind the cafeterialike hermeneutics is operative in some of the following examples. Paul, in writing his first and second letters to the Corinthian church, said at the end of each letter: "Greet one another with a holy kiss!" Both remarks are in the imperative mood. But how many Christians follow Paul's directive today? Virtually none! Western, especially American, cultural values strongly deter strangers and nonrelatives from kissing one another in public, particularly so in the case of males kissing males. So culture has moved millions of modern Christians to ignore a clear, unambiguous biblical command. There is no exegetical difficulty in those two passages whatsoever; the problem is totally cultural.

---

[54]Yet there were times when Luther did seem to know that the Mosaic theology of the Old Testament era did not apply to people of his day. On one occasion he said: "Moses' law cannot be valid simply and completely in all respects with us. We have to take into consideration the character and the ways of our land when we want to make or apply laws and rules." See his "On Marriage Matters," *The Christian in Society, Luther's Works,* vol. 46, trans. and ed. Robert Schultz (Philadelphia: Fortress Press, 1967) 291.

In 1 Corinthians 11:5 Paul, influenced by his culture, says a woman who prays or prophesies with her head uncovered "dishonors her head; it is the same as if her head were shaven." But what theologian—even an ultraconservative one—tries to enforce Paul's assertion today by having women in a Sunday morning worship cover their heads? None, of course. Again, culture has moved theologians and church leaders to ignore a clear biblical directive. Moreover, why is the command for women to have their heads covered less important than the next reference in 1 Corinthians 14:34: "The women should keep silent in the churches. For they are not permitted to speak, but should be subordinate, as even the law says."

Is the reference to keeping women silent in church easier to enforce ecclesiastically because there is still considerable sexism in society as a whole, whereas the veiling of women today would be too much of a cultural anachronism? It would appear to be so. The wearing of a veil or some other mandatory head covering in Western society has been discontinued for centuries, but the right for women to speak in public is a relatively recent phenomenon. It was not until the 1850s that Susan B. Anthony became the first woman to speak at the New York State Teachers Convention. Her public speaking shocked even the women who made up two-thirds of the convention.[55] When Catherine Beecher in the 1840s toured New England to promote female education, her speeches had to be read in public by her brother.[56] For a woman to speak in public was seen as rude and insubordinate; it was going against God's design for man. And, of course, the right for American women to express themselves at the ballot box did not occur until 1920 when the Nineteenth Amendment of the Constitution of the United States became law.

---

[55]Una Stannard, *Mrs. Man* (San Francisco: Germain Books, 1977) 58.

[56]Ibid., 57.

CHAPTER 3

WOMAN AS "EVIL"

One need not study the cultural and religious views pertaining to woman for very long to discover that she has been closely linked to evil. For instance, in Western cultures the female's "place" commonly is on the left side of the male. When viewed superficially, the left side may not mean anything to most people. Yet there is a significant meaning in this position. The word "left" comes from the Latin word "sinister," a word that today means wicked or evil. The male side is "right," namely, proper or correct.

Linking woman to evil is especially evident in the labels that are applied to her vis-à-vis man. Derogatorily, she is called a "shrew." The man, however, is seen as "shrewd." In the English language there is no male counterpart for "bitch," which is so readily applied to an unliked woman. Even the expression "son of a bitch," a derogatory remark directed at some unliked man, really blames his mother for his behavior. The word "witch," another female designation, never has a wholesome meaning. The male counterpart "wizard," though, fares considerably better. A man is complimented when someone in the business world calls him a "financial wizard." A sexually loose woman is referred to as a "slut" in common parlance. No such word exists for a sexually deviant male. To call him a "playboy" or "stud" is to compliment him.

Associating woman with evil has been an age-old practice, deeply embedded in many cultures. The Greek poets were fond of equating woman with evil. Euripides (480–406 B.C.) has Hippolytus say: "Why hast thou given a home beneath the sun, Zeus, unto woman, specious curse to man?" (*Hippolytus* 616-17). Andromache, a woman who had internalized the values of men, says: "Strange that God hath given to men slaves for the venom of all creeping pests, but none hath ever yet devised a balm for venomous woman, worse than fire or viper'' (*Andromache* 269-73). Here we have a good example of how women have internalized male prejudice.

Another influential Greek poet, Aeschylus (525?–456 B.C.), in his play *The Suppliant Maidens* has the chorus declare: ''Evil of mind are they [women], and guileful of purpose, with impure hearts, recking naught of altars more than carrion birds'' (748-49). Aristophanes (448?–385? B.C.) in one of his plays writes: ''I grieve for the sake of womankind, because the men account us all to be sly, shifty and rogues'' (*Lysistrata* 10-11). The male chorus of this ancient Greek play declares: ''For women are a shameless set, the vilest of creatures going'' (368-69). In another of Aristophanes' plays, he has women rightly criticizing Euripides for insulting them. One of the women makes bold: ''But there is he [Euripides], calling us double-dealers, false, faithless, tippling, mischief-making gossips, a rotten set, a misery to men'' (*Thesmophoriazusae* 394-95). The great epic writer, Homer, has Agamemnon saying: ''One cannot trust women'' (*The Odyssey* 11).

Among the Romans, we find Tacitus (first century A.D.) picturing women as dominating and cruel (*Annuals* 3.33). Seneca, a philosopher and statesman, saw human anger as a womanish and childish weakness (*De Ira* 1.19.3). And Juvenal, the satirist, said: ''There is nothing a woman will not permit herself to do'' (*Satires* 6.457).

Views like these, in which women were seen as ''dominating,'' did not minimize the ancient male belief (noted in chapter 1) that men were naturally aggressive, active, and dominant and that women no longer were passive and submissive. Not at all. They only show that the negative views that so many men had (and still have) of women sometimes led to contradictory statements.

She Introduced Evil

The ancient, agrarian-oriented males not only pictured woman as evil, but they were also convinced beyond a shadow of doubt that she introduced evil into man's world. This belief was widespread and well established in the ancient past.

Greek men believed evil was introduced by the beautiful woman, Pandora. Zeus, the chief of the gods on Mount Olympus, became angry with Prometheus for stealing fire from the gods and giving it to mortal men. In his anger Zeus ordered Hephaestus (the god of smiths) to fashion a creature

WOMAN AS "EVIL"   41

that would be both beautiful and evil, one that every male would desire. So he created woman. Hephaestus succeeded so well in fashioning his creation that even the Olympian gods marveled at her beauty. The Graces adorned her with necklaces; Aphrodite gave her qualities of love; the Seasons crowned her with flowers and golden animals; Hermes gave her an inquisitive mind and a deceitful nature. Her final gift was a large, sealed jar, given to her by Zeus. Possessing all these gifts, she was named Pandora (the all-gifted one) and sent to Earth. Hephaestus presented her to Epimetheus, who was warned by his brother, Prometheus, not to accept a gift from Zeus. Epimetheus, however, could not comprehend how a creature so beautiful and gifted could possibly be a source of evil. He not only accepted her; he took her as his wife.

Soon after the wedding, Pandora became curious about the contents of her sealed jar. Unbeknownst to her, the jar was filled with evil by Zeus. She broke the seal and lifted its lid, permitting all the evils (sorrow, sickness, pain, loneliness, envy, hatred, greed, fear, distrust, deception, and so forth) to escape. Only one item remained, having become caught under the rim of the lid. This item was Hope, which Pandora was unable to get back into the jar.

This Greek myth, which goes back to about 800 B.C., explained the existence of evil among human beings. But the myth explained more than this: it also made woman—her beauty notwithstanding—responsible for the numerous evils that plagued the human race. Hesiod, the Greek poet (eighth century B.C.), wrote that Zeus "made the beautiful [woman] evil to be the price for the blessing" (*The Theogony* 585).

Whether it is the Pandora myth or some other account, it soon becomes evident that blaming woman for ushering in evil is an ancient male explanation. The Genesis account has Adam saying: "The woman whom thou gavest to be with me, she gave me fruit of the tree, and I ate" (Genesis, 3:12). Jesus Ben Sirach, the author of Ecclesiasticus (an apocryphal book of the Old Testament, second century B.C.), says: "From a woman sin had its beginning and because of her we all die" (Ecclesiasticus 25:24). Other rabbis, before, during, and after Christ, explained the one-time Hebrew custom of having women walk in front of the corpse at a funeral in this manner: "Because they [women] brought death into the world." Woman's menstruation was explained: "Because she shed the blood of Adam . . ." (*Genesis Rabbah* 17:8).

Another religious document of Hebrew literature, *The Book of Adam and Eve,* even blames Eve for humans and animals feeling enmity toward each other. *The Book of the Secrets of Enoch* (written in the first century A.D.) bluntly faults Eve for having brought death into the world: "And I put sleep into him and he fell asleep. And I took from him a rib, and created him a wife, that death should come to him by his wife." Similar statements can be found in other Hebrew literature that reflect the male's negative view of woman between 200 B.C. and A.D. 500.

Where and when the male picture of woman as the one who introduced evil, even death, really began may never be known for certain. One thing, however, is quite evident, namely, that this male myth not only appears to be virtually as old as ancient recorded history, but it is also deeply woven into the cultural fabric of many societies. As noted above, the Greek men had their Pandora myth; and, somewhat similarly, the Hebrew rabbis, and the church fathers after them, had Eve, whom they saw as having ushered in evil.

Some analysts such as Elizabeth Gould Davis and Wolfgang Lederer, on the basis of data that are weak, believe that the male version of laying the origin of evil at the doorstep of woman is the result of a "patriarchal revolt" that occurred in the Near East around 2,000 B.C. Prior to that revolt the world supposedly had gynocracies that had no reason to fault their own sex for the introduction and personification of evil.[1] Salvatore Cucchiari sees a gender revolution having occurred sometime between 3,500 and 12,000 B.C. This revolution ushered in prejudices against woman, such as the idea of her having introduced evil.[2]

The Greeks and the Hebrews were not alone in believing that woman introduced evil. Far across the seas in North America, some men also mythologized about woman having introduced evil. The Blackfoot Indians had a legend saying that the Creator, Na-pi (meaning old man), created man and woman out of clay, but it was the folly of woman that introduced death.[3]

---

[1]Elizabeth Gould Davis, *The First Sex* (Baltimore: Penguin Books, 1971) 133-47. Wolfgang Lederer, *The Fear of Women* (New York: Grune and Stratton, 1968) 153-68.

[2]Salvatore Cucchiari, "The Gender Revolution and the Transition from Bisexual Horde to Patriarchal Band: The Origins of Gender Hierarchy," in Sherry B. Ortner and Harriet Whitehead, eds., *Sexual Meanings: The Cultural Construction of Gender and Sexuality* (New York: Cambridge University Press, 1981) 31-80.

[3]Andrew Lang, *The Making of Religion* (London: Longman, Green and Company, 1898) 260.

The Montagnais Indians in Quebec, at least as far back as 1634, explained the introduction of evil by a myth that closely resembled the Greek Pandora myth.[4]

Seeing woman as the originator of evil became a theme thoroughly woven into much of Christian theology, primarily through the pronouncements of the early church fathers. Irenaeus (second half of the second century), whose name means "the peaceful one," did not see woman as very peaceful. He argued, "Having become disobedient, she [Eve] was made the cause of death, both to herself and to the entire human race" (*Against Heresies* 3.22). Irenaeus's words sound remarkably similar to those of Jesus Ben Sirach, cited earlier. Tertullian (A.D. 150?–220?), a contemporary of Irenaeus whom the German scholar Leopold Zscharnack called "an enemy of women," was even harsher than Irenaeus. Said Tertullian: "You [Eve] are the devil's gateway . . . you are the first deserter of the divine law. You are she who persuaded him whom the devil was not valiant enough to attack. You destroyed so easily God's image, man. On account of your desert, that is death, even the Son of God had to die" (*On the Apparel of Women* 1.1). The Alexandrian church father Origen (A.D. 184–254) asserted: "What is seen with the eyes of the creator is masculine, and not feminine, for God does not stoop to look upon what is feminine and of the flesh" (*Selecta in Exodus* 17.17). Ambrose (A.D. 340–397), the spiritual tutor of St. Augustine, believed that "she [Eve] was first to be deceived and was responsible for deceiving the man." Again, he said, "She [Eve] . . . made her husband a partaker of the evil of which she was conscious" (*Paradise,* chaps. 4 and 6). St. Chrysostom (died in A.D. 407) preached: "The woman [Eve] taught once, and ruined all" (*Homilies on Timothy* 9). In another homily he reportedly said: "What else is woman but a foe to friendship, an unescapable punishment, a necessary evil, a natural temptation, a desirable calamity, a domestic danger, a delectable detriment, an evil of nature."[5] Still another church father, St. Augustine—who after his "playboy" days were over, bequeathed his sexual fears and hangups to Christian theology for centuries following him—said that the Flood was caused by woman. He asserted: "And the calamity [the Flood], as well as

---

[4]Henry Youle Hind, *Explorations in the Interior of the Labrador Peninsula,* vol. 1 (London: Longman, Roberts, and Green, 1863) 61.

[5]Cited in Heinrich Kramer and James Sprenger, *The Malleus Maleficarum,* trans. Montague Summers (New York: Dover Publications, 1971) 43.

the first [the Fall], was occasioned by woman, though not in the same way"
(*The City of God* 15.22). Isidore of Seville (A.D. 560–636), an archbishop
in the church, stated that Eve meant life or disaster—life because she was
the origin of being born; disaster because through her transgression she became the cause of dying (*Etymologiae Libri* 7.5). Martin Luther, a one-
time Augustinian monk, believed that because of what Eve did, "we can
hardly speak of her without shame."[6]

The Temptress

The patriarchal culture of the agrarian societies not only saw woman
as having introduced evil into the once-sinless and evil-free world, but
woman also personified evil by her very existence or presence, especially
as a temptress. The Talmud records Rabbi Johanan saying: "When the ser-
pent copulated with Eve, he infused her with lust" (*Yebamoth* 103b).
Woman's "lust" was not confined to herself. Rather her lust was something to which she frequently exposed man, distracting him from noble
pursuits. It was Eve's role as temptress that caused Adam to fall, and ever
since then woman has tempted man. The "seductive" nature of woman
prompted the Hebrew rabbis to enjoin men: "Do not converse much with
women, as this will ultimately lead you to unchastity" (*Nedarim* 20a).

The Hebrew Talmud provides still another example of how the female
body was seen as a constant temptation to the male. Rabbi Hisda taught:
"A woman's voice is a sexual excitement" (*Berakhoth* 24a). Women's
voices were not the only concern, for "if one gazes at the little finger of a
woman, it is as if he gazed at her secret place" (*Berakhoth* 24a). Rabbinic
theology also did not permit a man to walk behind a woman. Why? Because the woman would tempt the man sexually. It was for this reason the
rabbis maintained: "Better go behind a lion than behind a woman." Again,
"Whoever crosses a river behind a woman will have no portion in the future world. . . . Because the woman in crossing will naturally lift up her
dress" (*Berakhoth* 61a).

The seductive nature of woman was perceived as very real to the Hebrew male. This seductiveness, to a large degree, lay behind the veiling of
women so that men and even angels would not be attracted to their uncovered hair or face (*Testament of Reuben* 5).

---

[6]Martin Luther, *Lectures on Genesis*, vol. 1 of *Luther's Works*, trans. George Schick,
ed. Jaroslav Pelikan (St. Louis: Concordia Publishing House, 1958) 118-19.

The stereotypic view that man had of woman as a seductive siren is apparent in other rabbinic literature. One man was never to be left alone with two women, whereas one woman could be left with two men (*Kiddushim* 4:12). The pious rabbis apparently thought men had more reason to fear seduction than women had to fear rape. Yet, one must ask: which is more likely to occur?

The above rabbinical utterances, and others, concerning the so-called seductive character of woman evolved during what is commonly known as the oral-law period of the rabbinic era. The rabbinical teachings, however, did not develop in an environment of cultural isolation; rather, they were shaped by cultural definitions and formulations of neighboring societies. One need only read some of the Babylonian and Assyrian literature regarding sexist perceptions of women to see the similarities and parallels found in Hebrew writings. For instance, the Babylonian culture that preceded the rabbinical writings pictured woman as a seductive siren: "Woman is a pitfall, a hole, a ditch."[7]

The Greeks, another society that influenced the theology of the rabbis, expressed similar sexist prejudices regarding the perceived sexual passions and evil nature of women. Aristotle taught that women lacked the natural capacity for virtue (*Rhetoric* 1361A, 5). Euripides said: "Women were the best devisers of evil" (*Medea* 408–409). Greek men, says Philip Slater, were terrified of women, whom they perceived to be statuesque, passionate, and seductive.[8]

Sexist expressions and definitions from Roman culture undoubtedly also helped shape the rabbinic view of woman. Ovid wrote: "In us [sexual] desire is weaker and not so frantic; the manly flame knows a lawful bound" (*The Art of Love,* 1.281-82). At another time, Ovid also said that the man in pursuit of sexual love was to "corrupt her with promises, corrupt her with prayers; if she be willing, you will gain your end with ease" (*The Art of Love* 1.355-56). These latter words are hardly complimentary to the human male. Yet, it was always the woman that was the sexual temptress. Juvenal, in one of his satires, declared that a mother could not give her daughter wholesome instruction. Said he: "Teach her decent ways, when

---

[7]W. G. Lambert, *Babylonian Wisdom Literature* (Oxford: Clarendon Press, 1960) 147.

[8]Philip Slater, *The Glory of Hera: Greek Mythology and the Greek Family* (Boston: Beacon Press, 1968) 164.

there's no decency in her? Not a chance in the world. Like mother, like daughter'' (*Satire* 6.240-41).

East of the Greeks and Romans, in India, men viewed women similarly: "It is the nature of women to seduce men . . . for that reason the wise are never unguarded. . . . For women are able to lead astray in this world not only a fool, but even a learned man" (*Laws of Manu* 2.213-15).

The sexist cultural values and definitions regarding the "seductive" nature of woman were soon absorbed by the postapostolic Christians after the first half of the second century, especially by the church fathers and countless clergy following them. Most of the church fathers were reared in the Greco-Roman culture. Moreover, they were well versed in the literature of the Greek and Roman poets and philosophers. Thus it is not surprising to read perceptions of woman that are very similar to those whom the church fathers in other contexts sometimes called "pagans." Clement of Alexandria (A.D. 150–215) believed and taught that every woman should blush because she is a woman. He also said that a veiled woman would not cause a man to fall into sin (*The Instructor* 3.11). Tertullian wrote, "It is right that the face which was a snare to them [angels] should wear some mark of a humble guise and obscured beauty" (*Against Marcion* 5.8).

Penny Schine Gold has shown that in France during the twelfth century the Cistercian abbots barred women from coming in contact with men in the monastery because they were seen as potential contaminators.[9] Even the "female religious," or the woman who chose to remain a virgin, "never escaped the male assumption that she was a danger, a source of contamination, and that, in addition, her sex made her incapable of resisting the temptation of any contact with the male or the world."[10]

The Harlot

Given centuries of cultural biases, let someone utter the word "harlot" or "prostitute" and what comes to mind? A man will think of a woman assuming that role. Even many women think that way. The biased male culture has socialized them to the same level of stereotypic thinking so that

[9]Penny Schine Gold, *The Lady and Virgin* (Chicago: University of Chicago Press, 1985) 84.

[10]Eleanor C. McLaughin, "Equality of Souls, Inequality of Sexes: Woman in Medieval Theology," in Rosemary Radford Ruether, ed., *Religion and Sexism: Images of Women in Jewish and Christian Traditions* (New York: Simon and Schuster, 1974) 244.

they, like the men, fail to see that the word "prostitute" can also refer to male behavior.

Throughout history the word "harlot" or its synonym, "prostitute," has not only been seen as a female role, but it has also been equated with evil. One finds this emphasis in religious and nonreligious literature. I shall cite only a few religious instances.

In the Old Testament "harlot" or "harlotry" is frequently used to convey the evils of Israel's unfaithfulness to Jehovah. It is also used as a symbol of injustice. Isaiah assailed Jerusalem: "How the faithful city has become a harlot, she that was full of justice" (Isa. 1:21). Ezekiel and Jeremiah make similar use of the term.

By equating female harlotry with spiritual unfaithfulness and social evils, the Old Testament prophets reflected a cultural heritage that predated the existence of Israel. Long before Jeremiah accused the Israelites of harlotry, the ancient Near Eastern cultures of Assyria, Babylon, and Akkadia had assigned the lowest social value to the female harlot or prostitute. She was often more despised than the menial slave.[11]

A harlot in the patriarchal cultures of the Near East was "evil" because she was not faithful to one man, her lord. Sexual unfaithfulness especially was abhorrent to the patriarchal mind-set because it placed the entire patriarchal inheritance system in jeopardy. The patriarch gave his name and property only to *his* son(s), not to the son(s) of some other father. A child born as a result of a wife's unfaithfulness was totally the property of the intruding male. Such a child was not considered to be the wife's, not even half hers. Woman—the ancients believed—only provided the "soil" in which man planted his seed as a miniature child for nine months. (This understanding of conception is known as the homunculus concept. See chap. 5 for an extended discussion of this ancient agrarian belief and the role it played in shaping the definition of woman as inferior to man.)

The unfaithful wife was evil, not merely because she shared her body with another man, but because her sexual act had the potential of bringing another man's child into her husband's domain. So serious was the offense of an unfaithful, adulterous wife that the ancient Romans, for example, paraded the unfaithful wife in the nude on a donkey, allowing the crowds to

---

[11]Vern L. Bullough, *The History of Prostitution* (New York: University Books, 1964) 22.

attack her with insults, hoots, and expectoration. After being publicly hu-
miliated, she was assigned to a permanent life of prostitution.[12] The Babylonians drowned the adulterous wife, and the Hebrews stoned her to death.

In spite of the fact that the female prostitute symbolized evil in patriarchal societies, harlotry or prostitution was not really condemned or outlawed. This stance was operative in the Old Testament too. The patriarchal
Hebrews—who were apparently influenced by preceding and surrounding
cultures—uttered an occasional reprimand against it, but "the normal
practice was to accept prostitution as a fact of life without any moral condemnation," says Bullough.[13] That there was no social or theological disgrace attached to the occasional act of consorting with a prostitute is plainly
evident in the account of Genesis 38, where Judah is described as having
a sexual encounter with his daughter-in-law, Tamar, who had disguised
herself as a harlot.

Previously she had been rebuffed by Judah's son, Onan, who refused
to impregnate her, even though he appeared to have enjoyed the pleasure
of having sexual intercourse with her. Whenever he consorted with her, he
practiced coitus interruptus. Evidently, he did not want to assume the levirate obligation of siring offspring for his departed brother, Er, who was
Tamar's deceased husband. The Genesis writer says that God slew Onan,
apparently for not assuming his levirate responsibilities. After Tamar's
second husband also died, Judah apparently saw some evil omen accompanying this woman. He did not want his third son to take her as a wife,
so he told Tamar to remain a widow.

Having thoroughly accepted the patriarchal legitimacy of the ancient
levirate custom, Tamar did not let herself be put aside. She was determined to leave an offspring for the lineage of Judah. So one day she threw
off her garment, veiled herself as a prostitute, and then stationed herself at
the roadside, where she knew Judah would pass by on the way to shear his
sheep. Judah, not recognizing her as Tamar, thought her to be a harlot.
Before she could proposition him, he asked her: "Come, let me come into
you." In addition, Judah said he would pay her by giving her a baby goat.
Tamar responded by asking for some items of surety until she received the

[12]Paul Lacroix, *History of Prostitution*, vol. 1, trans. Samuel Putnam (New York: Cov-
ice, Friede Publishers, 1931) 217-19.

[13]Bullough, *Prostitution*, 25.

young goat. So before she let Judah have his pleasure, he had to give her his signet, with its cord, and his walking stick.

Later when Judah sent his servant with a young goat to Tamar, the servant returned with the message that the roadside was not the site of any harlot. This report disturbed Judah because others would hear that he did not pay the harlot for her service. Therefore, it was not socially or theologically disgraceful for the Hebrew male to interact sexually with a prostitute, but it was socially disrespectful not to pay her. In fact, Judah was prepared to let Tamar keep his signet and cane so that no one would think he was unfair.

The Judah-Tamar incident not only reveals the acceptability of prostitution among the ancient Hebrews; it also portrays the existence of a double standard. No regret, no shame, no sin was felt by Judah for having had sex with a prostitute.

When Judah heard that his daughter-in-law Tamar had played the role of a prostitute and had become pregnant, he became morally indignant and demanded that she be executed as an adulteress. Her act was a violation of the patriarchal ethic. So as she was brought out to be executed, she revealed Judah's pledge items and announced that it was he who had impregnated her. When Judah saw that Tamar had not become pregnant by someone outside his family, her "evil" act immediately evaporated. The patriarchal ethic had not been violated, and that is what mattered most. Prostitution, or sex outside of marriage, that did not affect the patriarchal value system was of no moral concern.

When a son was warned by his father, the patriarch, about obtaining sexual pleasure from a prostitute, it was not that prostitution was condemned per se, but that such behavior—especially if engaged frequently—would eventually result in financial, social, physical, and personal ruin.[14] Note the Sumerian father telling his son: "Night and day I am tortured because of you [my son]. Night and day you *waste* [emphasis added] in pleasure."[15] The Egyptians warned young men: "Look not upon her [the harlot] when she comes, and know her not, She is the vortex of deep water, whose whirling is unfathomable."[16] Very similar are the words of King Solo-

---

[14]Lederer, *Fear of Women*, 161.

[15]Samuel Noah Kramer, *History Begins at Sumer* (Garden City: Doubleday, 1956) 15.

[16]James H. Breasted, *A History of Egypt* (New York: Charles Scribner's, 1959) 85.

mon, a man who had 700 wives and 300 concubines. He cautioned his sons: "Do not stray into her [the prostitute's] paths; for many a victim has she laid low" (Proverbs 7:24).

The evil of prostitution in agrarian-patriarchal cultures did not lie in the fact that it violated a monogamous relationship. The wide practice and acceptance of multiple wives and concubines plainly shows that such was not the case. One reason for seeing prostitution as evil lay in the potential of making a man a prodigal. Proverbs 7 makes this very clear. Another possible reason for defining prostitution as evil was that many prostitutes apparently were married. Proverbs 7:19 has a prostitute saying: "My husband is not home; he has gone on a long journey." For a wife to have sex outside marriage was always evil because it was an act of adultery, even though such behavior was not necessarily wrong if done by the husband.

Among the ancients, adultery was always defined in terms of the woman's marital status, not the man's. A married man could only commit adultery when he had sex with another man's wife. If he sexually consorted with an unmarried woman, he could not be charged with adultery. It was only the wife who had to be faithful to the husband. Robert Graves and Raphael Patai, two Hebrew scholars, say it well when they note that there was "no stigma attached in early Judea to men who lay with prostitutes— so long as these were not the property of a husband, or father, or in a state of ritual impurity."[17] The Hebrew attitude toward prostitution may have been derived from the Hittite culture, because among the Hittites men were not punished for cohabiting with prostitutes.[18]

When the prodigal theme relative to prostitution was not stressed, the Hebrew attitude toward the world's "oldest profession" was quite neutral, even accepting. The story of the harlot Rahab is a case in point. Joshua sent two spies to Jericho. They lodged ("lay") with Rahab, the prostitute. Rahab hid the spies as the men of Jericho came to take the spies captive. In return for Rahab's protection, the spies promised to protect her, her father, mother, brother, and sisters. The spies told Joshua their experiences in Jericho, including their having lain with Rahab. Joshua showed no dismay or discontent with their prostitute connection. In fact, he promised to keep the commitment made to Rahab by his spies. When the Hebrews de-

---

[17]Robert Graves and Ralph Patai, *Hebrew Myths: The Book of Genesis* (Garden City: Doubleday and Company, 1964) 246.

[18]E. Neufeld, *The Hittite Laws* (London: Luzac and Company, 1951) 54-56.

stroyed Jericho, they did indeed rescue Rahab and her family. After the rescue she "dwelt in Israel to this day," according to Joshua 6:25. There is no evidence that she ceased being a prostitute.

Centuries of male-dominated cultures pictured woman as the evil one in the prostitution syndrome. It was always the woman's fault when men obtained sexual favors from her. Theologians and nontheologians alike blamed the woman for ruining men. Martin Luther, for instance, said: "I would have such venomous, syphilitic whores broken on the wheel and flayed because one cannot estimate the harm such filthy whores do to young men who are so wretchedly ruined and whose blood is contaminated before they have achieved full manhood."[19]

Although theologians blamed women for the evils of prostitution, ironically there were times when they saw prostitution serving a beneficial service. St. Augustine, even though he condemned prostitution, once said: "Take away the prostitutes from human life, and everything will be disturbed by lust" (*De Ordine* 2.4.12). Thomas Aquinas essentially echoed Augustine by saying that prostitutes served a social function. They were like city sewers in that they drained off the filth and stench. And Martin Luther also sounded like Augustine when he said in 1543 that the hasty removal of the bordellos in the city of Halle might do more harm than good. "It may cause injury to the good if this evil [prostitution] is eradicated prematurely."[20]

Woman as Witch

Woman not only introduced evil into the one-time male "paradise"; she not only personified evil in the sex act as a temptress; she not only played the role of harlot; she was also a witch. Even today the word "witch" betrays the force and fury of male bigotry.

Although the Old Testament said, "You shall not permit a witch to live" (Exod. 22:18), it was not until the Middle Ages that theologians became obsessed with the thought that witches were to be hunted, tortured, and burned at the stake. Witches were seen as one prominent way in which the "evil" of woman manifested itself. The paranoid attitude that the church's leaders developed toward witches apparently was absorbed from

---

[19]Martin Luther, *Luther: Letters of Spiritual Counsel,* trans. and ed. Theodore G. Tappert (Philadelphia: Westminster Press, 1955) 293.

[20]Ibid., 294.

the cultures of pre-Christian Europe. The Germanic tribes, the Visigoths, and the Lombards all had an excessive fear of witches.[21]

This male fear led to the Council of Salzburg in A.D. 799 approving bodily torture of witches. For about 700 years after, sporadic witch hunts and persecutions occurred throughout Western Europe. Then on 5 December 1484, the fear of witches was intensified by Pope Innocent VIII's papal bull *Summis Desiderantes Affectibus*. This "Witches Bull," as it has been called, appointed two Dominican monks, Heinrich Institoris [Kramer] and Jakob Sprenger, as inquisitors to rout the "abominable heresy." These two monks wrote a 275-page book in 1486, condemning witchcraft. They called it *The Malleus Maleficarum*. Note the feminine ending of the last word in the title!

In May 1487 the theological faculty of the University of Cologne gave its approval to this Dominican work. The volume soon became a handbook on witchcraft throughout Europe, with theologians considering it to be the ultimate authority. It went through numerous printings during its 100 years of pervasive influence. It left its mark not only on theologians before the Reformation, but also on men like Luther and Calvin during and after the Reformation.

With utmost seriousness, *Malleus Maleficarum* described in graphic detail how witches dried up cows' milk, caused hailstorms, killed and ate children in the raw flesh, rode through the air, and removed men's genitals. Here is an account regarding the latter:

> In the town of Ratisbon a certain young man who had an intrigue with a girl, wishing to leave her, lost his member; that is to say, some glamour was cast over it so that he could see or touch nothing but his smooth body. In his worry over this he went to a tavern to drink wine; and after he sat there for awhile he got into conversation with another woman who was there, and told her the cause of his sadness, explaining everything, and demonstrating in his body that it was so. The woman was astute, and asked whether he suspected anyone; and when he named such a one, unfolding the whole matter, she said: "Of persuasion is not enough, you must use some violence, to induce her to restore your health." So in the evening the young man watched the way the witch was in the habit of going, and finding her, prayed her to restore to him the health of his body. And when she

---

[21]Julio Caro Baroja, *The World of Witches* (Chicago: University of Chicago Press, 1964) 49-50.

maintained she was innocent and knew nothing about it, he fell upon her, and winding a towel tightly round her neck, choked her, saying: "Unless you give me back my health, you shall die at my hands." Then she being unable to cry out, and with her face already swelling and growing black, said: "Let me go, and I will heal you." The young man then relaxed the pressure of the towel, and the witch touched him with her hand between the thighs, saying: "Now you have what you desire." And the young man, as he afterwards said, plainly felt, before he had verified it by looking or touching, that his member had been restored to him by the mere touch of a witch.[22]

Following this account, *Malleus Maleficarum* relates an incident that a Dominican priest heard in a confession. The priest is reported to have said:

One day . . . while I was hearing confessions, a young man came to me and, in the course of his confession, woefully said that he had lost his member. Being astonished at this, and not being willing to give it easy credence, since in the opinion of the wise it is a mark of light-heartedness to believe too easily, I obtained proof of it when I saw nothing on the young man's removing his clothes and showing the place. Then, using the wisest counsel I could, I asked whether he suspected anyone of having so bewitched him. And the young man said that he did suspect someone, but that she was absent and living in Worms. Then I said: "I advise you to go to her as soon as possible and try your utmost to soften her with gentle words and promises;" and he did so. For he came back after a few days and thanked me, saying that he was whole and had recovered everything. And I believed his words, but again proved them by the evidence of my eyes.[23]

Bizarre as these accounts may appear to the twentieth-century reader, they were taken as the gospel truth by individuals of the fifteenth century. Theologians, who were better educated, also believed that witches could remove and restore a man's genitals. One needs only to note Luther's words in this regard. Said he: "Next there are witches, i.e., the wicked devil's whores who steal milk, influence the weather, ride on he-goats and broomsticks, travel on clouds, shoot people, make lame and paralyze, torture children in their cradles, bewitch genitals."[24]

---

[22]*Malleus Maleficarum*, 119.

[23]Ibid.

[24]Martin Luther, "The Gospel for the Festival of the Epiphany," *Sermons II, Luther's Works,* vol. 52, ed. and trans. Hans J. Hillerbrand (Philadelphia: Fortress Press, 1974) 182.

The twentieth-century reader of *Malleus Maleficarum* may be tempted to dismiss its accounts of witchcraft (as believed by Kramer, Sprenger, Luther, and others) to be mere superstition. But to the medieval and Reformation-era theologians, witchcraft was very real. They were governed by an Aristotelian Weltanschauung. The words of the sociologist W. I. Thomas come to mind, namely when situations or phenomena are defined as real, they have real consequences. The theologians of the past had no doubt about the evil reality of witches, and so the consequences were real too.

Almost every page of *Malleus Maleficarum* points to woman as being evil and preoccupied with witchcraft. Here are a few examples as found on the pages noted after each citation:

> Therefore let us now chiefly consider women; and first why this kind of perfidy [witchcraft] is found more so in fragile a sex than in men. (p. 41)
> [W]omen are naturally more impressionable, and more ready to receive the influence of a disembodied spirit; and that when they use this quality well they are very good, but when they use it ill they are very evil. (p. 44)
> [N]early all the kingdoms of the world have been overthrown by women. (p. 46)
> All witchcraft comes from carnal lust, which is in women insatiable. (p. 47)
> [T]he devils do these things [kill children in the womb] through the medium of women, and not men. (p. 66)
> But it is common to all of them [witches] to practice carnal copulation with devils. (p.99)
> [I]n the diocese of Basel at the town of Dann, a witch who was burned confessed that she had killed more than forty children. (p. 140)
> St. Augustine speaks in his *De Civitate Dei,* Bk. XVIII, Chapter 17, where he tells of the tavern women who changed their guests into beasts of burden. (p. 174)

The fear and paranoia that gripped male theologians with reference to what they defined as witchcraft reveals a deep, subconscious fear of women on the part of men. To make this observation is not to be guilty of exaggerated Freudianism. A number of pages in *Malleus Maleficarum* clearly reveal this deep-seated fear, especially the descriptive accounts of witches removing or bewitching male genitals. Kramer and Sprenger reflected a widely held belief that witches often attacked the human male where he was most vulnerable: his genitals. In response to the question whether witches can, with the help of "devils," actually remove a man's penis or whether they do so by some glamour or illusion, the authors responded: "There is no doubt that certain witches can do marvellous things with regard to male organs" (p. 58). Again, "Witches are not content with such practices in respect of the genital member, . . . but they can frequently take away the generative power itself, so that a woman cannot conceive, and a man cannot perform the act even when he still retains his member" (p. 80). But one of the most bizarre beliefs with regard to the power of witches was the conviction that they were able to collect penises and place them in birds' nests. Note the words of the *Malleus*: "And what then is to be thought of those witches who in this way sometimes collect male organs in great numbers, as many as twenty or thirty members [penises] together, and put them in a bird's nest, or shut them up in a box, where they move themselves like members, and eat oats and corn, as has been seen by many and is a matter of common report?" (p. 121).

The perceived evil of feminine witchcraft was present in still another bizarre belief, namely that women as witches would assume the role of *succubi*, demons who would lie on the bottom during the sex act. Those lying on top were called *incubi* (p. 112).

In addition to the male fear that women gave themselves to the incubi, male theologians also feared that young maidens often lost their virginity to the incubi. Again, *Malleus Maleficarum* says: "Incubus devils will not only infest those women who have been generated by means of such abominations, or those who have been offered to them by midwives, but that they try with all their might, by means of witches who are bawds or hot whores, to seduce all the devout and chaste maidens in that whole district or town" (p. 114).

Virginity was highly valued in patriarchal societies. A virgin was to be deflowered by her husband only. Thus if a young maiden could lose her virginity through witchcraft, it was indeed a threat to the male ego and the patriarchal definition of reality. So it is not surprising that Kramer and Sprenger wrote the way they did about the patriarchal understanding of witches and their perceived powers.

As one studies the history of witchcraft, it soon becomes apparent that by comparison men were rarely accused of being sorcerers or wizards. Apparently, the devil in the majority of instances preferred to employ women to accomplish his evil goals. Thus in the minds of men, witches are women. This belief stretches back to ancient Sumeria (c. 3,000 B.C.). The Sumerian socioreligious culture said that devils often took on the form of a woman.[25]

Witchcraft not only threatened the male ego; it also threatened the entire patriarchal system with its accompanying economic, social, and ecclesiastical power structure. Thus it was not enough to condemn verbally the evils of feminine sorcery. The heresy of witchcraft had to be expunged. In order to accomplish this goal, the *Malleus* lay on the bench of every judge, on the desk of every magistrate, says Montague Summers.[26] Why? So judges and magistrates would indeed recognize the gravity and depravity of this feminine evil and punish the guilty with all severity. The latter portion of *Malleus Maleficarum* instructs judges about the kind of sentences that they were to hand down to apprehended witches. One such instruction reads: "She shall be condemned to the fire as convicted"(p. 249).

Upon reading the theologically sexist pronouncements concerning women as witches in *Malleus Maleficarum* of the pre-Reformation era or the statements made by theologians after the Reformation, it soon becomes evident that, except for the one reference in Exodus 22:18, it was not the Bible that shaped this sexist theology in the Western Church. Rather, centuries of institutionalized male fears developed a theology that said it was God-pleasing to persecute and even to burn witches at the stake. As Margaret Murray has aptly shown, the medieval belief in witches was essentially the remains of a pagan religion.[27]

The witchcraft hysteria that gripped European ecclesiastics resulted in hundreds of thousands of executions. Before these women were executed, they were commonly tortured. Both acts received plenty of legitimation that came from parish priests as well as from theological professors. Luther definitely had a fear of witches and did not hesitate to say that witches were "the devil's harlots and, when apprehended, are rightfully burned at the stake."[28] Calvin too preached against the evils of witches, even ad-

---

[25]Arthur Frederick Ide, *Woman in the Ancient Near East* (Mesquite TX: Ide House, 1982).

[26]Montague Summers, introduction to 1948 edition of *The Malleus Maleficarum*, trans. Montague Summers (New York: Dover Publications, 1971) viii.

[27]Margaret A. Murray, *The Witch-Cult in Western Europe* (New York: Oxford University Press, 1971 [1921]).

[28]Martin Luther, "On the Councils and the Church," *Church and Ministry III, Luther's Works*, vol. 46, trans. Charles M. Jacobs (Philadelphia: Fortress Press, 1966) 172.

vocating mass executions for all witches. "Calvin, when remodeling the laws of Geneva, preserved and fiercely prosecuted those against witches."[29]

The witch hunts, tortures, and executions that were carried out in the name of God by clergy and other ecclesiastical leaders revealed all the horrors of inhumanity imaginable. The devil and his evil angels, who manifested themselves in evil women, had to be attacked in the most brutal way known to mankind. W. E. H. Lecky recalls that iron bridles with prongs were commonly thrust into the accused woman's face. She was then chained to a wall in such a way so that she could not lie down to rest. She was frequently kept in this state for days, "while men were constantly with her to prevent her from closing her eyes for a moment of sleep."[30] These witch bridles can still be seen in some European museums, especially in Scotland.

Robert Pitcairn shows that witches were tortured also by inserting their legs in iron frames.[31] These frames were periodically heated over a brazier. Others had their legs broken daily for days on end so that more than a dozen fractures per leg were often inflicted. Still others were tortured by withholding water from them. Men believed a witch would never confess while she had water to drink. Another method was to employ the "Pricking Test." Men thought witches had certain insensitive spots. Pricks were meant to find those spots in order to prove a woman was a witch. Frequently an accused woman was stripped and searched for moles and scars that were considered to be marks of the devil. Others were searched for supernumerary teats that demons reportedly sucked to feed themselves. Frequently an accused woman was also subject to thumbscrews, leg vices, whipping stocks with iron spikes, scalding hot baths, and made to sit on a prayer stool that was covered with sharp pegs. Indeed here the words of W. E. H. Lecky come to mind: "The physical suffering of such a process was sufficient to overcome the resolution of many."[32]

T. C. Lethbridge once said, "It is a curious piece of irony that the church, which had suffered so much persecution itself, should have been the organization which treated witches with even greater brutality, and

---

[29]Pennethorne Hughes, *Witchcraft* (Baltimore: Penguin Books, 1965) 175.

[30]W. E. H. Lecky, *History of the Rise and Influence of the Spirit of Rationalism in Europe*, vol. 1 (New York: George Braziller, 1955 [1865]) 146.

[31]Robert Pitcairn, *Criminal Trials in Scotland*, vol. 1 (Edinburgh: Wm. Tait, 1833) 376.

[32]Lecky, *Spirit of Rationalism*, 146.

shows how terribly it had wandered from the teachings of its great master."[33] Thoughts like these evidently failed to stir the consciences of prejudiced men. Nor did it occur to the clergy, to whom "all the complaints
and information were made," that these torturous acts were more evil and
demonic than the imagined witchcraft of the falsely accused, defenseless
women.[34]

Often, as Carolyn Merchant has shown, the vast majority of women
accused of witchcraft—for example, in England—came from the lower
socioeconomic level of society.[35] William Monter has found similar evidence with regard to witch-hunts in France and Switzerland.[36] Apparently
the devil found it easier to make witches out of women who came from the
lower socioeconomic segment of society.

The atrocities that were committed by the church's leaders in their fa-
natical witch-hunts did not become more humane with the Protestant Reformation. Lecky says, "The history of witchcraft in Protestant countries
differs so little from its history in Catholic ones, that it is not necessary to
dwell upon it at much length."[37] George Rosen argues similarly: "The
Reformation brought no change in the persecution of witches. If anything,
the situation became worse."[38]

Both sides—Catholics and Protestants—were influenced by centuries
of similar cultural prejudices against women. Both parties accepted the
sexist belief that woman introduced evil into the male world and both believed that the devil worked through witches to perform many of his evil
deeds. Thus there was no difference in how Protestants or Catholics treated
alleged female sorcerers. To question the commonly held beliefs and practices concerning witchcraft was unheard of. Therefore, when Reginald Scot
published his *Discoveries of Witchcraft* in 1584, in which he argued that
witchcraft was full of "erroneous novelties and imaginary conceptions,"

[33]T. C. Lethbridge, *Witches* (New York: Citadel Press, 1968) 16.

[34]Pitcairn, *Criminal Trials,* 50.

[35]Carolyn Merchant, *The Death of Nature: Women, Ecology and the Scientific Revolution* (San Francisco: Harper & Row, 1980) 138.

[36]E. Williams Monter, *Witchcraft in France and Switzerland* (Ithaca: Cornell University Press, 1976) 118.

[37]Lecky, *Spirit of Rationalism,* 119.

[38]George Rosen, *Madness in Society* (Chicago: University of Chicago Press, 1968) 12.

he took a heretical stand. The book was a counterblast to the widely accepted *Malleus Maleficarum*. But, given the cultural mind-set of that day, Scot's arguments were soon belittled. In direct response to Scot, none other than King James I (who authorized the King James Bible) wrote a book entitled *Demonologie*. The king defended the ancient beliefs and practices concerning witchcraft as they applied to women. His mind-set was similar to that of the Hebrew rabbis who preceded him by 1500 years. The latter taught that "Women are addicted to witchcraft" (*Yoma* 83b).

Why, one is compelled to ask, was woman seen in so many ancient cultures as the one who introduced evil, as being a temptress, a harlot, and as a witch who served as the devil's handmaiden? This question is particularly significant when one considers that it is woman who brings gentleness and tranquility to the male world. It is the woman who for centuries served as midwife, healer, and comforter, trying to calm the physical and psychological evils of the world. Impartial observation of history shows woman to be more of an opponent of evil than is man. Women traditionally have not planned and waged wars, attempting to annihilate one another across centuries as have men. Women often have tried to serve as peacemakers, an inclination that even the sexist Greek poet Aristophanes (in the fourth century B.C.) conveyed (sort of tongue-in-cheek) in his drama *Lysistrata*. Throughout history women have been more devout and religious in comparison to men. Mountains of social research have corroborated this phenomenon. Yet the male myth that sees woman being the initiator and representative of evil persists.

If becoming sexually aroused is evil, then woman is not the evil one here either. It is not the woman who is quickly aroused sexually. Even a man defined as "handsome" does not excite a woman in the same way as a "beautiful" woman will excite the average man. Yet it is she who has been (and still is) seen as the temptress or the harlot, about whom men like to make negative, sexually slanted jokes.

Biosocial Resentment and Envy

Woman alone gives birth to children, nurses them, and is their primary nurturer in their early, formative years. Moreover, the social and economic roles that commonly have been defined as the province of the male have never been performed exclusively by men. Subconsciously, men are aware of this fact. Even in hunting and gathering societies, woman is not a passive entity. She not only plants and gathers food, but she also contributes to the processing of the food that is brought home. Anthropological research also shows that there are numerous instances where woman even participates in the actual hunting and killing of animals. In short, the male has never had an exclusive social or economic role that woman could not participate in too. Nor does the man have a monopoly in his highly treasured possession of physical strength, because some women are larger and stronger than some men.

In the presence of woman's monopolistic functions, men unconsciously developed a biosocial resentment as a defense mechanism. This phenomenon did not reveal itself in simple, undisguised resentment or envy, but in the form of picturing woman as evil. Awareness of woman's monopoly was psychologically repressed and overshadowed by institutionalizing and socially legitimating male values that had the effect of creating self-fulfilling prophecies. Women were defined and treated as evil, a definition that in turn compelled many women to assume inferior positions and roles, such as harlot, temptress, and witch. Moreover, women internalized the values pertaining to these roles as being "feminine," appropriate to their sex.

The natural superiority of woman, to employ Ashley Montagu's expression,[39] not only shows itself in childbirth and early nurturance activities, but it also demonstrates itself in the sex act. The male definition of woman as weak and inferior is suddenly transferred to the man as he completes the sex act, where he must give and extend a part of his anatomy—his penis—to the woman. Moreover, after he has reached orgasm, he temporarily loses his potency. But not so with the woman. She does not give; she only receives. Nor can she become sexually impotent. Thus it is not difficult to understand how such effects have aroused the human male's resentment, especially since he for hundreds of years defined himself as biologically and socially superior to woman.

Womb Envy. Man's resentment or envy also shows itself in other ways. Some fifty years ago, Felix Boehm observed in his psychoanalytic practice that many men envied and unconsciously emulated the act of childbirth. He called the phenomenon "parturition envy."[40] Karen Horney said es-

[39]Ashley Montagu, "The Origin of Subincision in Australia," *Oceania* 7 (1937): 193-207.

[40]Felix Boehm, "The Femininity Complex in Man," *International Journal of Psychoanalysis* 11 (October 1930): 456.

sentially the same thing four years earlier when she, in 1926, rejected Sigmund Freud's concept of "penis envy." Instead, she discovered that boys and men were often given to "womb envy." They showed "envy of pregnancy, childbirth, and motherhood, as well as of the breast and the act of suckling."[41]

The observations by Horney and Boehm have been corroborated by Bruno Bettelheim's empirical research. He found that boys in the Orthogenic School in Chicago admitted being envious of girls having breasts and mothers being able to have babies. The boys said they disliked the girls as a result and even dreamed of cutting off the girls' breasts as well as tearing out their vaginas.[42] A few years prior to Bettelheim's study, Edith Jackson in 1950 found that boys wished they could someday give birth to a child.[43]

These findings in part remind one of the Greek male writers who wrote about Zeus, a male god, who gave birth to Athena from his head and to Dionysus from his thigh. Similarly, the ancient Hittites said their god, Kumarbi, gave birth to two children.

The human male's desire (whether conscious or unconscious) to be a mother, says Una Stannard, shows itself in the social practice of assigning the man's surname to the wife and children borne by her. It is also evident when a man says, "She is the mother of my children."[44]

Another example of womb envy is the practice of couvade, a birth rite in which the father of the newly born child imitates various birth activities that commonly are experienced by the mother. Among the Basques, for example, the father confined himself to bed, requiring care while the mother, who had just given birth, resumed her household duties. In other societies the father, along with the mother, refrains from work and certain foods, just before and after the birth of the child.

The couvade has not been an isolated cultural practice. Moreover, it seems to be as old as recorded history. Historians and social scientists have found it in various parts of Europe, Africa, India, China, and South America. It was also found among some of the Greco-Romans before the birth

---

[41]Karen Horney, "Flucht aus der Weiblichkeit," *Internationale Zeitschrift fuer Psychoanalysis* 12 (1926): 360-74.

[42]Bruno Bettelheim, *Symbolic Wounds* (New York: Collier Books, 1962).

[43]Edith Jackson, "Development of the Wish for a Child in Boys," *Psychoanalytic Study of the Child* 5 (1950): 139-52.

[44]Una Stannard, *Mrs. Man* (San Francisco: Germain Books, 1977) 328.

of Christ. In the third century B.C. the Greek writer Apollonius Rhodius
spoke about the Tibareni people: "When wives bring forth children to their
husbands, the men lie in bed and groan with their heads close bound; but
the women tend them with food, and prepare child-birth baths for them"
(Argonautica 2.1011). The ancient historian Diodorus of Sicily wrote about
the Corsicans in the first century B.C.: "When the wife is about to give birth
she is the object of no concern as regards her delivery, but it is her husband
who takes to bed, as though sick, . . . for a specific number of days, feign-
ing that his body is in pain" (Diodorus of Sicily 4.14).

The male desire to be a mother has also been reported by relatively recent anthropological research. D. M. Hayano found that the natives of the
Eastern Highlands of New Guinea believed a man's pregnancy (distension
of the abdomen) occurs by the fetus entering through and up the penis[45];
and Anna S. Meigs has found institutionalized beliefs regarding male
pregnancy among the Hua in the highlands of Papua in New Guinea.[46]

In the light of these data, it is difficult to deny the reality of womb envy
among many men. Moreover, it is quite possible that all men to some degree harbor within their subconscious the desire to be a mother. In a male-
dominated culture, such a possibility will obviously be quickly denied by
most men. Their sexist socialization experience does not allow for such
thinking, and when it occurs, it must be quickly suppressed. The cultural
definition of "maleness" in this instance does not permit men to be honest
in their most private thoughts. Thus when men deny the concept of womb
envy, it does not necessarily—even among the scoffers—rule out its subconscious or conscious existence.

Menstruation Envy. Individuals who have given little or no thought to
the psychosocial dynamics of the human male's thinking and behavior
probably find it difficult to believe that men in a number of societies show
their envy of women in still another way, namely by imitating menstruation. For instance, some natives in central Australia, the Qatu in the New
Hebrides, the Abelam, the Arapesh, the Hua, and Wogeo Islanders of New
Guinea—to cite only some—have socially institutionalized the various male
menstruation practices. Among some men menstruation is imitated by

---

[45]D. M. Hayano, "Misfortune and Traditional Political Leadership among the Tuana
Awa of New Guinea," *Oceania* 45 (1974): 18-26.

[46]Anna S. Meigs, "Male Pregnancy and the Reduction of Sexual Opposition in a New
Guinea Highlands Society," *Ethnology* 15 (October 1976): 393-407.

making incisions of the penis, often slitting the penis on the underside from the orifice to the scrotum. This incision not only produces a flow of blood in the genital area, which makes the man think he is like a menstruating woman, but it also causes loss of control in his urine flow, thereby forcing him to squat like a woman when he has to urinate. Ian Hogbin, in his book *The Island of Menstruating Men,* shows that the Wogeo men even see themselves as superior to women as a result of their penile incisions.[47] Why superior? Well, women bleed by nature whereas men voluntarily cleanse (bleed) themselves! It is truly amazing to see what painful efforts some men will resort to in order to convince and unknowingly delude themselves, all with the aim of being superior to woman.

Nor are the Wogeo men the only ones who have institutionalized their envy of female menstruation. The Hua men, mentioned above in connection with womb envy, engage in bloodletting of their lower back and buttocks to imitate menstruation, according to Meigs.[48] Other institutionalized practices of men imitating menstruation have been noted by K. E. Read, M. R. Allen, and S. Lindenbaum.[49]

Psychosocial Projectionism

The fact that men have almost universally pictured woman as evil appears to be the result of what social scientists call social projection, specifically psychosocial projection. Relative to defining woman as evil, it is the process whereby men unknowingly attribute their own thoughts, attitudes, characteristics, and feelings to women.

Every honest man knows that it is he, not woman, who has sex on his mind when he sees an attractive or "sexy" woman. "It [the man's penis] rises at the sight or even at the thought of a woman. This helplessness on the part of the man to control his most cherished possession . . . infuriates him to the point of wishing to punish the sex that has such power over what

---

[47]Ian Hogbin, *The Island of Menstruating Men* (San Francisco: Chandler, 1970).

[48]Meigs, "Male Pregnancy," 393-407.

[49]K. E. Read, "Nama Cult of the Central Highlands of New Guinea," *Oceania* 23 (1954): 1-25; M. R. Allen, *Male Cults and Secret Initiations in Melanesia* (Melbourne: Melbourne University Press, 1967); S. Lindenbaum, "Sorcerers, Ghosts, and Polluting Women: An Analysis of a Religious Belief and Population Control," *Ethnology* 11 (1972): 241-53.

belongs to him.''[50] His weaknesses have been (and still are) unconsciously projected onto woman.

The one-time custom of requiring woman to be veiled becomes more understandable when one learns that a woman's hair and face commonly stirred a man's sexual desires in the ancient era. In this regard, citing the Jews as an example, Raphael Patai says: "The libido of the ancient Jews was readily aroused. . . . Women, when out of doors, had to wear garments which modestly hid the contours of their bodies, but even so men were forbidden to walk behind a woman in the street lest they be aroused to licentious thought or act.''[51]

The patriarchal norm of veiling women was not confined to the Jews. The church fathers also enjoined women to be veiled, and even gave reason why. Clement of Alexandria (A.D. 150–215) said woman is to "be entirely covered, unless she happens to be at home. For that style of dress is grave and protects from being gazed at . . . nor will she invite another to fall into sin by uncovering her face" (*The Instructor* 3.11). Tertullian (A.D. 160–220?), the Latin church father, said every woman should wear a veil or all men would be vulnerable when seeing her unveiled (*On the Veiling of Virgins* 16).

There is considerable irony in noting that it always was the woman's fault when a man was sexually aroused by her not being veiled. The ancient men were completely unaware that they were projecting their weaknesses onto women. Centuries of cultural sexism not only blinded men from seeing their deceptive and fallacious thinking, but in the case of the church fathers their erroneous thoughts were also woven into Christian theology. It was a theology that was believed to have come from God himself. Here the irony became tragedy!

Sex and its enjoyment, to most of the church fathers, was sinful and evil, even in the married state. Arnobius of Sicca (died A.D. 327?) saw married sex as filthy and "horrid" (*The Case against the Pagans* 4.19, 21). He thought the human sex organs were unsightly. Jerome wrote: "The activities of marriage itself, if they are not modest and do not take place under the eyes of God as it were, so that the only intention is children, are filth and lust" (*Epistle to Galatians* 3). Sexual intercourse, he said, was unclean and sinful (*Against Jovinianus* 1.20). In this same work he also declared: "The wise man should

---

[50]Davis, *First Sex*, 152.

[51]Raphael Patai, *The Jewish Mind* (New York: Charles Scribner's Sons, 1977) 500.

love his wife with cool discretion. . . . Nothing is worse than to love your own wife as if she were your mistress" (*Against Jovinianus*). St. Ambrose, the mentor of Augustine, contended that although marriage was good, it nevertheless contained something that made even married people blush, namely the sex act (*Concerning Virginity*).

Augustine was even more explicit on the sinfulness of sex in marriage. It became sinful after the Fall. Before the Fall the human male would have been able to impregnate his wife without a penile erection and without sin! Said he: "The man, then [before the Fall], would have sown the seed, and the woman received it, as need required it, the generative organs being moved by the will, not excited by lust." Again, he made bold to say: "So in those days [before the Fall] the wife could receive into the womb her husband's seed without rupture of the hymen" (*The City of God* 14.24, 26). Augustine said the erect penis was the instrument that passed on the first sin (*Sermons* 151:5). Sex, even in marriage, was a concupiscent act. Even Pope Gregory the Great (died in A.D. 604), who had more humane views regarding women than many other church fathers, once stated: "The carnal company between man and wife is for the sake of the procreation of children, not satisfaction of lusts" (Bede's *Opera Historica* 1.145). And as late as the twelfth century, Albertus Magus said in his *De Bono*: "Continence in marriage is a good condition, but not an excellent one, since it is more excellent in widowhood and most excellent in virginity."

Defining sex as evil, however, did not make it disappear from daily life. In fact, the desire for sex did not even leave those who condemned it. The mere presence of women kept that "sinful" desire alive. Thus the church fathers tended to see sex as woman's fault. For instance, St. Jerome (A.D. 342–420), who experienced numerous sexual temptations, once said women, especially those who assumed leadership roles in religion, were "miserable, sin-ridden wenches" (*Epistola* 132). Another time he boldly stated: "The devil . . . can always deceive man through woman" (*Homily 73 on the Psalms*). St. Augustine, like Jerome, argued: "I know nothing which brings the manly mind down from the heights more than a woman's caresses and the joining of bodies without which one cannot have a wife" (*The Nature of the Good*, chap. 18). St. Ambrose saw Eve's seductiveness as the origin of all evil and lies (*De Paradiso* 10.46, 47). And more than 100 years before Ambrose, Augustine, and Jerome one finds Gregory of Thaumaturgus (who was converted by Origen) saying that "a person may find one man chaste among a thousand, but hardly ever a woman" (*Metaphrasis in Ecclesiasten*, 7:29).

In the context of psychosocial projectionism, Bernard Prusak said it very well when he recently wrote: "Puzzled by the power of the sexual drive and the mysteries of generation and birth, authors in a patriarchal society killed two birds with one stone. They explained the *de facto* existence of evil by indicating woman as its source, and thereby also had both a theological explanation and the justification for maintaining the cultural facts of male dominance and female subservience."[52]

Projecting the human male's sexual weakness onto the woman seems to have been a large factor in shaping the physical structure of the Hebrew synagogue. The Hebrews, before and during the rise of early Christianity, did not permit women to worship with men in the same area of the synagogue. Women were segregated by a *michetza,* a separate room or gallery, behind and below the space occupied by men.[53] The Hebrew men were distracted by the visual presence of women, so they compelled them to take their place in a different part of the synagogue, a practice that apparently began with the era of the second temple, according to Solomon Schecter.[54] Gail B. Shulman says: "The idea of separate quarters for women in the synagogue arose not as a result of woman's ability to participate in the service, but to put away these distractions, these impure but nonetheless tempting beings."[55]

Since many of the early Christians worshiped frequently and regularly in Jewish synagogues, the practice of sexually segregating women from men during worship activities undoubtedly left its mark on many of the early church fathers. The synagogue practice not only reinforced the male projection process of seeing woman as the evil seductress, but it also in part helped shape a sexist theology among the church fathers in the postapostolic age.

Some Comments

In defining and perceiving woman as "evil," men have for centuries been engaged in one of the biggest deceptions recorded in human history.

---

[52]Bernard P. Prusak, "Woman: Seductive Siren and Source of Sin? Pseudepigraphal Myth and Christian Origins," in Ruether, *Religion and Sexism,* 97.

[53]Patai, *Jewish Mind,* 365.

[54]Solomon Schecter, *Studies in Judaism* (Philadelphia: Jewish Publication Society of America, 1911) 316.

[55]Gail L. Shulman, "View from the Back of the Synagogue," in Alice L. Hageman, ed., *Sexist Religion and Women in the Church* (New York: Association Press, 1974) 158.

It is a deception that still lingers in the minds of many men and male-dominated languages. This deception has been so strong that not only have men believed it for centuries (and many still do), but they have even succeeded in getting countless women to accept the myth that woman has been the primary introducer of evil.

Defining and seeing woman as evil was not just confined to statements. Public art and statues depicted this biased conception of woman as well. One very revealing work of this kind can be seen on the south side of the Cathedral of Worms in West Germany. Attached to the exterior of the cathedral, about thirty feet above the ground, is the statue of *Frau Welt* (worldly woman). Her nude body portrays beauty from the front, but her back is covered with ulcers, scorpions, and worms. Such was the medieval concept of woman. She was beautiful indeed, but that beauty was inseparable from evil.

Given that modern behavioral-science concepts were unknown to men in days gone by, it is perhaps understandable why they were not able to see their view of woman as erroneous. But what about today and tomorrow? Will thoughtful, justice-seeking men—including theologians—seriously attempt to remove all vestiges of woman being perceived and defined as evil? If they want to be serious conveyors of the truth, they have no choice but to help expose the processes of negative psychosocial projection (womb envy and psychosocial resentment) that not only have created a false understanding of woman but a false understanding of man as well. One does not socially or psychologically enhance one's own worth by demeaning that of another. As a social creature, the human male has virtually endless opportunities for engaging in complementary roles vis-à-vis woman. He need not engage in negative projection that has its basis in agrarian-patriarchal cultures. The human being, unlike the nonhuman, is not governed by blind instincts, but has the capacity for creative acts and roles. Thus men are not limited to deriving meaning from biologically related functions. Men need not see women as their competitors or enemies because women have biological abilities (e.g., giving birth and breast feeding a child) that men do not possess. Woman is not the opposite sex to man, nor is man the opposite sex to woman. Rather, each is complementary to the other. The sooner this concept is understood the sooner the picture of woman as evil will fade out of existence. Womb envy, biosocial resentment, and negative projections have no place in harmonious relationships between man and woman, who have been created as equals.

CHAPTER 4

WOMAN AS "INFERIOR"

Virtually every culture has in some way defined woman as biologically, intellectually, socially, or spiritually inferior to man. Defining woman as inferior with respect to these characteristics has been widely believed and institutionalized, in varying ways, in most of the world. Even in democratically oriented cultures, woman is still in many ways treated as man's inferior.

The Biological "Inferiority" of Woman

Aristotle, who left his abiding mark on Western culture and also on many Christian theologians, definitely saw woman as a biologically inferior being. Said Aristotle, "The female is as it were a deformed male" (*Generation of Animals* 2.737a:27). Aristotle's mentor, Plato (427?–347 B.C.), resorted to his reincarnation beliefs to argue that woman was inferior. He declared: "Men who proved themselves cowardly and spent their lives in wrong doing were transformed, at their second incarnation, into women" (*Timaeus* 91a).

Hippocrates, the famous Greek physician who preceded Aristotle by almost 100 years, contended that the male fetus began moving in his mother's womb at three months after conception, whereas the female fetus moved at four months. Some 500 years later, the anatomist Galen, who influenced centuries of Western biological and medical thought, said: "The female is less perfect than the male" (*On the Usefulness of the Parts of the Body* 14.6-7).

Belief in the biological inferiority of woman and the superiority of man was not confined to the Greeks. The Romans also believed in the slower fetal development of the human female. Pliny the Elder said that fetal movement begins forty days after conception for the human male and at

ninety days for the female.[1] The Talmud says the male fetus begins moving at forty-one days and the female at eighty-one.[2] This erroneous and
sexist belief, which today causes college students to laugh when they hear
it mentioned for the first time, was tenaciously held to and taught for
hundreds of years as a fundamental conviction regarding the inferiority of
woman. In other words, her inferiority already showed itself in her mother's womb. Thus Thomas Aquinas in the thirteenth century not only repeated the Talmud's fallacy of fetal movement, but he also regurgitated
Aristotle's prejudice about woman as a deformed male. Unhesitantly, he
wrote and theologized: "Woman is defective and misbegotten."[3]

The ancients rarely depicted the biological or physical inferiority of woman
in the light of her possessing less physical strength or in the light of her being
smaller in stature. She was inferior biologically to man because she lacked
the male's physical perfection, which in part was linked to the erroneous belief that the female fetus developed more slowly in the womb. That was how
the culture of men defined woman as a biologically inferior creature.

Like many other false definitions, this one was not without "evidence"
that made that faulty definition look factual. For instance, culture dictated that
a female was to be married by age twelve or thirteen. A wife at that age was
easily seen as inferior, especially when her husband was twenty or older. In
addition, women became pregnant frequently. High rates of pregnancy, cou-
pled with primitive or no reliable medical knowledge, resulted in high fe-
male-mortality rates during pregnancy and at the time of childbirth. Such high
death rates easily led men to conclude that women were indeed weaker than
men. In some instances the female mortality rate was accentuated because girls
were given poorer nourishment than boys, a fact recorded in the fifth century
B.C. by Xenophon in his *Constitution of the Lacedaemonians*. Even in the
Middle Ages, male infants in parts of Europe were breast-fed for periods twice
as long as female babies.[4]

[1]Roger Forbes, *The Midwife and the Witch* (New Haven: Yale University Press, 1966)
54.

[2]Julius Preuss, *Biblisch-talmudische Medizen* (Berlin: S. Krager, 1921) 451.

[3]Thomas Aquinas, *Basic Writings of St. Thomas Aquinas,* ed. Anton C. Pegis (New
York: Random House, 1948) 880.

[4]Emily Coleman, " Infanticide in the Early Middle Ages," in S. M. Stuard, ed., *Women
in Medieval Society* (Philadelphia: University of Pennsylvania Press, 1976) 55.

The relatively high mortality rates for women, vis-à-vis men, in the ancient world confirmed the simplistic belief that women were biologically inferior to men. One authority notes that the average longevity in the classical era of Greece was forty-five years for men and thirty-six years for women.[5] Another study shows tombstone evidence indicating that during the early centuries of Christendom, men outlived women by anywhere from four to seven years.[6] It was not until after the Middle Ages that woman's longevity began to rise with the appearance of an urban economy, a phenomenon that slowly began to change woman's fate.

Instead of seeing the shorter life span of woman as the result of social inequalities and institutionalized prejudice that needed correction, men saw it as confirming their belief that woman was biologically inferior to man. Male logic also argued that woman's biological inferiority was a reflection of the "natural order." And the male theologians, unknowingly influenced by their existing culture, saw women's biological inferiority as part of God's "created order." For instance, St. Albertus Magnus (thirteenth century), in his work *De Animalibus Libri,* said that woman was born from a weaker seed than man.

The biological inferiority of woman was so deeply entrenched in ancient male-oriented cultures that contrary evidence was not even noticed by learned men. They certainly must have known that the deaths of male fetuses in miscarriages outnumbered those of female fetuses. In fact, this difference was in all probability even more pronounced centuries ago, when famines were more common and the amount and quality of nutrition was less stable than today. Demographic studies show that the incidence of male fetuses experiencing prenatal death, vis-à-vis female fetuses, increases with the decline of nutritional conditions. In India, for example, where nourishment is inferior to that of the United States, the sex ratio at birth is 98.7 males to 100 females.[7] In the United States the sex ratio at birth is 105.7 males to 100 females.

---

[5]J. Lawrence Angel, "Paleoecology, Paleodemography, and Health," paper delivered at the Ninth International Congress of Anthropological and Ethnological Sciences (Chicago, 28 August to 8 September 1973). The information from Angel's paper is cited by Sarah B. Pomeroy, *Goddesses, Whores, Wives, and Slaves: Women in Classical Antiquity* (New York: Schocken Books, 1975) 227.

[6]David Herlihy, "The Natural History of Medieval Women," *Natural History* 87 (March 1978): 56-57.

[7]Ashley Montagu, *The Natural Superiority of Women* (New York: Collier Books, 1974) 85.

Research also shows that many more males than females are conceived; according to some estimates, it is about 120 to 150 males compared to 100 females. But as has just been seen, by the time of birth the number of males is greatly reduced so that in the United States it is only a fraction higher than that for females.

In addition to prenatal death rates being higher for boys, there is also the differential of the infant mortality rate (death during the first year of life). Demographic research shows about three boys dying for every two girls.

These data make it impossible to believe that women are biologically inferior to their male counterparts. Yet the belief persists, as it has for millennia. Moreover, women have all too often, and for too long, been taken in by this male myth. N. J. Berrill has said it well: "Men and boys are troublesome creatures, but being larger, stronger, and louder than the females they have succeeded in putting over the biggest bluff the earth has ever seen."[8] What is more, the bluff became imbedded into the culture of countless societies and in time shaped a theology regarding women.

The biological inferiority of woman was in part explained by a faulty biological understanding. The male fetus, it was argued, resulted from the semen that came from the father's right testicle and developed in the right side of the mother's womb. The female fetus came from the man's smaller, left testicle and developed in the left side of the mother's womb.[9] Numerous theologians believed this explanation, including Martin Luther's influential coworker Phillip Melanchthon (*De Anima* 420). This widely held belief went back at least to Empedocles and Democritus (fifth century B.C.).

Centuries of sexist cultural beliefs not only shaped the theologians' views of women as inferior; it also shaped the chauvinistic views of individuals who saw themselves as free from the "prejudices" of clergy. These individuals often have been referred to as "freethinkers." Yet, when it came to perceiving women, the freethinkers were frequently as sexist as the theologians. The forces of culture affected both groups in similar ways, at least with regard to how they viewed woman as biologically inferior to the human male. There is plenty of irony here, since neither side liked the other.

---

[8]N. J. Berrill, "Women Should Run the World," *Maclean's Magazine,* 15 February 1958, 8.

[9]George W. Corner, *Anatomical Texts of the Earlier Middle Ages* (Washington: The Carnegie Institute of Washington, 1927) 85.

The American freethinker and critic H. L. Mencken said in his book *In Defense of Women* (a title that sounds nonsexist): "The female body, even at its best, is very defective in form; it has curves and very clumsily distributed masses."[10] As is well known, Sigmund Freud saw woman as biologically inferior in that she was created without a penis, a phenomenon that he believed led every woman to penis envy. Otto Weininger, the Austrian philosopher, in his book *Sex and Character* saw man as mind and woman as matter. He argued that the body of a woman, as opposed to that of the man, possessed no soul. Marquis de Sade did not even see woman as being good for cannibalistic purposes. Said he: "And in company with all cannibal tribes, I believe that the flesh of women, as the flesh of all female animals, is necessarily inferior to that of the male species."[11] Charles Darwin said: "Man is more powerful in body and mind than woman."[12]

Woman as Intellectually "Inferior"

Closely related to the age-old belief that women are biologically inferior to men is the conviction that women are also intellectually inferior to men. Much recorded evidence shows the depth and breadth of this myth. Several hundred years before the birth of Christ, Plato, in discussing the education of men and women, asked: "Do you know, then, of anything practiced by mankind in which the masculine sex does not surpass the female on these points?" (*Republic* 5.455c). Aristotle saw man's "superior" intelligence as a reason for ruling over women (*Politics* 1254b:12). Roman culture limited the rights of women on the grounds of imbecility, says Robert Bierstedt.[13] And the Hebrew rabbis said: "Women are light-minded" (*Shabbat* 33b).

The agrarian cultural beliefs present in Greek and Roman societies with regard to woman's intellectual "inferiority" were not lacking among the church fathers. St. Chrysostom (A.D. 347–407), quite influential in the early church, made bold to say: "The [female] sex is weak and fickle" (*Hom-*

---

[10]H. L. Mencken, *In Defense of Women* (New York: Alfred A. Knopf, 1924) 36-37.

[11]Marquis de Sade, "Juliette," in Simone de Beauvoir, ed., *The Marquis de Sade* (London: John Calder, 1962) 171.

[12]Charles Darwin, *The Descent of Man and Selection in Relation to Sex* (London: John Murray, 1891) 901.

[13]Robert Bierstedt, *The Social Order* (New York: McGraw-Hill, 1970) 373.

ilies on Timothy, Homily 9). A contemporary of Chrysostom, Cyril of Alexandria, was a bishop whose monks seized Hypatia and tore her body to pieces in the church for teaching men mathematics and philosophy in the school of Plato and Plotinus. Woman, man's "inferior," was not to teach men. Socrates Scholasticus, the fifth-century historian, said that Hypatia did not "feel abashed in coming to an assembly of men."[14] Such behavior had to be crushed.

Seeing women as intellectually inferior to men was believed for centuries after Cyril of Alexandria. For centuries theologians wrote dogmatically about woman's intellectual inferiority. Thomas Aquinas, a theologian of no small influence, also saw the intellectual inferiority of woman as a basic fact of life. He said that women were not perfect enough in wisdom. Thus public teaching could not be entrusted to them (*Summa Theologica* 2a-2ae, 177, 2). Nor did Martin Luther really show much improvement, even though he said favorable things about women at times. Yet the fact remains that on numerous occasions he too reflected centuries of sexist values, which he wove into his theology. "Men," said he, "have broad shoulders and narrow hips, and accordingly possess intelligence. Women have narrow shoulders and broad hips and a wide fundament to sit upon" (*Table Talks* 55). Another time, when talking about the Fall, he said: "Adam was wiser than Eve."[15] Luther also believed that "a man is nobler than woman."[16]

Earlier I noted that the male-perceived biological inferiority of women was shared alike by theologians and freethinkers. This was also true regarding woman's perceived intellectual inferiority. Once more culture created strange bedfellows out of two very different groups. Jean Jacques Rousseau, whose book *Emile* in 1762 was thought to contain "an abominable doctrine"—according to the archbishop of Paris, Christophe de Beaumont—wrote: "All little girls dislike learning to read and write, but they are always willing to learn to use the needle" (*Emile* 5). This statement by Rousseau shows how cultural practices develop into beliefs that people see as biological givens. In other contexts, Rousseau demonstrated awareness of this process of distortion. Ear-

---

[14]Socrates Scholasticus, *The Ecclesiastical History,* ed. Philip Schaff (Grand Rapids: Eerdmans Publishing Co., 1957) 160.

[15]Martin Luther, "Lectures on I Timothy," *Commentaries on I Corinthians 7, I Corinthians 15, Lectures on I Timothy, Luther's Works,* vol. 28, ed. Hilton C. Oswald (St. Louis: Concordia Publishing Company, 1973) 278.

[16]Martin Luther, "Commentary on I Corinthians 7," *Luther's Works,* 28:16.

lier in *Emile,* he noted that it was erroneous to explain all wickedness and evil by idly repeating the old phrase, "Such is man." Rousseau countered this by saying: "Yes, such is the man you have made." But when it came to recognizing the phenomenon of little girls' opting "to use the needle," he failed to see that they did so as the result of culture rather than as the result of inborn biological tendencies.

The German philosopher Arthur Schopenhauer proclaimed: "Women are defective in the powers of reasoning and deliberation."[17] Time and time again Schopenhauer degraded woman's intelligence, clearly revealing his unawareness of how culture had forced woman to appear less intelligent. To corroborate his opinions, he said that woman's inferior mental capacities accounted for the Greeks' excluding women from their theaters. He also recalled Rousseau's utterance, namely that "women have, in general, no love for any art; they have no proper knowledge of any; and they have no genius."[18]

Charles Darwin, who stirred the anger of many theologians, was as sexist as anyone. He argued: "The chief distinction in the intellectual powers of the two sexes is shown by man's attaining to a higher eminence, in whatever he takes up, than can woman—whether requiring deep thought, reason, or imagination."[19] Citing Galton's *Hereditary Genius,* Darwin tried to verify his perception of woman's intellectual inferiority by saying, "If men are capable of a decided pre-eminence over women in many subjects, the average of mental power in man must be above that of woman."[20] Friedrich Nietzsche, who in many ways laid the foundation for Hitler's evils, expressed his belief concerning woman's inferior mental ability rather crudely: "When a woman has scholarly inclinations there is generally something wrong with her sexual nature."[21]

So pronounced was the conviction that women were intellectually inferior to men that not only clergymen and freethinkers echoed centuries of previous cultural prejudices, but so did physicians and educators—right into

---

[17]Arthur Schopenhauer, "Of Women," in Will Durant, ed., *The Works of Schopenhauer* (New York: Frederick Ungar Publishing Company, 1928) 449.

[18]Ibid., 452.

[19]Darwin, *Descent of Man,* 566.

[20]Ibid.

[21]Friedrich Nietzsche, *Beyond Good and Evil,* trans. Helen Zimmern (New York: Russell and Russell, 1964) 21.

the twentieth century. Dr. Ralph W. Parsons contended that college-educated women suffered more from digestive disorders and were more likely to experience mental problems. His views were published in the *New York Medical Journal* in 1907. William H. Walling, another physician, espoused the position that too much mental stimulation was harmful for pubescent girls.[22] A one-time president of the Oregon Medical Society, F. W. Van Dyke, said that hard study took away a woman's beauty and would lead to hysteria, neurasthenia, dyspepsia, astigmatism, dysmennorrhea, as well as stifle sexual desire. He also wrote that educated women had arrested development of the pelvis, which would harm the fetus by decreasing its head and brain capacity. This "medical" observation led him to say that women should not pursue higher education. After all, a woman is longer and more fondly remembered for being a good mother rather than for being a college graduate, said he.[23] A gynecologist, William E. Darnall, said the husband of an educated woman would "discover too late that he has married a large outfit of headaches and spine aches, instead of a woman fitted to take up the duties of life."[24] These sexist views portraying woman as intellectually inferior were not propounded by quacks, but by leading physicians of their time. Moreover, their beliefs were published in reputable medical journals.

The argument for woman's lesser intelligence was sometimes linked to her "inferior" biological makeup. For instance, George J. Engelmann, a physician, maintained that woman's menstrual cycle made her unfit for higher education.[25] Still another physician, who wrote a popular textbook on gynecology, advised with regard to women pursuing higher education that "each menstrual period should be passed in the recumbent position until her system becomes accustomed to the new order of life."[26]

[22]William H. Walling, *Sexology* (Philadelphia: Puritan Publishing Company, 1904) 207.

[23]F. W. Van Dyke, "Higher Education a Cause of Physical Decay in Women," *Medical Records* 67 (1905): 296-98.

[24]William Edgar Darnall, "The Pubescent Girl," *American Gynecological and Obstetrical Journal* 18 (June 1901): 490.

[25]George J. Engelmann, "The American Evil of Today: The Influence of Modern Education on Functional Development," *Transactions* (American Gynecological Society) 25 (1900): 8-45.

[26]Thomas A. Emmett, *The Principles and Practices of Gynecology* (Philadelphia, 1879) 21.

The so-called inferior mental ability of woman—held by physicians and others—was not based on controlled scientific data. In fact, according to Ashley Montagu, it was not until 1903 that the first scientific study was undertaken relative to intelligence of the sexes.[27] Today, while some differences may be found—sometimes in favor of women and sometimes in favor of men—no reputable physician or scientist would assert that men have a higher native intelligence than women.

The Social "Inferiority" of Woman

Not only has woman been seen as biologically and intellectually inferior to man, but she has also been defined as man's social inferior. Precisely when this widespread male perception of woman began in history is difficult to say with certainty. There are, however, some clues.

Sumerologist Samuel Noah Kramer thinks that the social-inferiority belief regarding women did not exist prior to 2400 B.C. After 2400 B.C., however, woman no longer was able to practice polyandry, own or control vast amounts of property, receive economic rewards equal to man, hold equal rank with him, or perform spiritual exercises equal to man.[28] Kramer's observation is supported by H. W. F. Saggs, who says "that in the very beginning of Sumerian society women had a much higher status than in the heyday of the Sumerian culture."[29] Among the Egyptians, woman's subordination did not occur at one point in history and continue without interruption. Jacques Pirenne believes that the social inferiority of woman did not become institutionalized until 2270 B.C. and that the phenomenon suffered at least two reversals, one from 1580 to 1085 B.C. and another from 663 to 525 B.C.[30]

The male-oriented culture of the Fertile Crescent area evidently made its impact on the Hebrews, who defined woman to be of lesser social worth in various portions of the Old Testament. Exodus 21:7 permitted the Hebrew father to sell his daughter into slavery, but no such law existed rel-

---

[27]Montagu, *Natural Superiority of Women*, 142.

[28]Samuel Noah Kramer, *The Sumerians: Their History, Culture, and Character* (Chicago: University of Chicago Press, 1962).

[29]Ibid., 187.

[30]Leonard Swidler, *Women in Judaism: The Status of Women in Formative Judaism* (Metuchen NJ: Scarecrow Press, 1976) 5-7.

ative to the son. Deuteronomy 21:10-14 permitted the Hebrew soldier to use a captured woman for his pleasure, and if after some time she no longer gave him "delight," he was at liberty to let her go.

Wives in Hebrew culture were also socialized to call their husbands by their names and titles, a practice that clearly reflected woman's lower social status. One common form of address used by a wife was *"ba'al,"* meaning master or lord of woman.[31] Another word she would use was "rabbi," meaning teacher.[32] But more commonly, she called her spouse *"adon"* (lord). This is the word Sarah used in reference to Abraham in Genesis 18:12. The Hebrew woman addressed her husband as "a slave addressed his master, or a subject his King."[33]

The birth of a daughter was not considered important by an Old Testament man. The desire was always for a son to be born. Even the wives had internalized this male value. In Genesis 29 and 30 Leah and Rachel (Jacob's two wives) compete with each other as to who would give Jacob the largest number of sons. It was especially important to have the first-born be a son. Numerous places in the Old Testament attest to this preference. In fact, few people realize that when they read references to "children" in translations of the Old Testament that the Hebrew texts commonly speak only about "sons." For instance, in Deuteronomy 6:7 the King James translation commands the Israelites to teach the Commandments "diligently unto your children." The Hebrew text, however, does not say "children"; it only speaks about teaching the sons. Translators have misread this text and many others as well.

Among the Greeks the social inferiority of woman, according to Vern L. Bullough, became culturally established by the ninth century B.C.[34] By the Athenian era in the fifth century B.C. the Greek man expected women to "prepare the meals, run their household and stay out of sight."[35] So inferior was the Greek woman's social status that she could only leave her house when she

---

[31]Johannes Leipoldt, *Die Frau in der Antiken Welt und im Urchristentum* (Leipzig, 1954) 43.

[32]Raphael Loewe, *The Position of Women in Judaism* (London, 1966) 23.

[33]Roland de Vaux, *Ancient Israel: Its Life and Institutions* (New York: McGraw-Hill, 1966) 39.

[34]Vern L. Bullough, *The Subordinate Sex* (Baltimore, 1974) 50ff.

[35]C. M. Bowra, *Classical Greece* (Chicago: Time Inc., 1965) 85.

was accompanied by an escort, usually her husband or someone designated by him.[36] If a Greek woman in the fifth century B.C. left her house without her husband's approval, she aroused his anger, according to Aristophanes' play *Thesmophoriazusae*. Women in Athens "had far less freedom than men to move about the city."[37] The wife was primarily her husband's housekeeper and the mother of his children. She had no formal education. Women who were fairly well educated were mistresses, the *hetaerae*, not the wives. Only *hetaerae*, not wives, were permitted publicly to listen to the male philosophers in the arcades or in the council of an all-male decision-making group known as the Areopagus.[38]

The low social standing of the Athenian wife extended far beyond her not being permitted to have a meaningful social life in public or in the presence of men. Even as a child she was considered to have low social value. Hilarion's words come to mind here. He told his wife before she was about to give birth that if the infant was born a male to let it live, but if it was a female to "cast it out."[39] The Greek scholar Philip Slater sums up the social inferiority of the Greek woman exceedingly well: "The male child was . . . of vital importance [even] to the wife—her principal source of prestige and validation. Yet how much she must have secretly resented the callous and disparaging male attitude toward female children who were an economic liability, a social burden."[40] "A [Greek] husband always had the right to repudiate his wife, even without showing cause," says Flaceliere.[41] Woman had the social status of a slave.[42] She could not, according to Euripides' tragedy *Medea*, divorce her husband, whereas he could do so anytime. Small wonder that Medea sor-

---

[36]Charles Albert Savage, *The Athenian Family: A Sociological and Legal Study* (Baltimore, 1907) 29.

[37]G. W. Botsford and E. G. Sihler, eds., *Hellenic Civilization* (New York: Octagon Books, 1965) 336.

[38]William H. Sanger, *The History of Prostitution* (New York: Eugenics Publishing Company, 1939) 54.

[39]A. Deissmann, *Light from the Ancient East* (New York: Doran, 1927) 168.

[40]Philip Slater, *The Glory of Hera: Greek Mythology and Greek Family* (Boston: Beacon Press, 1968) 29.

[41]Robert Flaceliere, *Love in Ancient Greece*, trans. James Cleugh (New York: Crown Publishers, 1962) 116.

[42]F. A. Wright, *Feminism in Greek Literature: From Homer to Aristotle* (Port Washington NY: Kennikat Press, [1923] 1969) 1.

rowfully wrote: "Surely, of all creatures that have life and wit, we women are of all unhappiest" (*Medea* 231-32).

Even in Sparta (seventh century B.C.) where women, unlike in other societies, were allowed to compete against men in athletic events, men still kept their wives "under lock and key," says Plutarch (*Lycurgus* 15.8). The Greek woman, especially in Athens, could rarely leave her husband's house. Attending a funeral of a close relative was one of the few times she could leave the home. Flaceliere cites Menander, who expressed the Greek mind: "A respectable wife ought to keep indoors. Only good for nothing women frequent the street."[43] Only among the Epicureans was there a semblance of equality between the sexes. So negatively skewed was the life of the Greek woman that F. A. Wright believes that strong discrimination against women, along with the practice of slavery, "brought about the decay first of Athens and then of Greece."[44]

In Roman society, where woman had somewhat more freedom than the Hellenistic woman, she nevertheless still lived most of her life in an inferior social role. "Women [in Rome] could not plead in court; the amounts they legally inherited were limited; and a woman could not, for example, leave money to her children if they were under her husband's *patria potestas*."[45] Moreover, "Women were never associated in their husband's occupations, knew little of their affairs, and were less closely attached to their interests than even their bondmen."[46] A woman could even be divorced for going out in public without wearing a veil, according to Plutarch's *Romulus*.

While Roman women were permitted, unlike their Greek counterparts, to be present at the meal when men ate, they nevertheless bore definite marks of social inferiority. They did not even possess a separate name of their own, distinctive from their father, while they were under his control. If the father's name was Flavius, the daughter commonly was called Flavia. If his name was Claudius, she was named Claudia. When there were several daughters, they would be named Claudia Unus, Claudia Secunda, Claudia Tertia, and so forth.

---

[43]Flaceliere, *Love in Ancient Greece,* 118.

[44]Wright, *Feminism in Greek Literature,* 1.

[45]O. A. W. Dilke, *The Ancient Romans: How They Lived and How They Worked* (Dufour Editions, 1975) 49.

[46]Charles Merivale, *The Fall of the Roman Empire: A Short History of the Last Century of the Commonwealth* (London, 1853) 226.

If a father had only two daughters, the names would be Claudia Maior and Claudia Minor.

The agrarian perception of woman as a socially inferior creature was not just confined to Greco-Roman culture. In ancient China "girls were generally regarded as much less valuable than boys. . . . One proverb stated in effect that the most beautiful and gifted girl was not so desirable as a deformed boy."[47] Fu Xuan, a Chinese poet, expressed the Chinese social conception of the human female very well when he said: "No one is glad when a girl is born and by her the family sets no store."[48] These Chinese views were remarkably similar to the views the Hebrews had during the rabbinic era (c. 400 B.C.–A.D. 500). The rabbis said: "At the birth of a boy all are joyful, but at the birth of a girl all are sad" (*Niddah* 31b). The *Book of Rites,* a Confucian source, did not permit married sisters to eat with their brothers at the same table.

Another example of woman's social inferiority in China was the country's one-time practice of foot binding, a sexist custom that reportedly existed for almost a thousand years. Foot binding commonly began when a girl was five years old. A long cotton bandage, several inches wide, was tightly wrapped around both feet, forcing the four small toes of each foot under and up against the fleshly part of the foot. In time the toes stopped growing and became stunted. In the process the heel was forced down, pushing the instep outward, all of which made the foot look like a clenched fist. The big toe, says Forman, was left free, but it was forced into the front part of a small shoe.[49] Foot binding frequently caused severe infection. "The flesh often became putrescent during the binding and portions sloughed off from the sole; sometimes one or more toes dropped off," in the words of a Christian missionary.[50] Frequently gangrene set in, leading to leg amputation or even death.[51]

Why did this cruel sociocultural custom exist? There is only one answer to this question: It existed to please men. It made an "inferior" being look

[47]Kenneth Scott Latourette, *The Chinese: Their History and Culture* (New York: Macmillan Company, 1964) 574.

[48]Cited in Elizabeth Croll, *Feminism and Socialism in China* (New York: Schocken Books, 1980) 22.

[49]Harrison Forman, *Changing China* (New York: Crown Publishers, 1948) 199.

[50]Howard S. Levy, *Chinese Footbinding: The History of a Curious Erotic Custom* (New York: W. Rauls, 1966) 26.

[51]Forman, *Changing China,* 199.

more desirable. A woman whose feet were not small, as a result of not having been bound, was "disgraced and it was impossible to get a desirable husband for her," according to Latourette.[52] One observer noted that the results of bound feet was "pleasing in men's eyes. . . . Looking at a woman with bound feet walking is like looking at a rope-dancer, tantalizing to the highest degree."[53]

As so frequently happens, cruel customs are often highly valued in many societies, even by those who endure the cruelty. So it was with foot binding. When some Christian missionaries in the nineteenth century on occasion unbound the feet of some girls, the girls would rebind them when alone.[54] The male perception of what made the female "beautiful" was deeply internalized early in life. The girls also knew that their peers and their mothers would exert inescapable social pressures upon them to conform.

Moving to the Fertile Crescent area, one notes that women were assigned other forms of social inferiority, forms that left their mark on the Hebrew theologians of the rabbinic era and also on the church's theologians, for example, the church fathers.

The Hebrew rabbis firmly believed in the reality of woman's low status. "Happy is he," declared one rabbinic teaching, "whose children are males, and woe to him whose children are females" (*Kiddushim* 82b). Josephus, a first-century Pharisee, accurately reflected the then-existing sexist thought by saying: "The woman, says the Law, is in all things inferior to man. Let her accordingly be submissive" (*Apion* 2.201). And the inferiority of woman was summed up most strikingly in the Hebrew prayer: "Blessed [art Thou] who did not make me a woman" (*Menahot* 43b).

Woman as Spiritually "Inferior"

The impact of ancient culture went beyond defining woman as man's biological, intellectual, and social inferior. It also shaped the male perception of woman as a spiritual being. The Hebrews had no divine command in the Old Testament to instruct girls or women. When Deuteronomy in chapters four, six, and eleven commands the Hebrew fathers to teach the statutes, ordinances, and commandments of God to their offspring, it

---

[52]Latourette, *Chinese*, 576.

[53]Lin Yutang, *My Country and My People* (New York: Halcyon Press, 1935) 167.

[54]M. E. Burton, *Notable Women of Modern China* (New York, 1912) 20.

does not include daughters. Only the sons were to be taught religious teachings. The exclusion of females from religious education in the Old Testament is never explained. To teach daughters or females was a very serious violation in the eyes of the Hebrews. The oral law in Jesus' day firmly declared: "Let the words of the Law be burned rather than committed to women. . . . If a man teaches his daughter the Law, it is as though he taught her lewdness" (*Sotah* 3:4).

Other spiritual inequalities in the Hebrew religious culture become apparent when one notes that only the males, not females, underwent circumcision, a prominent religious practice. Circumcision made one become an heir to the privileges and blessings of the God of Abraham. Where the omission of females from this rite left women spiritually is not known. The Hebrew theologians and priests did not discuss this matter.

Parenthetically, it should be noted that to talk about female circumcision is not an attempt to be facetious. I have found that many men, upon first hearing about female circumcision, usually smile and laugh audibly. It is a laugh of ignorance. They are unaware of what they do not know. The literature pertaining to female circumcision is quite abundant. In fact, it stretches back to the Greek historian Herodotus, who in the fifth century B.C. already mentioned female circumcision.

Hebrew women could not be counted to make up a quorum (*minyan*) for a public worship gathering to be held in a synagogue. Rabbinic law required ten men to be present. Nine men and one or more women did not suffice (*Aboth* 3:6). Once a quorum was present, the men engaged in worship. They alone were the ones who chanted or sang in the synagogue service.[55] The women were required to be veiled and silent.

In the previous chapter we saw how many church fathers, consistent with Greco-Roman culture, saw woman as evil and as the originator of evil as well. In the spiritual sense, prominent and influential theologians said woman, in contrast to man, was not created in the image of God. St. Augustine, who probably influenced Christian theology more than any other church father, said the image of God in woman was inferior to that of the man. Apart from her husband, the woman did not possess the image of God (*On the Trinity* 12.10).

Isidore, an archbishop of Spain in the sixth century, taught that woman was in the image of man because she was made from man. Man, on the other

---

[55]Raphael Patai, *The Jewish Mind* (New York: Charles Scribner's, 1977) 365.

hand, was in the image of God (*Sententiae* l0.4-6). A twelfth-century teacher in the church, Peter Abelard, based his belief about woman not having the image of God on 1 Corinthians 11:7. Said he: "As man, according to the Apostle [Paul], is in the image of God, so woman is in the image of man" (*Introductio ad Theologiam* 1.col. 991). Also in the twelfth century, Ernaud of Bonneval in his *Hexameron* portrayed man as having the higher rational soul (*spiritus*), whereas woman represented the lower rational soul (*anima*) among humans. In the thirteenth century Thomas Aquinas taught that God's image is not found in man in the same way it is present in woman because man is both the beginning and the end of woman, similar to God's being the beginning and the end of creation (*Summa Theologiae* 1a, 93:5).

The spiritually inferior argument, as applied to women by some prominent Christian teachers of theology, at times reflected some unusual and unsound logic. Heinrich Kramer and Jacob Sprenger in *Malleus Maleficarum* (discussed in chap. 3), in speaking about the etymology of the Latin word *femina,* said: "*Femina* comes from *fe* and *minus* , since she is ever weaker to hold and preserve the faith. And this as regards faith is of her very nature" (p. 46). From this specious argument one sees the powerful influence of sexist culture upon teachers in the church and how it shaped their opinions regarding woman's spiritual makeup. To say that *femina* etymologically means "faithless" is going to great lengths to build a case for man's superior spirituality. The argument by Kramer and Sprenger seems to have no basis in scholarly literature. The best Latin dictionaries do not even hint at any such etymology.

Were these two Dominican monks perhaps influenced by Peter Abelard? It was he who three centuries earlier argued that the Latin word *mulier* (woman) indicated a deficiency of the spirit (*Exposito in Hexameron* 760-61).

If woman was not really made in the image of God, it was not stretching sexist logic to conclude that she also was not really human. Such conclusions, of course, existed. One bishop, according to Carl von Hefele, argued at the second council of Macon in A.D. 585 that "women could not be seen as human without qualification."[56] The council fortunately did not accept the bishop's position. Yet, the argument for woman's lack of humanity did not end in the sixth century. In 1595 Valens Acidalius, in Germany, published a document of fifty-one theses entitled *Disputatio nova contra mulieres, qua pro-*

---

[56]Carl Joseph von Hefele, *Conciliengeschichte*, vol. 3 (Freiburg: Herder'sche Verlagshandlung, 1877) 41.

batur eas homines non esse. Many of these theses declared that women were not human. A couple of theses, says Manfred P. Fleischer, "linked them [women] with dogs and demons."[57] The document's putative author was a physician, Valens Acidalius, the son of a Lutheran pastor who signed the Lutheran Book of Concord. The *Disputatio,* according to Fleischer, was in print for 174 years in spite of its having been attacked by Simon Gediccus, a Lutheran theologian whose rebuttal received support from the theological faculties of Wittenberg and Leipzig.[58]

The thought of women not being human to the same degree as men, or not being created in the image of God was not just confined to Acidalius and those who enjoyed reading his theses. John Donne (1573–1631), the British poet and chaplain to King James I, wrote: "Man to God's image, Eve to man's was made. Nor finde wee that God breath'd a soule in her."

More recently, a noted German Lutheran theologian, Emil Brunner, said something reminiscent of Acidalius's *Disputatio.* According to Brunner, "It is certain that the Creator has created the mental and spiritual nature of woman different from that of man."[59]

The Subordination Myth

The fact that woman has been perceived for ages, from one culture to the next as biologically, intellectually, socially, and spiritually inferior has led to strong beliefs and practices regarding her "lesser" nature. In defense of this conviction, theologians have been very adept at citing biblical references to keep woman subordinate and submissive. To fulfill this mandate means that woman must, of course, obey man. It also means that she cannot teach in the church, especially not in worship settings.

The belief that woman is to obey man has its roots in agrarian-patriarchal cultures that structured life in such a manner so that the woman was economically, socially, and religiously dependent on man's "superiority." In ancient Greece the obedience to man is conveyed by an ancient fragment: "A good wife's duty 'tis . . . Not to command, but to obey her spouse; most mischie-

---

[57]Manfred P. Fleischer, " 'Are Women Human?'—The Debate of 1595 between Valens Acidalius and Simon Gediccus," *Sixteenth Century Journal* 12 (1981): 108.

[58]Ibid.

[59]Emil Brunner, *The Divine Imperative* (New York: Macmillan, 1937) 375.

vous a wife, who rules her husband.''[60] As noted above, among the Greeks
"a husband always had the right to repudiate his wife, even without showing
cause.''[61] The Greek wife or mother was not just subordinate to her husband,
but also to her son(s). Telemachus told his mother, Penelope: "Nay, go to
thy chamber, and busy thyself with thine own tasks, the loom, the distaff, and
thy handmaidens ply their tasks . . . since mine is the authority in the house"
(*The Odyssey* 1.356-60). The woman of Lacedaemon said: "When I was a
girl, I was taught to obey my father, and I obeyed him; and when I became a
wife, I obeyed my husband.''[62] The Greek poets frequently used the term *des-
pot* to express the institutionalized belief that man was the woman's lord. For
instance, Euripides has Medea say that husbands are the "despots" of wives
(*Medea,* 236).

Nor was the situation much better in Rome when it came to woman's
role vis-à-vis the son or husband. As has already been noted above, the
Roman woman came under the patriarchal institution and law known as
patria potestas and *manus,* which gave the man total control over his
daughters, wife, or any other woman. Table V, one of the Twelve Tables
of Roman law, required that a woman be under a guardian if she had no
father or husband to obey.[63] Roman law also demanded that the wife worship her husband's gods. Cato tells us that the Roman wife did not have
the right to tell her husband's slave what to do (*Aulus Gellius Noctium Gellius* 17.6.10). And Seneca (first century A.D.) said: "Man is born to rule
and woman to obey."

The situation was not much different for the Jewish woman during the
rabbinical era (c. 400 B.C.–A.D. 400). This view was summed up well in
the first century by Josephus: "Let her [woman] be submissive, not for her
humiliation, but that she may be directed; for the authority has been given
by God to the man" (*Apion* 2.201). Given this view of woman's subordination, it is not surprising to note that the Hebrew woman was obligated
to wash her husband's face, hands, and feet (*Kethuboth* 59b, 61a.). Even

---

[60]Cited in Mitchell Carroll, *Women of All Ages and in All Ages* (Philadelphia: Rittenhouse Press, 1907–1908) 259.

[61]Flaceliere, *Love in Ancient Greece,* 116.

[62]James Donaldson, *Woman: Her Position and Influence in Ancient Greece and Rome
and among the Early Christians* (New York: Longmans and Green, 1907) 32.

[63]Andrew Stephenson, *A History of Roman Law* (Boston: Little, Brown and Company,
1912) 129, 361.

before the rabbinic era, the subordination of the Hebrew woman appears to have been well established. For instance, at the time of Moses the husband had veto power over his wife's vows, according to Numbers 30:12; her vows had little or no value apart from her husband's approval.

The early fathers of the church were not far behind the Hebrews, Greeks, and Romans in terms of seeing and treating woman as man's subordinate. Clement of Alexandria, mentioned above, believed that a man's beard was a sign of his superiority over woman (*The Instructor* 3.3). Epiphanius of Salamis (A.D. 315–403), a bishop, taught that the devil was unable to tempt Adam because of Adam's superiority, so he turned to Eve, whom he was able to seduce because of her ignorance. Hence ignorance was not only a feminine quality, but also reason for woman to be subordinate (*Adversus Octoginta Haereses* 1.643).

Theologians within the Judeo-Christian tradition for the last 2,000 years or so found Genesis 3:16 very convenient to defend their subordination beliefs regarding woman. Most modern Bible versions, including the King James, translate this reference as: "Your desire shall be for your husband and he shall rule over you." Because woman (Eve) was the first to sin, she became subordinate to man for all time.

The culture of sexism influenced the interpretation and translation of Genesis 3:16. The Hebrew text contains the word *teshuqa,* which today is commonly translated as "desire." However, the oldest translation of the Old Testament, the Greek Septuagint of about 285 B.C., translates *teshuqa* as "turning" (*apostrophe*), not "desire." Other ancient versions or fragments that also render *teshuqa* as "turning" are the Syriac Peshitto (A.D. 100), the Old Latin (A.D. 200), the Sahidic (A.D. 300), the Bohairic (A.D. 350), and the Ethiopic (A.D. 500).

Most modern English translations render *teshuqa* in Genesis 3:16 as "desire." The early English Bibles, however, translated *teshuqa* as "lust." For example, the Coverdale version of 1535 and the Cranmer Bible of 1539 are cases in point. However, in Song of Solomon 7:10 these two Bibles translated *teshuqa* as "turning."

The use of "lust" for *teshuqa* seems to reflect a rabbinic influence that dates back to the Babylonian Talmud of the fifth century A.D. It appears to be the first known work to interpret *teshuqa* to mean "lust." Such a translation, of course, is very much in keeping with the concept of seeing woman as evil, discussed in chapter 3.

The link between the early English versions of the sixteenth century and rabbinic theology of the Babylonian Talmud with regard to Genesis 3:16 seems to have been Pagnino, the Italian monk who studied under the rabbis.[64] Thus when in 1528 Pagnino published his Latin version of the Bible, he rendered *teshuqa* as "lust." Undoubtedly the Coverdale and the Cranmer Bibles were influenced by Pagnino's understanding of *teshuqa*, and so the word "lust" found its way into their translations. This mistranslation of Genesis 3:16 led Richard Simon to say: "Pagnino has too much neglected the ancient versions of Scripture to attach himself to the teachings of the rabbis."[65] In the light of how the ancient versions translated *teshuqa*, this criticism seems accurate.

To translate *teshuqa* as "lust" or "desire" rather than "turning" makes a very significant difference; it portrays woman in a negative light. It makes her dependent or subordinate to man. It communicates the thought that only woman desires to be with man—sexually or otherwise—and that man has no real need or desire to be with woman. The reciprocity and mutuality of the sexes, if realized at all by the patriarchal culture, certainly was not a significant thought pattern. Thus it is not surprising to see the mistranslation of Genesis 3:16 take the form that it did, and still does.

There is still another sexist element in most English translations of Genesis 3:16. The second half of this reference reads: "and he *shall* rule over you." The Hebrew wording—more correctly conveyed by the Septuagint and other ancient versions—reads: "and he *will* rule over you." Substituting the word "shall" for "will" changes the meaning significantly. The statement has now switched from the simple future tense to the volitional form. It also makes the statement prescriptive, a direct command from God. Such a translation ignores the fact that the future tense in Hebrew, unless dictated by the context, does not imply or require a sense of obligation. Evidently the cultural force of sexism led the male translators to overlook this grammatical rule. The ancient belief that woman was inferior to man and therefore submissive to him unconsciously changed the translators' interpretation.

---

[64]Katherine Bushnell, *God's Word to Women* (Oakland CA: published by the author, 1923 [?]) sec. 142. This work has been reprinted by Ray B. Munson, North Collins NY. Bushnell's book first drew my attention to different translations of *teshuqa*.

[65]Cited by Bushnell, *God's Word to Women*, sec. 142.

Alphonse Mingana, a twentieth-century linguistic expert in Semitic languages and a curator of Oriental manuscripts at the John Rylands library, Manchester University, concerning the insertion of "shall" in place of "will," said: "The future tense or aorist never implies in the Semitic languages a sense of obligation. This remark highly befits the sentence 'He shall rule over thee.' "[66] Another respected scholar and grammarian, James Hope Moulton, with regard to "shall" versus "will," said: "Speaking generally, it may fairly be claimed that unless volitive force is distinctly traceable from the context, it would be better to translate by the futuristic form."[67]

When Genesis 3:16 is read "and he will rule over you," it makes the message conditional upon Eve's turning away from God to Adam. In other words, if she continues to turn to man, then he will rule over her. It is not an inevitable or God-given command that results from the innate nature of woman; it is a matter of woman's choice.

The familiar translation of "he shall rule over you" has for centuries been read and heard in very sacred and holy settings, so that the mistranslation has created a self-fulfilling prophecy. The inferiority and submissiveness of woman has been seen as God's command by woman as well as by man. Thus even today the argument of woman's inferiority still exerts a powerful impact among those who from childhood have heard the incorrect word "shall" instead of "will" as it pertains to Genesis 3:16.

Among Christian theologians the argument for the subordination of woman has not just been confined to Genesis 3:16. The forces of cultural sexism have unconsciously prompted clergy also to find "proof texts" in the New Testament that reportedly declare woman everlastingly to be subordinate to man in all societies. Three references in particular have had great appeal. One passage is 1 Corinthians 11:3: "But I want you to understand that the head of every man is Christ, the head of a woman is her husband, and the head of Christ is God." Another text is found in Ephesians 5:22-24: "Wives, be subject to your husbands, as to the Lord. For the husband is the head of the wife as Christ is head of the church, his body, and is himself its Savior. As the church is subject to Christ, so let wives also be subject in everything to their husbands." Still another passage—loved by

---

[66]Cited by Bushnell, *God's Word to Women*, sec. 273.

[67]James Hope Moulton, *A Grammar: New Testament*, vol. 1 (Edinburgh: T & T Clark, [1906] 1949) 151.

male chauvinists—is found in 1 Peter 3:1: "Likewise you wives, be submissive to your husbands.''

The latter two references in no way speak about woman's behavior in the
church. To apply these references to a church context reveals a rather strange
hermeneutic, one that many theologians still are fond of using. When it comes
to keeping woman silent and subordinate in church, biblical passages can be
employed apparently even when the context only talks about family life—the
family life of the Greco-Roman era, at that. It is as though the end—keeping
woman in her place—justifies employing these passages.

These New Testament passages and related ones convinced thousands
of theologians that man not only is woman's superordinate, but that this
role was so decreed by God for the remainder of human history. It was part
of God's created order. Listen to the words of Marcus Dods, a British
theologian who, with reference to 1 Corinthians 11:3, argued: "This subordination of the woman to man belongs not merely to the order of the
Christian Church, but it has its roots in nature.''[68] A Roman Catholic theologian declared: "Man is called by the Creator to this position of leader
[over woman], as is shown by his entire bodily and intellectual make-up.''[69]
H. A. W. Meyer, in his commentary on Corinthians, used Paul's directive
about wearing a head covering (probably a veil) to argue that woman was
under man's power. The whole context, said he, "points to the authority
of the husband over the wife.''[70]

Henry Alford, who wrote a widely used New Testament commentary, told
his readers that 1 Peter 3:1-7 spoke of woman's "whole course of obedience.''[71] In connection with Ephesians 5:22, John Exell—in his *Biblical Illustrator,* a widely used commentary— maintained: "Submission is required
of the wife towards her husband.''[72] He also added: "Wives must reckon it
their unquestionable duty to be subject to their husbands.''[73] Such citations

---

[68]Marcus Dods, *The First Epistle to the Corinthians* (New York: A. C. Armstrong and
Son, 1905) 151.

[69]Augustine Rossler, "Woman," in *The Catholic Encyclopedia,* vol. 5 (New York:
Encyclopedia Press, 1913) 688.

[70]Heinrich August Wilhelm Meyer, *Critical and Exegetical Hand-Book to the Epistles
of the Corinthians,* vol. 6 (New York: Funk & Wagnalls, 1884) 252.

[71]Henry Alford, *The Greek New Testament* (Chicago: Moody Press, 1958) 358.

[72]John Exell, *The Biblical Illustrator* (Grand Rapids: Baker Book House, 1954) 571.

[73]Ibid.

abound in the theological books and articles. The ones cited here are but a sample of how theologians and clergy have seen woman as subordinate to man.

These biblical passages, along with the ethic of sexism so thoroughly embedded in ancient cultures, led theologians to formulate in written form woman's subordination in the marriage vows, a practice that began in the Reformation era. Until rather recently, it was common in American Protestant churches to have the bride promise to "obey" her husband in the years ahead. Now one finds that more and more conservative churches are omitting the word "obey" from the wedding ritual.

The removal of the promise to obey has, of course, not been without sharp criticism. For instance, at least one American denomination's official publication opposed such deletions. In the view of that publication churches that no longer used the word "obey" were engaged in an unbiblical practice.[74]

To be sure, the three New Testament passages (1 Cor. 11:3; Eph. 5:22-24; 1 Pet. 3:1) at one time probably meant to convey a subordinate role for women in some regions. The church, which gave women essential equality in the apostolic era (see chap. 10 for more detailed information), could not immediately dispense with all sexist practices of the Greco-Roman culture. Not to maintain some of the ancient patriarchal customs, when the church already ignored many others, would have made the Christian religion too offensive and perhaps even have given rise to additional persecution, of which there was already too much.

The New Testament writers surely were fully aware of the significance of *manus* and *patria potestas*. Both of these Roman institutions (discussed at greater length in chap. 6) meant "the wife [could] never, in point of law, be the mistress of the house, nor [could] she share the headship of the family with her husband."[75] M. I. Finley says: "Save for relatively minor exceptions, a [Roman] woman was always in the power of some man—of her paterfamilias or of her husband or of a guardian."[76]

Christianity, during the apostolic era and for a brief period after, gave freedom to women that was incongruent with the Greco-Roman culture. A few illustrations are in order. When Celsus, the second-century critic of

[74]Ludwig Fuerbringer, "Frauenemancipation," *Der Lutheraner* 59 (July 1903): 232.

[75]Rudolph Sohm, *The Institutes of Roman Law* (Oxford: Clarendon Press, 1892) 366.

[76]Moses I. Finley, "The Silent Woman of Rome," *Horizon* 7 (Winter 1965): 59.

Christianity, argued that Christianity was primarily attractive to slaves and
women, he was not casting idle words to the wind. Primitive Christianity
did indeed appeal to women, given the many centuries of discrimination
against them. Many women, separate from their husbands or fathers, became Christians. Such behavior was repugnant to the Greco-Roman culture. The Roman institution of *manus,* along with other requirements, meant
woman was to worship her husband's ancestral gods.[77] This latter view is
underscored by Plutarch in the first century. He contended a man's wife
was to worship and honor only the gods that her husband believed and
worshiped. She was to shut the door tightly on other strange rituals and
unacceptable superstitions (*Conqiuqalia Praecepta* 140 D). This law, which
had been in existence for hundreds of years, was flaunted by many women
who found Christianity attractive.

The newly found freedom for women began with Jesus. It was he who
drastically departed from the sexist, socioreligious practices of his time. Behavior that we today expect and accept on the part of women in Western society was unthinkable 2,000 years ago. It was Jesus who not only welcomed
the emancipation of women but even encouraged it. In the words of John Ferguson, he "treated women with respect and seriousness rare in his age."[78]

While chapter 9 discusses the liberating acts of Jesus relative to women,
it needs to be noted here that he placed woman above the ancient laws and
taboos. For instance, he was not shocked or embarrassed when a woman who
had been issuing blood for twelve years touched him (Mark 5:25-34). According to Leviticus 15 such a woman was "unclean." Yet he approvingly
spoke to her, saying: "Go in peace and be healed of your disease." It is also
noteworthy that he did not see himself as having become temporarily unclean.
Leviticus 15:19 clearly specified that when someone came in contact with a
woman who had a "discharge of blood," that person was unclean for the rest
of the day. One can only imagine the social consternation Jesus must have
provoked by his behavior vis-à-vis the "unclean" woman.

Luke 13:11-13 portrays yet another example of Jesus showing his unusual concern for women. One day while he was in the synagogue, Jesus
summoned a woman who had had an infirmity for eighteen years. Un-

[77]Jerome Carcopino, *Daily Life in Rome,* trans. E. O. Lorimer (New Haven: Yale University Press, 1940).

[78]John Ferguson, *Jesus in the Tide of Time: An Historical Study* (London: Routledge
and Kegan Paul, 1980) 41.

doubtedly she had to come from the segregated woman's gallery of the synagogue to be healed by him. A woman in the synagogue was not permitted to interact with the worshiping men, but Jesus ignored this religious norm. Moreover, he even talked to her, thereby violating yet another religious rule. Nor was he upset when this woman publicly began praising God. She was breaking the oral law of the rabbis. That law said, "The voice of a woman [in public] is shameful" (*Berakhoth* 24a). A woman was not even permitted to speak as a witness in a criminal trial.[79] Such behavior would have violated her subordinate role.

While it was bad enough for Jesus to defy the socioreligious culture by interacting with "unclean" women and permitting them to speak in public, there was even more to upset the male chauvinists. To define woman as subordinate frequently led men to see her as a sex object, especially when, for some unfortunate reason, she became sexually promiscuous. While such a woman provided sexual gratification for many men, she was not afforded social courtesies or respect in public. Again, Jesus was different. On one occasion, having accepted a Pharisee's "dinner" invitation, he approvingly let a prostitute anoint his feet (Luke 7:36-50). For Simon, the Pharisee, such behavior was too much. One just did not relate so accommodatingly to a woman, especially a prostitute! The fact that so many men could not do without prostitution—a social institution created by men—was irrelevant to Jesus' critics.

The church's theologians, who say they follow Jesus, not only overlook that Jesus did not see women as subordinate, they also fail to see the cultural or situational context of Ephesians 5, 1 Corinthians, and 1 Peter 3. They also ignore the fact that the Greek word for obey (*hypakoo*) is never used by Paul in terms of the husband-wife relationship. He uses it only with regard to slaves and children. Evidently the sexist cultural values and practices prevented theologians from seeing that these and similar references were written for particular local circumstances and not as timeless, universal commands of God meant for all situations or cultures.

Sexist theologians throughout the ages, especially modern ones, have failed to ask themselves why so many other biblical references are not seen as equally prescriptive for all times and cultures. For example, 1 Timothy 3:4-5 demands a "bishop [clergyman] must manage his own household

---

[79]Joseph Baumgarten, "On the Testimony of Women in 1 Q Sa," *Journal of Biblical Literature* 76 (1957): 266-69.

well, keeping his children submissive and respectful in every way. For if
a man does not know how to manage his own household, how can he care
for God's church?'' Yet, it is rather easy to find sexist theologians or clergy
who are divorced or whose children have become pregnant out of wed-
lock. At the end of 1 and 2 Corinthians St. Paul, in the imperative, tells
the Christians: "Greet one another with a holy kiss.'' Yet, one does not
find even the most conservative American Christians taking these references seriously. Why not? Obviously culture has led them to ignore Paul's
clear command. First Corinthians 5:9-13 asks the Christians in Corinth not
to associate with non-Christians. Again, what theologian or clergyman,
despite taking the submission of woman literally and legalistically, follows the wishes of Paul with respect to avoiding non-Christians?

First Timothy 2:9 tells the women in the Ephesus congregation not to
groom themselves with braided hair, gold or pearls, or costly attire. Apart
from the compliance of women in the Old Order Amish society or Hutter-
ite communities, this passage is completely ignored by others—even by
ultraconservative clergymen.

These are only a few examples—many more could be cited—that
chauvinistic clergy, who say that they teach the "whole Bible," reinterpret or do not take many clear biblical references very seriously. That many
such passages are no longer taken literally indicates that modern cultural
values and beliefs have spelled significant theological change with regard
to women. Such changes, however, often betray the absence of any her-
meneutical grounds. Culture simply changed the clergy's theological practices without there being conscious awareness on their part. On the other
hand, the retention of certain sexist interpretations indicates not only that
many ancient cultural beliefs are still equated with God's will, but that sexist theologians practice a "cafeteria theology" by choosing only biblical
passages that meet their taste.[80]

The perceived inferiority of women has had its effects throughout history. The words of Vern L. Bullough can hardly be improved: "Men have
been generals, kings, writers, composers, thinkers, and doers; women have
been wives, mistresses, companions, friends and helpmates. . . . As in-

---

[80]Alvin J. Schmidt, "Fundamentalism and Sexist Theology," in Marla J. Selvidge, ed.,
Fundamentalism: What Makes It So Attractive? (Elgin IL: Brethren Press, 1984) 104.

dividuals, with few exceptions, women did not count. They were mothers, wives, daughters, sisters, proper, and forgotten."[81]

Behind the belief that women are inferior lie centuries of cultural prejudices that have been (and still are being) reinforced by selectively citing given passages from the Bible. Jesus' refusal to relate to women as inferior beings has not been (and still is not) recognized by countless theologians and clergy who carry his name. It is as though they never read the Gospels. During most of the Christian church's existence, the "inferiority" of woman was also internalized by women, even by those who were not ordinary women. Let us note but one example. St. Hildegard of Bingen (twelfth century A.D.), a prominent female abbess who had considerable influence on medieval monasticism, likened man to the soul and woman to the body. She saw the soul as heaven and the body as earth.[82] Nor has the theology of the Virgin Mary altered woman's inferior status within the church. Penny Schine Gold says:"Unlike the Virgin Mary, the living, human woman could never, it seems, totally divest herself of a kind of sexual aura implicit in her femaleness."[83] Elizabeth Schuessler Fiorenza says the Mary myth has "its roots and development in a male, clerical, and ascetic culture and theology." Fiorenza further notes that this myth is a theology of woman, preached by men to women, and one that serves "to deter women from becoming fully independent and whole human persons."[84]

---

[81]Vern L. Bullough, *The Subordinate Sex* (Urbana IL: University of Illinois Press, 1974) 3.

[82]Lina Eckenstein, *Woman under Monasticism* (New York: Russell and Russell, 1963) 275.

[83]Penny Schine Gold, *The Lady and the Virgin* (Chicago: University of Chicago Press, 1985) 113.

[84]Elizabeth Schuessler Fiorenza, "Feminist Theology as a Critical Theology of Liberation," in William K. Tabb, ed., *Churches in Struggle: Liberation Theologies and Social Change in North America* (New York: Monthly Review Press, 1986) 57, 59.

CHAPTER 5

WOMAN AS "UNCLEAN"

The male definition of woman as "unclean" has a longstanding record with many effects, one being that women themselves, to a large degree, have accepted this unfortunate definition. The fact that women have been (and really still are) culturally conditioned to spend relatively large amounts of money and time to cover up or remove their "uncleanness" with perfumes and cosmetics is evidence enough to show that the "unclean" perception of woman is far from the mere history of some unusual culture.

Menstrual Taboos

When one surveys the various taboos that cultures have imposed on people, there is one that is conspicuous: the menstrual taboo. Among the Hindus a woman's son must avoid his mother during her menstruation because she is thought to be mysteriously dangerous, a bloodstained witch.[1] The Laws of Manu in the Hindu religion say that a man's vitality diminishes if and when he approaches a menstruating woman. In southern Nigeria a menstruating woman may not prepare her husband's meals, and she is commonly confined to a separate room, according to P. A. Talbot.[2] Among the Caribs in British Guiana it is believed that food prepared by a menstruating woman will make men ill.[3]

---

[1]G. M. Carstairs, *The Twice-Born* (Bloomington: Indiana University Press, 1961) 158.

[2]P. A. Talbot, *Life in Southern Nigeria* (New York: Macmillan and Company, 1923) 228.

[3]Hutton Webster, *Taboo: A Sociological Study* (Stanford: Stanford University Press, 1942) 86.

The Carrier Indians of British Columbia had newly menstruating girls live in a hut of branches in the wilderness, essentially isolated for three or four years. It was believed that even a glimpse of them would defile an observer, especially a male. She was not permitted to walk on a path or step into a river for fear of polluting either one. While exiled, she was covered with a headdress of tanned skin that veiled her face and breast. "Her arms and legs were loaded with sinew bands to protect her from the evil spirit with which she was filled. She was herself in danger and she was a source of danger to everybody else."[4] The Dene Indians, another Canadian tribe, saw a menstruating woman as "the very incarnation of evil, a plague to be avoided at all costs, a being with whom all contact, however innocent and indirect, entail[ed] exceedingly dreadful consequences."[5]

Numerous other cultural taboos are found recorded in the anthropological literature. For instance, the Chippewa girl or woman who had her "period" had to eat alone and not talk to a man or a boy. Eskimo girls, upon having their first menstrual experience, were seen as unclean for forty days. These girls also had to let their hair cover their faces. A Uganda Bantu woman makes her husband "sick" by touching him when she has the menses. Among the Hadza of East Africa a menstruating woman avoids certain activities for fear of polluting what she touches.[6]

These are but a few illustrations of how woman has been defined by men as "unclean" in some non-Western societies. For an extended portrayal and discussion of varying menstrual fears and taboos, the reader may wish to consult *The Curse* (1976), by Janice Delaney, Mary Jane Lupton, and Emily Toth.

A woman's menses also was abhorrent to the Hebrew men of the Old Testament era. Leviticus 15:19 states: "When a woman has a discharge from her body, she shall be in her impurity for seven days, and whoever touches her shall be unclean until the evening." Not only did one become unclean by touching a menstruating woman, but if one touched her bed, or any item upon which she sat during this time, the result was also un-

---

[4]Ruth Benedict, *Patterns of Culture* (Boston: Houghton Mifflin Company, 1934) 28.

[5]A. G. Morice, "The Canadian Dene," *Annual Anthropological Report* (Toronto, 1905) 971.

[6]Mary Douglas, *Natural Symbols: Explorations in Cosmology* (New York: Vintage Books, 1975) 132-33.

cleanness. Such a "polluted" person, husband or whoever, had "to wash his clothes and bathe himself in water," according to Leviticus 15:22.

Leviticus 20:18 warns men, saying they would be cut off from the people if they were to engage in sexual intercourse with a menstruating woman. A menstruating woman in the Old Testament, as well as in the rabbinic era, "could not touch food or dishes to be used by those who ate in such a state," says Jacob Neusner.[7] Such a woman was also not permitted to prepare meals for her family during this time.

Some time after Leviticus, the oral law of the rabbis (now essentially recorded in the Talmud) became operative among the Hebrews. That law expanded the male perception of woman's uncleanness. Niddah 5:1 of the Hebrew Talmud asserts: "All women convey uncleanness (by the reason of blood) in the antechamber [vagina], for it is written, 'and her issue in her flesh be blood.' " Theodor Reik, a Jewish scholar, has shown that "under Talmudic law, a [Hebrew] man should not pass anything to a menstruating woman nor she anything to him."[8] The Hebrew woman had to purify herself by means of a ritual bath call *mikvah*.

Although Jesus was in no way bothered by the ancient patriarchal definition of woman's so-called uncleanness (see chap. 4, where mention is made of the woman who, with an issue of blood, touched him), the same cannot be said of many theologians in the early church and even later.

Dionysius of Alexandria, a third-century church father, said that a menstruating woman was prohibited from receiving the Lord's Supper and from approaching the altar, the "Sancta Sanctorum" (*Epistola Canonica ad Basilidem Episcopum,* canon 2). Also in the third century, the *Apostolic Tradition of Hippolytus* said: "If a woman is menstruous, she shall be set aside and baptized on some other day." About a hundred years or so later one finds another church father, St. Jerome, declaring: "Nothing is so unclean as a menstruating woman" (*Commentariorum in Zacharium Prophetam* 3, col. 1517).

For a long time many theologians in Christendom believed menstruation was a curse inflicted on women because of Eve's sin.[9] It was a belief

[7]Jacob Neusner, *Judaism: The Evidence of the Mishnah* (Chicago: University of Chicago Press, 1981) 66.

[8]Theodor Reik, *Pagan Rites in Judaism* (New York: Farrar, Straus and Company, 1964) 81.

[9]Vern and Bonnie Bullough, *Sin, Sickness, and Sanity: A History of Sexual Attitudes* (New York: New American Library, 1977) 119.

that Christians evidently inherited from their Hebrew heritage. Theodor
Reik says that it was the ancient rabbis who first saw woman's menstruation as the result of Eve's transgression in the Garden of Eden.[10] Linking
menstruation to Eve's sin is, of course, still done when people—even
women—refer to menses as "the curse."

It was agrarian sexism that shaped not just the theological prejudices
of Dionysius and Jerome but also some of the decisions made by the church
councils. Thus in the latter half of the fourth century the Synod of Laodicea said in its forty-fourth canon: "Wives should not approach the altar."[11] In A.D. 485 the Synod of Rome barred women from approaching
the baptistery.[12] One hundred years later, the Synod of Auxerre in France
declared: "A woman may not touch the communion palla."[13] Also in the
sixth century one finds the Syriac church not permitting women, during
their menstrual cycle, to participate in communion.[14]

Theological sexism had not lost favor by the latter part of the eighth
century because in A.D.789 the Synod of Aachen, in its seventeenth canon,
asserted: "Women may not approach the altar, according to canon 44 of
Laodicea."[15] In the early ninth century the so-called "Reform" Synod of
Paris in 829 issued a canon, similar to previous church canons, saying that
women were not to come to the altar or to touch communion ware. This
synod said: "In some provinces it happens that women push themselves
into the altar area where they handle the holy vessels, giving to the believers the priestly vessels, and even extend the body and blood of the Lord to
the people. Such a practice is horrible and must not continue."[16]

In England during the latter part of the tenth century, one finds the forty-
fourth canon of the so-called Canons of Edgar (named in honor of King
Edgar, who reigned from 959–975) saying: "It is right that no woman come

---

[10]Reik, *Rites,* 85.

[11]Carl Joseph von Hefele, *Conciliengeschichte,* vol. 1 (Freiburg: Herder'sche Verlagshandlung, 1873) 771.

[12]Hefele, *Conciliengeschichte,* (1875) 2:611.

[13]Hefele, *Conciliengeschichte,* (1877) 3:46.

[14]Arthur Voobus, *Syrische Kanonessammlungen* (Louwain, 1970) 1:267.

[15]Hefele, *Conciliengeschichte,* (1877) 3:666.

[16]Hefele, *Conciliengeschichte,* (1879) 4:63.

near the altar while mass is being celebrated."[17] Another Anglo-Saxon theological ruling declared: "We . . . command that at those hours in which the priest sings the mass no woman approach near the altar, but let them stand in their places. . . . Women should bear in mind their infirmities and the tenderness of their sex, and therefore they shall dread to touch any of the holy things belonging to the services of the church."[18]

Not only were women discriminated against by keeping them from the altar and from receiving communion, but even when they were allowed to commune, they had to receive communion differently from men. As early as A.D. 578 a church canon specified: "*Ne liceat muliere nude manu eucharistiam accipere*" (A woman may not receive the communion bread with her bare hand).[19]

The practice of not allowing a woman to receive the communion bread in her bare hand was not just confined to one or two isolated places or times. Maskell, in his *Ancient Liturgy of the Church of England,* shows that in the Anglo-Saxon church, from the ninth century onward, women were only permitted to receive the Eucharist if their hands were gloved.[20] No such rule or requirement ever existed for men. Evidently, the "uncleanness" of woman made it necessary for theologians to make sure that no woman's hand would make the communion bread unclean. Clearly, culture had shaped not only their perception of woman, but it also shaped a theology concerning her nature and role in the church's life. Given such theological opinions and practices, one is reminded of the words Jesus spoke to the Pharisees. He said: "In vain do they worship me, teaching as doctrine the precepts of men" (Matt. 15:9). One might substitute the word *culture* for the word *men* in Jesus' statement, since Jesus also saw culture shaping the theological beliefs and teaching of the religious elite.

Although today most churches no longer bar menstruating women either from receiving communion or from the altar, the ancient menstrual taboo

---

[17]Cited by D. Whitelock, M. Brett, and C. N. L. Brooke, eds., *Councils and Synods with Other Documents Relating to the English Church,* vol. 1 (Oxford: Clarendon Press, 1981) 328-29.

[18]Benjamin Thorpe, *Ancient Laws and Institutes of England,* vol. 2 (London: G. Eyre and Spottiswoode, 1840) 407.

[19]Hefele, *Conciliengeschichte,* 3:46.

[20]William Maskell, *The Ancient Liturgy of the Church of England* (Oxford: Clarendon Press, 1882) 187.

has not disappeared entirely. As late as 1957 a Catholic handbook issued for seminaries said menstruating women could receive the Lord's Supper, but they could not, in this biological state, participate in liturgical functions at the altar.[21] In many conservative Lutheran churches women were not permitted to take the communion ware, which they had cleaned, to the altar in preparation for the next service. That act had to be performed by the male officers known as elders. Whether this curb on woman's church activities was prompted by the old belief of her being unclean or because she was not to be involved in pastoral functions is not clear. I personally know of one upper-middle-class Lutheran congregation in an American city that in the 1950s still did not permit women to place the communion ware on the altar. And as recently as 1970 the Catholic church barred women lectors from the sanctuary during their menstrual periods.[22]

The fear of menstruating women that prevailed among the church's clergy for more than a thousand years was only once or twice interrupted by a voice of common sense. In the seventh century Pope Gregory I was asked if menstruating women were permitted to attend church and also receive the Eucharist. Unlike some of the church councils and theologians before and after him, he replied in the affirmative. Said he: "The monthly courses of women are not their fault because nature causes them."[23] This is the only contrary voice that I was able to find. An exhaustive search might reveal one or two additional voices similar to Gregory's. However, given the centuries of cultural fear and prejudices that were associated with a woman's menses, it seems unlikely that even a handful of sympathetic ecclesiastical leaders existed in the many centuries of the church's life.

One wonders how much the erroneously perceived uncleanness of woman, stemming from primitive beliefs, influenced the medieval church to have married clergy dismiss their wives. For instance, the Synod of London in 1102 and in 1108 did not allow priests to administer Mass unless they first dismissed their wives.[24] Evidently, the "uncleanness" of the wives would have made the clergy unclean, so they had to dismiss them.

---

[21]Dominic M. Prummer, *Handbook of Moral Theology*, trans. G. W. Shelton (New York: P. J. Kennedy, 1957) 270.

[22]Albertus Grath, *Women and the Church* (Garden City: Image Books, 1976) 135.

[23]Bede, *Opera Historica* (London: Wm. Heinemann, 1930) 137.

[24]Hefele, *Conciliengeschichte* (1886), 5:292.

It is rather ironic to hear even a modern woman refer to her menses as "the curse." In employing this expression, such women are echoing an ancient myth that was created by fear-ridden male cultures. If the woman's menstruation ever was a curse to anyone, it was primarily so to the males, whose social and religious norms prevented them from having sexual intercourse during this time; it was the masculine culture that conjured up various fears and inhibitions regarding the presence of blood during menses.

The Roman philosopher Pliny, in the first century, showed the seriousness with which men took the mythological beliefs concerning a woman's menses. Without any apparent doubt, he wrote: "Contact with it [menstrual blood] turns new wine sour, crops touched by it become barren, grafts die, seeds in garden are dried up, the fruit of trees falls off, the bright surface of mirrors in which it is merely reflected is dimmed, the edge of steel and the gleam of ivory are dulled, hives of bees die, and a horrible smell fills the air; to taste it drives dogs mad and infects their bites with an incurable poison" (*Natural History* 8.64).

As recently as the eighteenth century many Portuguese and Germans believed that if the hair of a menstruating woman were to be buried, a snake would arise from it.[25] The mythology of "the curse" appears to have been taken even more seriously by men in cultures where hunting is (or was) an important source of the people's food supply.[26] The belief that a woman's menstrual period deters successful hunting is a topic that one can hear men talk about even in present-day urban settings, where hunting obviously is not even a sport for most men, much less an important means of obtaining food. This old male prejudice, however, is not supported by empirical research. For example, one experimental study by Nunley showed that it is not female menstrual blood but the presence of any kind of blood that deters successful hunting. Human blood evidently alerts animals to the presence of human beings, whom they then elude.[27]

Physiologically, a woman's menstrual period never was a curse, reportedly something she must endure because of Eve's sin in the Garden of Eden. Menstruation for women is as natural and normal as is the growth

---

[25]Reik, *Rites*, 85.

[26]Michio Kitahara, "Menstrual Taboos and the Importance of Hunting," *American Anthropologist* 84 (1982): 901-903.

[27]M. Christopher Nunley, "Response of Deer to Human Blood Odor," *American Anthropologist* 83 (September 1981): 630-34.

of facial hair to men. The "curse" was simply the product of women's having unwittingly accepted and internalized sexist male values and beliefs that became enshrined in culture upon culture. The various sexist beliefs that made the "curse" seem real will not disappear overnight. For instance, in 1970 Dr. Edgar Berman, a physician, Democratic party official, and personal friend of former Vice President Hubert Humphrey, was brash enough to assert that a woman's menstrual cycle and menopause disqualified her for key executive jobs. He put it in this way: "If you had an investment in a bank, you wouldn't want the president of your bank making a loan under these raging hormonal influences at that particular period."[28]

When Congresswoman Patsy T. Mink of Hawaii requested Hubert Humphrey to ask for Berman's resignation from the Democratic party's Committee on National Priorities for his sexist remarks, Berman replied that Mink's letter was an expression of a woman's "raging hormonal imbalance."[29] When a man acts angry about some occurrence, it is not seen as the result of a hormonal imbalance. But when a woman expresses just and appropriate anger, she is either hysterical or suffering from a hormonal imbalance. The fear and horror, prompted by ignorance, that men have attached to woman's menses became imbedded in the culture of numerous societies. M. Esther Harding has argued that the menstrual taboo was likely the first taboo that men imposed on women.[30] In fact, it may well have been man's first success in conveying the myth of woman's inferiority, a myth that woman all too often had to accept in the agrarian, patriarchal societies. The cultural forces compelled her, given her frequent pregnancies and small children to nurse.

Woman's "uncleanness," perceived to stem from her menstrual cycle, was frequently reinforced by religious values. These values undoubtedly aggravated the problem for woman in that it made men feel justified in their prejudicial and discriminatory views of woman's "impurity." The Hebrew rabbis used the word *niddah* to describe woman's menstrual uncleanness. In fact, the Talmud has a book called *Niddah* that largely deals with

---

[28]Christopher Lyon, "Role of Women Sparks Debate by Congresswoman and Doctor," *New York Times,* 26 July 1970, p. 35.

[29]Ibid.

[30]M. Esther Harding, *Woman's Mystery* (London: Longman's, Green and Company, 1935) 43.

woman's perceived uncleanness. The word *niddah* was derived from *na-dah*, which means to expel. Often it meant that woman was to be expelled from conventional social interaction or discourse. Here is an example: Theodor Reik recalls an experience from his Jewish childhood, when his grandfather, while sitting at the table, said to his wife: "*Mach den Tisch rein!*" (Clean the table.) At first Theodor thought, as his grandmother got up, that she would wipe the table. But no, she went to another room and stayed there. Only later did he learn that "clean the table" meant leave the table because she had her menstrual period.[31]

The widespread—one is almost tempted to say universal—male fear of woman's menses has not just been reinforced by Jewish and Christian theology but by other religions too. The Koran, for example, says: "Separate yourselves therefore from women and approach them not, until they be cleansed. But when they are cleansed, go unto them as God hath ordained for you."

Childbirth "Uncleanness"

Although much emphasis was given to children's being a "blessing" in the Old Testament, the process of giving birth ironically was seen as an unclean act. The Hebrew woman had to undergo a mandatory, ritualistic purification after having given birth to a child (Lev. 12:1-8).

If the newly born infant was a girl, the mother was unclean for two weeks. Leviticus 12:5 reads: "If she bears a female child, then she shall be unclean for two weeks, as in her menstruation, and she shall continue in the blood of her purification for sixty-six days." If, however, the child was a boy, the mother was unclean only for one week, and the purification of the mother's blood comparatively took only thirty-three days to complete (Lev. 12:2-4).

Why the mother was considered to be unclean for a period twice as long with the birth of an infant daughter, as opposed to giving birth to an infant son, is nowhere explained in the Old Testament. The twentieth-century person—religiously oriented or not—is simply perplexed at this unexplained distinction. One is compelled to ask how such a distinction arose.

C. F. Keil and F. Delitzsch, two Old Testament exegetes of the nineteenth century, believed that Leviticus 12 reflected the ancient conviction that bleeding and watery discharge continued longer after the birth of a girl

---

[31]Reik, *Rites*, 81.

than after the birth of a boy.[32] This opinion was similarly expressed by Hippocrates, the Greek physician, in the fifth century B.C. In one of his works (*Regimen* 1.27), he argued that girls are more inclined to water and moisture than boys, who were more inclined to fire and drier substances. This ancient distinction, it need hardly be said, was of course in error, yet held to for centuries because of sexist cultural values.

The so-called uncleanness of childbirth was not just confined to the Hebrews of the Old Testament. It was not too long after Christianity had become legalized in the Roman empire that one finds Christian theologians increasingly reflecting ancient cultural prejudices pertaining to women. As noted in the previous chapter, the words and actions of Jesus were soon overshadowed by longstanding sexist values stemming from patriarchal stereotypes regarding women. So by the fifth century one finds St. Augustine saying that Leviticus 12:1-8 also applied to the Christian woman in childbirth (*Quaestionum In Heptateuchum* 3, col. 694f). His pronouncement is rather ironic because it was he who gave Christian theology the distinction of "ceremonial law" versus "moral law" in interpreting the Old Testament. This distinction, he taught, meant that Christians were no longer bound to the Old Testament's ceremonial laws, which, for example, commanded the Israelites to circumcise males, to tithe, not to eat fish without fins or scales, pork, or rabbit, not to wear clothing with mingled fabrics, and so forth. Christians were only bound to the moral law. "Thou shalt not covet" was a moral precept, whereas the examples just cited were ceremonial or symbolic laws (*Contra Faustus* 6.2).

Surely this distinction makes Leviticus 12:1-8 a ceremonial law. Yet the cultural forces of sexism overpowered Augustine so that he lost sight of his own theological model, which should have led him to say that childbirth was no longer unclean in the new covenant under Christ, who—according to Augustine and other Christians—fulfilled the law. But as we saw earlier, Augustine was no advocate of female equality.

Not just Augustine but others after him saw childbirth as unclean. The Arabic canons of Nicaea (the ninth canon) declared: "Women ought to abstain from entering the church and from partaking of holy communion for forty days after a birth; after which, let the woman carefully wash her garments and bathe her person and the child; then let her, together with her

---

[32]C. F. Keil and F. Delitzsch, *Biblischer Commentar ueber Die Buecher Moses,* vol. 2 (Leipzig: Doerffling and Franke, 1870) 98.

husband present him in the church at the steps of the altar . . . let the priest receive and say for her the prayer of purification and bless the child according to the prescribed ceremonies of the church."[33]

The first Prayer Book of King Edward VI in 1549 contained a ritual known as "The Order of the Purification of Women." The ceremony, dating back to medieval times and earlier, says Walker, took place "in the church porch (*anteostium*) . . . and after the prayers the woman was sprinkled with holy water, and the priest led her by the right hand into the church (*per manum dextram in ecclesiam*)."[34] Some medieval rites used Psalms 121 and 128. The English Prayer Book of 1549 omitted the latter psalm. The American version of the Book of Common Prayer used selected verses from Psalm 116, according to Walker.[35] This psalm speaks about thanking God for recovering from illness, not from having given birth to a child.

In 1552 the editors of the English Prayer Book changed the ritual's name from "The Order of the Purification of Women" to "The Churching of Women." This change was made in order not to give a wrong understanding, says Procter.[36] This change is significant in that it reflects once again how culture, however slowly, affects the church's theology. In Leviticus 12 the woman is clearly pictured as unclean and in need of being purified. The church, like St. Augustine and subsequent others, saw Leviticus as accurately portraying woman to be unclean as a result of childbirth. However, I have not been able to find any evidence that from Augustine (fifth century) to the time of Edward VI (sixteenth century), infant girls vis-à-vis boys were considered to be unclean twice as long. Why girls no longer made their mother unclean for twice the period of time is not clear. Whatever prompted the removal of that particular form of inequality, by 1552 English church leaders saw the word *purification* as improper so they gave the old ritual a new name.

Although some theologians evidently saw the word *purification* as inappropriate in that it conveyed an unclean perception of woman, sexist

---

[33]Samuel Cheetham, "Churching of Women," in William Smith and Samuel Cheetham, eds., *A Dictionary of Christian Antiquities* (London: John Murray, 1908) 390-91.

[34]Gwynne Walker, *Primitive Worship: The Prayer Book* (London: Longman's, Green and Company, 1917) 357.

[35]Ibid.

[36]Francis Procter, *A History of the Book of Common Prayer* (London: Macmillan and Company, 1880) 434.

practices associated with childbirth did not come to an end. For instance, the ''churching of women'' continued in many Protestant churches. The sixteenth-century Lutheran church in Germany had its counterpart to the English ritual. In its manual *Die Kirchenordnung der evangelischen luth-erischen Kirche Deutschlands in ihrem ersten Jahrhundert,* 1824, the Lutheran church called its rite of churching woman ''*Von Kirchgang und Einsegnung der Kinderbetterinnen*'' (Church Attendance and Consecrating the Childbirth Process). Although the Lutheran ritual said that its churching of women did not mean the law of Moses was still operative, it did not repudiate the ''unclean'' concept of woman in Leviticus 12. The Lutheran rite also added 1 Timothy 2:15, namely, ''Women will be saved through bearing children, if she continues in faith and love and holiness, with modesty.''

Ehrenfried Liebich, a Lutheran pastor in the eighteenth century, produced the German Hirschberger Bible. Liebich inserted his own comments between given references to this Bible edition. Following Leviticus 12:5, he commented on the Mosaic wording that portrays the mother to be unclean for sixty-six days if she bore a girl and thirty-three days if the infant was a boy. Liebich said that this difference is to remind people that it was the female sex that brought the foremost uncleanness—sin—into the world.

More than a hundred years after Liebich's Hirschberger Bible and the Lutheran ritual of churching women, one still finds some very decided sexist opinions regarding woman's uncleanness that hark back to Leviticus 12. In 1905 a widely used Bible commentary, *The Expositor's Bible* (24 volumes), has S. H. Kellog, a true-blue Calvinist, putting forth the same argument as Liebich. Kellog also made bold to say that the double time period of a woman's uncleanness at a girl's birth was an added reminder of woman's initial role in the fall of mankind into sin.[37]

In the 1950s the Moody Bible Press published *The Bible Self-Explained.* Similar to the Hirschberger Bible of the eighteenth century, it inserted comments between selected Bible references. For example, Genesis 3:16 is inserted after Leviticus 12:2. In doing so, this Bible edition indicated that woman, whether in childbirth or in her menstrual cycle, was unclean because Eve (woman's prototype) brought sin into human relationships.

---

[37]S. H. Kellog, ''The Book of Leviticus,'' *The Expositor's Bible,* vol. 2 (New York: A. C. Armstrong and Son, 1905) 322.

It is noteworthy to observe that for centuries cultural forces shaped the religious perception of woman as unclean. And it is even more interesting to note that in more recent times, in an era of growing feminine equality, cultural forces have prompted a redefinition of woman. The stringent, obsessive fears once attached to a woman's menses are slowly losing their force and presence. While uninformed and bigoted men may still be repelled by a woman's menstruation, they no longer see themselves as contaminated when coming in physical contact with a woman having her menstrual period as they once did, for example, in the Old Testament era. Similarly, the religious definition of woman becoming unclean in the act of childbirth has changed even more. Gone are the days of what theologians once called "the churching of women." Today many clergy—even those in fundamentalistic and conservative churches—have not even heard of this formerly religiously mandated custom. "The Churching of Women," once called "The Order of the Purification of Women" from the Middle Ages to the nineteenth century, took different forms as a result of the cultural forces that changed it from one society to another. The Lutheran ritual differed from the rite of the Church of England, and the American rite differed from its English ancestor. Moreover, there was no real resemblance to Leviticus 12 in these rituals. The patriarchal interpretation of Genesis 3:16, St. Augustine's views of woman with respect to her becoming unclean in childbirth, and other similar ones gave way to the culture of the day. Whether church leaders recognized it or not—and undoubtedly they did not—culture had slowly reshaped the definition of woman as unclean to one where the agrarian-patriarchal perception of woman was becoming less and less prominent.

CHAPTER 6

WOMAN AS "UNEQUAL"

The cultural mores in the agrarian era that defined woman as inferior socially, biologically, intellectually, and spiritually definitely affected concrete life situations. Different social customs and institutions, often reinforced by theologians and their chauvinistic theology, clearly demonstrated that woman was defined and treated as decidedly "unequal" vis-à-vis the human male.

The Virgin Bride and the Double Standard of Sex

Even today men in Western society still make a great deal of noise about the importance of marrying a virgin bride. Such noise harks back to centuries of sexist values and beliefs that were integrated into the social structure of agrarian societies, where patriarchal values held sway. Today the male desire to marry a virgin is largely an emotional phenomenon because in Western societies there is no longer the force of law or capital punishment behind the patriarchal craving for a "pure" woman at the time of marriage. In the past, however, it was quite different.

One effective way to assure that the bride was a virgin was to marry her while she still was essentially a child. That is precisely what the cultural mores provided and required in ancient times. Whether it was the Assyrians, the Babylonians, the Hebrews of the Old Testament era, the Greeks, or the Romans, a man ranging from nineteen to thirty years of age would marry a girl of twelve or thirteen. In some societies an agreement was made with the girl's father a year or two before she was twelve. For example, the influential church father, St. Augustine, says in his *Confessions* that at the age of thirty he contracted to marry a girl two years before the marriageable age; evidently she was only ten years old. Plutarch in his *Parallel Lives of Illustrious Greeks and Romans* says the Roman fathers commonly gave their daughters into marriage at age twelve or under. Justinian's *Institutions* corroborates Plutarch's report.

The male desire to have a virgin bride portrays a decided sexist posture, revealing an institutionalized double standard of sexual behavior. This standard is apparent in Deuteronomy 22:13-21, which shows that when the bride was found not to be a virgin, she was brought to her father's house, where she was then stoned to death. No such punishment existed for the nonvirgin groom at the time of marriage. In fact, it was unthinkable for anyone even to question the double standard of sexual behavior when it did not harm another man's property.

Another example of the double standard pertaining to a woman's virginity, or lack of it, is found in Deuteronomy 22:28-29. Here we find that when a man—single or married—deflowered a maiden, he was not stoned to death but rather merely required to pay her father fifty shekels of silver and then marry her.

Adultery and the Double Standard of Sex

In modern Western societies adultery is commonly understood to be the result of a husband or wife sexually cohabiting with a third party. So common is this understanding that it comes as a shock to many Christians and non-Christians today when they hear that for the greater part of history, including the sexual ethics of the Old Testament, such a view of adultery was unknown. Among the ancients adultery was defined on the basis of the woman's marital status. The man's status was irrelevant. A married man who enjoyed the sexual favors of a single woman could not commit adultery! A married woman, on the other hand, cohabiting with either a single or married man was *always* guilty of adultery. If a man—single or married—had sex with a married woman, then he too was guilty of adultery. The essence of the offense lay in having sex with a married woman, who was her husband's property. Man was never woman's property. Adultery in patriarchal societies was primarily a property violation.

In chapter 3 we noted that no social shame or condemnation was attached to a Hebrew male consorting with a prostitute. Relative to the time of Onan (mentioned in Genesis 38), Robert Graves and Raphael Patai provide additional evidence for this observation. They show there was "no stigma attached in early Judea to men who lay with prostitutes, so long as these were not the property of a husband or father, or in a state of ritual impurity."[1] Similarly, men in the Hittite society were not punished or ridiculed for enjoying sexual favors with prostitutes.[2] And in the classical era of Greek literature Demosthenes (388–322 B.C.), describing the Greek double standard, said: "Mistresses [*hetaerae*] we keep for the sake of pleasure, concubines for the daily care of our persons, but wives to bear us legitimate children and to be faithful guardians of our households" (*Against Neaera* 122). The Greek wife, like the wives in other male-dominated societies, would have suffered death had she consorted sexually with someone other than her husband.

Not only could the man in ancient societies consort with prostitutes without any social or theological reprobation, but he could also add to his sexual variety by gathering unto himself maids or concubines, especially if he had the material resources to do so. Having concubines was a widespread and accepted practice in the ancient cultures of the East, whether among the Semites, Greeks, or Romans. In Genesis 30 an account is given of how Jacob had sons from two household maids, Bilhah and Zilpah. Nowhere in the entire Bible is there any negative comment relative to Jacob's behavior.

Numerous other instances are recorded in the Old Testament where men had sexual intercourse with women who were not their wives. The culture of the ancient, patriarchal societies had made the double standard of sexual behavior a way of life. Nowhere do the priest or scribes in the Old Testament era ever question the culturally entrenched male ethic of woman being "unequal." But pity the poor wife if she ever had sex with another man! "A husband had freedom to fornicate, while a wife could be put to death for doing the same thing."[3]

The belief that it was considered sinful in the Old Testament for a man—married or not—to have sex with a prostitute is a good example of present-day culture, influenced by Christian values, leading well-meaning individuals to see something in the Old Testament texts that simply is not there. It also shows a lack of understanding of the values and practices of the pa-

---

[1]Robert Graves and Raphael Patai, *Hebrew Myths: The Book of Genesis* (Garden City: Doubleday & Company, 1964) 246.

[2]E. Neufeld, *The Hittite Laws* (London: Luzae & Company, 1951) 54-56.

[3]Vern L. Bullough, *The Subordinate Sex* (Urbana: University of Illinois Press, 1974) 23.

triarchal culture as found among the ancient Hebrews. To be sure, there are numerous references to the sinfulness of a harlot or prostitute in the Old Testament. For instance, there are accounts in Proverbs that speak about the evils of harlotry, but the emphasis is on how such a woman will take advantage of the man. Proverbs does not say that a man's extramarital sex act with such a woman was sinful or morally wrong.

In agrarian societies the values revolved around the patriarch, the head of the family unit or clan. Wife, child, or slave all were required to serve him: he was supreme. Laws reflected a patriarchal ethic. This ethic was quite evident in the procedures that were employed to prove an accused woman guilty of adultery, a sin that could only be committed against the husband.

The Assyrians and Babylonians had the woman accused of adultery undergo the river ordeal. She was thrown into the river, and if she drowned, she was guilty. If she did not drown, she was innocent. The Hebrews, apparently influenced by this cultural method of ascertaining a woman's guilt or innocence, also used a water test. Theirs, however, was not performed in a river, undoubtedly because the Hebrews had no rivers deep enough to drown someone. So they performed the "bitter-water test" (Num. 5:11-31). This test was conducted by a priest reciting a religious ritual, while the accused woman drank water that was mixed with dust from the tabernacle floor. The priest would also make her swear an oath, saying that if she was not guilty of having sinned sexually against her husband—whose property she was—she would suffer no ill physical effects. If the bitter water, however, caused her stomach to swell or her thigh or inner parts to waste away, she was pronounced guilty of adultery. She then became a "curse among her people" (Num. 5:27), but was not executed as Leviticus 20:10 and Deuteronomy 22:24 called for when a woman was guilty of adultery. Evidently, the death penalty was not part of the bitter-water test because the Hebrews required two eyewitnesses for conviction of a capital offense (Deut. 17:6). This law prevented taking the "guilty" woman's life as delineated in Numbers 5.

The glaring inequality of the bitter-water test is evident in that no such test existed for any man. Moreover, given the pervasiveness and the power of the ancient cultural mores that socially and religiously legitimated the double standard of sexual conduct, no woman would have dared accuse her husband of adultery. Cultural forces did not even permit her to think about her unequal status with respect to the injustice of the double standard. In a patriarchal culture where the wife was totally subordinate to her husband, only he was seen as being harmed by the wife lying with another man. By definition only the wife could be unfaithful, not her husband.

The Homunculus Myth

The ancient patriarchal societies drew many of their values and beliefs from their agrarian experiences. This was particularly true with regard to their understanding the conception or birth process. Having witnessed all kinds of seeds sprout in the soil and bring forth new plants, whether they entered the soil by natural means or were deliberately planted by human beings, it is understandable why the ancients in many societies saw the birth of humans and other animals coming forth from "seed" deposited by the male. Just as the soil served as the place where the seed of a plant received shelter and nourishment for it to germinate and grow, so too the uterus of the female (human or nonhuman) provided shelter and nourishment for the "seed" of the male to germinate and grow until it was ready to be born.

The female, like the soil, was considered to be passive. She contributed nothing biologically or genetically. Every biological quality and characteristic was derived from the male. In fact, it was believed that the "seed" of the human male contained a miniature human being (homunculus), and the "seed" of the nonhuman male contained a miniature animal (animalculus).

The homunculus myth is another example of how woman was seen as unequal relative to the man. The Greek playwright Aeschylus (525?–456 B.C.) expressed the homunculus position and woman's inequality by having Apollo say: "The mother of what is called her child is not its parent, but only the nurse of the newly implanted germ . . . whereas she, as a stranger for a stranger, doth but preserve the sprout" (*Eumenides* 658-661). Aristotle said: "Male is that which is able to concoct, to cause to take shape, and to discharge semen [seed] possessing the principle of the form. . . . Female is that which receives semen, but is unable to cause semen to take shape" (*Generation of Animals* 4.765b:10-11). Euripides, the Greek poet, had Orestes saying that his father is "my source of life," while his mother "did but foster me" (*Orestes* 553). Diodorus (first century B.C.), a Greek writer of history, thought the homunculus belief went back to the Egyptians, who thought "that the father is the sole author of procreation and the mother only supplies the fetus with nourishment and a place to live" (*Diodorus of Sicily* 1.80.4-5).

The above citations clearly show that agrarian experiences influenced and undergirded the ancient understanding of the human conception process. The Greek word *spermakos* and the Latin word *semin* both mean "seed." It was the male's ejaculated fluid that was likened to the seed of plants.

The homunculus concept was the culturally acceptable way of understanding the process of biological reproduction in ancient societies. The Old Testament calls the substance ejaculated by man *zera* ("seed"), for example, in Leviticus 15:16, 17, 18, and 32. Hebrew women were treated "as fields to be ploughed and sown."[4] *Genesis Rabba* (fifth century A.D.) has Jacob telling Reuben: "The ploughing and sowing I did in Leah should have been done in Rachel." This is similar to the way Aristophanes has Athenian speaking about the sex act: "I'd like to strip and plough my field" (*Lystrata* 1172).

Tertullian, the influential church father of the second century, in his *De Anima* said that woman "brings neither sperm nor pneuma, nor substance whereas the man produces pneuma and substance." Here it looks like Tertullian echoed the views of Aristotle, who said the "pneuma is enclosed within the semen" (*Generation of Animals* 2.736b: 37-38). A couple of centuries after Tertullian, St. Augustine showed himself a true homunculus believer by declaring, "God forms man of human seed," thus comparing the man's sexual emission with seed sown in the soil of the farmer (*On Marriage and Concupiscence* 2.29).

So firmly was the homunculus doctrine accepted in ancient societies that when the microscope made its appearance, this belief prevented even scientists from seeing what they really saw. In 1678 Anthony Leeuwenhoeck, the father of microbiology and a maker of microscopes, said he saw miniature dogs, rabbits, horses, and human beings when he examined their respective sperms under the microscope. In fact, his "findings" were published in the proceedings of a highly reputable scientific group, the Royal Society in London.[5] Ironically and unbelievably, Leeuwenhoeck's "obser-

---

[4]Graves and Patai, *Hebrew Myths*, 242.

[5]Royal Society, "Observationes D. Anthonii Leeuwenhoeck de Natis e Semine Genitali Animalculis," *Philosophy Transactions* (London, 1678). Some scholars believe that by 1716 Leeuwenhoeck seemed less certain of actually having seen miniature humans or animals in the respective sperms. See A. W. Meyer, *The Rise of Embryology* (Stanford: Stanford University Press, 1939).

vations" were confirmed by other scientists in noteworthy universities.[6] Dalenpatius in 1699 said he even saw the hands, feet, chest, and head of the human in the sperm of man.[7] Some scientists even made drawings of what they "saw." One such drawing, made by Hartsoeker in 1694, appears in A. W. Meyer's scholarly book *The Rise of Embryology* (1939).

These drawings were conveniently used by some theologians to demonstrate conclusively that birth control—the spilling of "seed" as in Genesis 38:8-10—was indeed a "wicked sin" because miniature human beings were being destroyed by not allowing conception to take place. Said Rabbi Meir: "Now it has been seen through the viewing instrument which is called a microscope that a drop of man's sperm, while yet in its original temperature, contains small creatures in man's image and likeness. . . . How strange the Talmudic idea that *hash-hatat zera* is 'like murder' seemed to the philosophers among us before the microscope was invented" (*Sefer Ha Brit* 1797).

That highly educated men of science believed they saw the homunculus in human sperm, and the animalculus in animal sperm, pointedly demonstrates that once given cultural beliefs have been accepted or legitimated for long periods of time, they lead individuals to see something that in reality does not exist. This ancient understanding, erroneous and unfortunate, has not yet completely disappeared from existence. Vestiges of the homunculus concept are still around. It is not uncommon to read in the newspapers of today that a wife "bore her husband x number of children." Even a college-educated woman can still be heard saying: "I gave birth to his two children." These are good examples of how some aspects of the agrarian-patriarchal culture is still with us.

The homunculus belief not only viewed woman as a totally passive, unequal instrument in the reproductive process, but it also blamed her if no pregnancy occurred. It was never the fault of the man. In part, the ancients justified the institution of polygamy or having concubines on the basis of the first wife's being "barren." The use that Jacob made of Rachel's and Leah's maids in Genesis 30 illustrates this practice quite well. The Talmud reveals that if a woman did not "bear" her husband a child within ten years of married life, the husband was to take a second woman.

---

[6]Richard Lewinsohn, *A History of Sexual Customs*, trans. Alexander Mayer (New York: Harper and Brothers, 1958) 202.

[7]Joseph Needham, *A History of Embryology* (New York: Abelard and Schuman, 1959) 205-206.

As noted, the ancient agrarian doctrine of the homunculus did not come to an end with the invention of the microscope. Basically, the belief remained for another 200 years. The first scientific step away from this sexist view of the conception process occurred when Karl von Baer in 1827 discovered the human ovum. But he too was still blinded by centuries of cultural sexism that saw woman as unequal to man in the reproductive act. He believed the ovum was passive until activated by the male sperm. That the ovum provided one half of the fetus's heredity content was unknown to him and other scientists of his day.

In 1877 the Swiss biologist H. Fiol took still another step away from the homunculus myth when he observed the entry of sperm into the ovum of a starfish. Understanding the fertilization process in human beings, however, took longer still. It was not until after 1900 that human chromosomes were studied in terms of inheritance, revealing for the first time that man and woman were equal in the conception and birth process. Each provides 23 chromosomes to the fetus. No longer could woman be seen as someone who merely provided shelter and nourishment for man's "seed." Science, in effect, had demolished the ancient agrarian myth that had defined woman as unequal to man.

The homunculus belief illustrates a truth often not recognized, namely, that when a cultural concept has been widely accepted—as the homunculus concept was—it can actually distort the perception of empirical reality, as it did with the scientists who "saw" miniature human beings under the microscope that in fact were not there. With the homunculus concept there was a reversal of the adage that "to see is to believe." Instead, belief led to "seeing."

Woman as Property: The Case of Adultery

The history of woman's inequality is conspicuous by the way the ancients, and generations following them, viewed adultery. As I noted earlier in this chapter, adultery was treated as a property offense. Vern Bullough expresses it very well: "Adultery was not a sin against morality, but a trespass against the husband's property."[8] The wife was the husband's property. No one could have sexual intercourse with her without the husband's consent—a very rare occurrence. The ancient Greeks would

---

[8]Bullough, *Subordinate Sex,* 23.

on occasion even give their wives to others on loan as one would loan out other items of property.[9]

The concept of adultery as a property offense in patriarchal societies applied even to a man's female servants or maids. For example, in *The Odyssey* Odysseus comes home after an absence of ten years. He finds that twelve of his servant women had sexual relations without his permission. So he commands his son, Telemachus, to kill all of them. It was a matter of disposing of damaged, unwanted property that the patriarch no longer valued.

The Greek male, like men in other societies of that time, could not commit adultery if he had sex with an unmarried woman. "Extra-marital love relationships were a matter of course for the Greek man."[10] Medea, in one of Euripides' plays, laments this double standard of sex: "If a man grows tired of the company at home, he can go out and find a cure for his tediousness. We wives are forced to look to one man only" (*Medea* 244-47). Flaceliere shows that "adultery by the husband, however open and recognized by public opinion, could not be cited by the wife as grounds for a marital separation. On the other hand, adultery by the wife rendered her repudiation obligatory. Refusal to dismiss her entailed the loss of civil rights of the husband."[11]

In Rome under Augustus (27 B.C.–A.D.14), the Roman institution of *patria potestas* permitted the husband of an adulterous wife to kill her.[12] The Romans saw adultery on the part of a wife as one of the most serious domestic crimes.[13] This view of woman persisted for centuries. Thus we read that *Lex Julia* (a Roman law operative during the sixth century of the Christian era) clearly stated that a wife had no right to bring charges against her husband in the event of adultery.

---

[9]Charles Albert Savage, *The Athenian Family: A Sociological and Legal Study* (Baltimore, 1907) 12.

[10]Verena Zinserling, *Women in Greece and Rome* (New York: Abner Schramm, 1973) 39.

[11]Robert Flaceliere, *Love in Ancient Greece,* trans. James Cleugh (New York: Crown Publications, 1962) 116.

[12]Sarah Pomeroy, *Goddesses, Whores, Wives, and Slaves: Women in Classical Antiquity* (New York: Schocken Books, 1975) 159.

[13]Wilhelm A. Becker, *Gallus,* trans. Frederick Metcalfe (New York: Longmans, Green and Company, 1920) 156.

The double standard regarding adultery was also the social norm among the Hebrews. "In Jewish [and Old Testament] law adultery was the intercourse of a married woman with *any* man other than her husband."[14] Deuteronomy 20:22 says: "If a man is found lying with the wife of another man, both of them shall die." Similarly, Leviticus 20:10 states: "If a man commits adultery with the wife of his neighbor, both the adulterer and the adulterous shall be put to death." Note, no mention is made of a husband lying with an unmarried woman. Genesis 30 clearly shows that Jacob had sexual relations with at least two maids. Jacob is by no means pictured as guilty of adultery. Rather, the sons of these two maids, as well as the sons of his two wives (Rachel and Leah) were counted as his legitimate offspring. Had Rachel and Leah had sexual intercourse with someone other than Jacob, they would have been stoned to death in Hebrew society. Jacob, however, could without legal or moral impunity consort with the maids of his wives. Why? Because they were his property. That was the patriarchal view of reality and fairness, and it was fully accepted by Hebrew socioreligious mores.

The double standard of sexual behavior did not only apply to actual sexual acts. It also applied to male suspicions. If a Hebrew man suspected his wife of having been involved in an adulterous act, he could compel her to undergo the bitter-water test. It was a harsh test. Numbers 5:11-31 graphically portrays the various elements that the accused wife had to endure. The account says that God told Moses:

> Say to the people of Israel, if any man's wife goes astray and acts unfaithfully against him, if a man lies with her carnally, and it is hidden from the eyes of her husband, and she is undetected though she has defiled herself, and there is no witness against her, and since she was not taken in the act; and if the spirit of jealousy comes upon him, and he is jealous of his wife, who had defiled herself; or if the spirit of jealousy comes upon him, and he is jealous of his wife, though she has not defiled herself; then the man shall bring his wife to the priest, and bring the offering required of her, a tenth of an ephah of barley meal; he shall pour upon it and put no frankincense on it, for it is a cereal offering of jealousy, a cereal offering of remembrance, bringing iniquity to remembrance.
>
> And the priest shall bring her near, and set her before the Lord; and the priest shall take holy water in an earthen vessel, and take some of the

---

[14]I. Abraham, *Studies in Pharisaism and the Gospels* (Cambridge: Cambridge University Press, 1917) 73.

dust that is on the floor of the tabernacle and put it into the water. And the priest shall set the woman before the Lord, and unbind the hair of the woman's head, and place in her hands the cereal offering of remembrance, which is the cereal offering of jealousy. And in his hand the priest shall have the water of bitterness that brings the curse. Then the priest shall make her take an oath, saying: "If no man has lain with you, and if you have not turned aside to uncleanness, while you were under your husband's authority, be free from this water of bitterness that brings the curse. But if you have gone astray, though you are under your husband's authority, and if you have defiled yourself, and some man other than your husband has lain with you, then" (let the priest make the woman take the oath of the curse, and say to the woman) "the Lord make you an example and an oath among your people, when the Lord makes your thigh fall away and your body swell; may this water that brings the curse pass into your bowels and make your body swell and thigh fall away." And the woman shall say: "Amen, Amen."

Then the priest shall write these curses in a book, and wash them off into the water of bitterness; and he shall make the woman drink the water of bitterness that brings the curse, and the water that brings the curse shall enter into her and cause bitter pain. And the priest shall take the cereal offering of jealousy out of the woman's hand, and shall wave the woman's hand, and shall wave the cereal offering before the Lord and bring it to the altar; and the priest shall take a handful of the cereal offering, as its memorial portion, and burn it upon the altar, and afterward shall make the woman drink the water. And when he has made her drink the water, then, if she has defiled herself and has acted unfaithfully against her husband, the water that brings the curse shall enter into her and cause bitter pain, and her body shall swell, and her thigh shall fall away, and the woman shall become an execration among her people. But if the woman has not defiled herself and is clean, then she shall be free and shall conceive children.

This is the law in cases of jealousy, when a wife, though under her husband's authority, goes astray and defiles herself, or when the spirit of jealousy comes upon a man and he is jealous of his wife; then he shall set the woman before the Lord, and the priest shall execute upon her all this law. The man shall be free from iniquity, but the woman shall bear her iniquity.

This test was not formally abolished until A.D. 70. Abolishing the bitter-water test, however, did not result in the removal of the double standard pertaining to adultery. For the most part, the double standard of sexual morality, including what was considered as adultery, continued to be believed, even if it was no longer punished or tested for in the traditional manner. However, about forty years before the bitter-water test was abolished, the old patriarchal view of adultery encountered a major obstacle, at least in Hebrew society. That obstacle was Jesus Christ's radical redefinition of adultery. He said that adultery could also be committed against the wife, not just against the husband (Mark 10:11). This new definition undoubtedly shocked Jesus' hearers because the Old Testament, with which they were familiar, spoke only of adultery being a sexual offense that was committed against the husband.

Jesus also made bold to say that a man could commit adultery in his heart by merely looking at a woman lustfully (Matt. 5:28). Whether the woman was single or married made no difference. Moreover, Jesus said nothing about a woman looking at a man lustfully. His words must have indeed shocked the patriarchs. It is not difficult to imagine the men asking: "How can a husband commit adultery against woman? No one has ever heard of such a thing!" Nor is it far-fetched to imagine the men saying: "What a radical, distorted view of adultery! That man is destroying our moral values!"

Jesus placed the burden of adultery squarely on the shoulders of the man, not on the woman. Apparently, he felt the ancient patriarchal mores were in dire need of correction. For example, Proverbs 7:18-19 has the woman trying to entice the man by saying: "Come let us take our fill of love till morning; let us delight ourselves with love. For my husband is not at home."

Although adultery in most Western societies is no longer seen in light of the patriarchal definition, but more in conformity with Jesus' view, it would be erroneous to conclude that the double standard of adultery ended with Christ's criticisms. Even many of the Christian church's theologians reverted to the patriarchal understanding of adultery. Frequently when the church fathers spoke about adultery, they focused only on the wife with no mention being made of the husband. Origen, for instance, argues: "The [divorced] wife will be considered adulterous if she, during the lifetime of her husband, joins up with another man" (*Testimony Ad Quirinum* 3.40). Nowhere does Origen say anything about a husband who remarries after divorce being guilty of adultery. The Synod of Arles (A.D. 314), in its tenth canon, stated: "To those who apprehend their wives in adultery . . . if possible the counsel is given that they should not take others so long as their own wives are alive, in spite of the fact that their wives are adulterous."

Again, no mention about adulterous men is to be found in this synod's deliberations. In fact, Carl von Hefele notes that this synod "did not regard the connection of a married man with an unmarried woman as adultery."[15]

St. Chrysostom (A.D. 347–407) saw extramarital affairs on the part of a husband to be adulterous, but the wife could not divorce him. A husband, however, was permitted to divorce his adulterous wife. The divorced husband was free to marry again, but not the wife (*Homilies on 1 Corinthians*). Another churchman, Ambrosiaster, circa A.D. 380, wrote: "A man may marry again if he has divorced his sinful wife, because he is not restricted in his rights as is the woman, because he is her head" (*Commentary on the Epistle to 1 Corinthians*). According to Socrates Scholasticus, a fifth-century church historian, Cyril of Alexander censured wives who married again after their husbands divorced them because of adultery. On the other hand, he failed to discuss the much more frequent occurrence of adultery by husbands (*Historia Ecclesiastica* 7.13-15). (Incidentally, Cyril's monks in A.D. 415 murdered Hypatia and then burned her flesh as they tore it from her bones. The monks killed Hypatia because she, as a mathematician and philosopher, contradicted Cyril's beliefs about women.)

Similarly, St. Jerome (A.D. 340–420) said it was wrong for a wife to dismiss her adulterous husband. Like some of the other church fathers, he, in his work *Ad Oceanum*, saw woman as morally equal to man but not legally. Jerome's view reminds one of today's sexist theologians, who see woman as equal to man legally but not theologically, when they insist that women are not to teach or even vote in the church.

The *Shepherd of Hermas* (an early-second-century Christian epistle that found its way into some of the early canons of the New Testament) asks whether a man sins by continuing to live with his wife whom he found in an adulterous act. Again, no question is asked whether a wife sins by continuing to live with her husband after he commits adultery.

The ninth canon of the Synod of Elvira (A.D. 305 or 306) prohibited a Christian woman from remarrying if she left her adulterous husband. If she did marry again, she was not, under normal circumstances, to receive the Lord's Supper until the man she left had died. Speaking about this canon, Victor Pospishil says: "A husband could remarry if his wife committed

---

[15]Carl Joseph von Hefele, *A History of the Christian Councils*, vol. 1, trans. Wm. R. Clark (Edinburgh: T & T Clark, 1894) 90.

adultery, while a wife could never remarry even if she was innocent and the husband guilty of misconduct.''[16]

These references from the church fathers and the councils indicate that the double standard relative to adultery—reinforced by the ancient concept of woman as property—countered Christ's view of adultery, namely, that the offense was equal whether committed by the wife or husband. Apparently theologians and church councils or synods found it easier to conform to ancient patriarchal values than to follow the teachings of the man whose name they appropriated unto themselves. The Council of Soissons (A.D. 744) in France permitted divorce when the reason was ''adultery of the wife, which gave the husband, but not the wife, the right to remarriage.''[17] The Council of Nantes (A.D. 875), in its twelfth canon, allowed the husband to dismiss his adulterous wife, but it did not permit him to take another wife. Again, it needs to be noted that no mention is made of a wife's being permitted to dismiss her adulterous husband. The Council of Ingelheim (A.D. 948) in Germany basically took the same stand as did Nantes.

These historical accounts of entrenched sexist theology bring to mind the words of the British jurist, Henry Sumner Maine. He said that the expositors of Canon Law had deeply injured civilization by the way they treated women less equally and less fairly than men.[18] The tragedy is that so many theologians did not have the sensitivity of the English jurist. Many are still insensitive.

Woman as Property: For Transfer or Sale

The concept of woman as property was not limited to how male-dominated cultures viewed adultery. Making woman man's property meant that she was also subject to sale or transfer. James Wellard shows that ''Assyrians [ca. 1000 B.C.] treated their own wives as they treated conquered peoples. . . . A wife and a man's children were his property: hence he could do what he liked with them.''[19]

Among the Athenians in the fifth century B.C., the wedding ceremony, according to William Hale, ''was simply an act of property convey-

---

[16]Victor J. Pospishil, *Divorce and Remarriage* (New York: Herder and Herder, 1967) 183.

[17]Ibid., 189.

[18]Henry Sumner Maine, *Ancient Law* (London: J. Murray, 1876) 163.

[19]James Wellard, *Babylon* (New York: Schocken Books, 1972) 145.

ance."[20] The bride who previously was the property of her father now became the possession of her husband. In fact, the twentieth-century American custom of the father giving the bride to the groom at the time of marriage—unknown to most people today—has its roots in the old patriarchal concept of woman being man's property. The Greek father, says Charles Savage, gave the bride away as early as 400 B.C.[21] Logically, one can only give away that which one owns or possesses as property.

In Roman society the social institution of *patria potestas* gave the father (the patriarch) complete authority and power over his entire family, including his slaves. Under *patria potestas* the son, unlike the daughter, would eventually gain freedom, either when the father died or when he granted the son emancipation. Then the son's wife, children, and slaves came under his *patria potestas*. A respectable daughter, however, could never gain freedom. When she was single, she came under the total control of her father's power, which served as the medium of property control relative to a woman's subjugation.[22] When she married, she not only came under the *patria potestas* of her husband, but, as his wife, she was also subject to his *manus*. This latter Roman law meant a married woman was under additional restrictions. Her freedom thus was curtailed by two very strong social institutions. As a wife, she "could in no wise repudiate her husband, while on the other hand, the husband's right to repudiate his wife was inherent in the absolute right [*manus*] which he possessed over her."[23] *Manus* gave the Roman man complete power over his wife.[24] For example, "If you were to catch your wife in an act of infidelity, you would kill her with impunity without a trial, but if she were to catch you, she would not venture to touch you with her finger, and indeed she has no right."[25] Whether single or married, she was always some man's possession or property.

---

[20]William Harlan Hale, *Ancient Greece* (New York: American Heritage Press, 1970) 190.

[21]Savage, *Athenian Family*, 55.

[22]M. I. Finley, "The Silent Woman of Rome," *Horizon* 7 (Winter 1965): 59.

[23]Jerome Carcopino, *Daily Life in Rome*, trans. E. O. Lorimer (New Haven: Yale University Press, 1970) 95.

[24]P. E. Corbett, *The Roman Law of Marriage* (Oxford: Clarendon Press, 1930).

[25]James Donaldson, *Woman: Her Position and Influence in Ancient Greece and Rome, and among the Early Christians* (New York: Longmans, Green and Company, 1907) 88.

The ancient Hebrews, similar to neighboring societies, also considered a woman to be the property of some male. In Deuteronomy 20:14 soldiers were told they could take enemy women as booty. And in Deuteronomy 21 the Hebrew soldiers were told they could take captive those women whom they considered "beautiful." A soldier could use such a woman sexually, but if after some time he no longer found "delight in her," he could let her go (Deut. 21:10-14). These examples show that the ancient cultural view of woman as man's property had become an integral part of the Hebrew socioreligious value system.

One of the Ten Commandments, given by Moses to the Hebrews, clearly pictures the wife as property. It reads: "You shall not covet your neighbor's wife, or his manservant, or his maidservant, or his ox, or his ass, or anything that is your neighbor's" (Exod. 20:17). Here the wife is definitely seen as property similar to the animals, all of which are man's possessions.

Mentioning this fact usually comes as a big surprise to people today, even to those who had once memorized this passage in Sunday school. Evidently the present-day Western culture, in which woman no longer is considered to be man's property, has prevented Sunday school students and countless church members, as well as their teachers, from really seeing and understanding that women among the Hebrews—as among other ancient societies—were the property of men. Modern church people overlook a very significant point here. Even many clergy and male seminary students miss this fact of history when they read or teach this commandment.

One might contend that when religious teachers in the Judeo-Christian context teach this commandment without drawing attention to the property concept of woman, they are unknowingly contributing to sexual inequality. That no real efforts have been made to draw attention to the sexual inequality fostered by this commandment (at least I am not aware of any) indicates that the property status of woman is not completely a thing of the past. Kate Millett argues that the "chattel status" of women is still operative today in many ways. According to her, the property status of women in a sense "continues in their loss of name, their obligation to adopt the husband's domicile, and the general legal assumption that marriage involves the female's domestic service and (sexual) consortium in return for financial support."[26]

---

[26]Kate Millett, *Sexual Politics* (Garden City NY: Doubleday and Company, 1970) 34-35.

With the idea of woman as property came wife purchasing and selling, a practice that even had the blessing of the church as early as the seventh century. In England one of the laws, ecclesiastically approved, read: "If a man buy a wife and the marriage take not place, let him give the money and compensate and make 'bot' to his 'byrgea,' as his 'borg-bryce' may be" (*The Laws of King Ine* article 31). Ecclesiastical approval of wife buying or selling was not confined to this one instance. In 1092 the Synod of Paris, Worcester, and Szaboles declared: "When a priest possesses a maid in place of a wife, he shall sell her and release her to the bishop's supervision."[27] In 1114 the Synod of Gran in Hungary said in its fifty-third canon: "When a wife of noble birth or aristocracy has left her husband for the third time, she receives mercy, but when she is from the common people, she is sold."[28] And the Germans, who considered the wife as negotiable property, sold them to the conquering Romans when it was expedient.[29]

The practice of buying and selling women continued for centuries. In 1732 in England, Fielding's Mr. Modern told his wife: "Your person is mine. I bought it [*sic*] lawfully in the church."[30] In fact, selling and buying wives in some scattered instances continued into the twentieth century.[31]

In many instances the selling of wives was preceded by advertising. One advertisement proclaimed that the subject was one who "can sow and reap, hold a plow, and drive a team . . . she is damned *hard mouthed* and headstrong. . . . Her husband parts with her because she is too much for him."[32] Sometimes before the wife was sold she was displayed by being led "through toll gates and villages, around the market or along the street to attract a crowd and ensure the public nature of the sale."[33] At times,

---

[27]Carl Joseph von Hefele, *Conciliengeschichte,* vol. 5 (Freiburg: Herder'sche Verlagshandlung, 1886) 204.

[28]Ibid., 324.

[29]Reinhold Bruder, *Die Germanische Frau im Lichte der Runeninschriften und der Antiken Historiographie* (Berlin: Walter de Gruyter, 1974).

[30]Lawrence Stone, *The Family, Sex and Marriage in England, 1500–1800* (New York: Harper & Row, 1977) 315.

[31]Samuel Pyeatt Menefee, *Wives for Sale* (New York: St. Martin's Press, 1981) 2.

[32]Ibid., 51.

[33]Ibid., 87.

says Menefee, she was sold at the same place where cattle were sold. Moreover, they were often sold like cattle in that they were fitted with halters.

The reality of wives as property is very evident in the following British stanza. It reads:

> Bought a wife on Sunday,
> Brought her home on Monday,
> Beat her well on Tuesday,
> Sick she was on Wednesday,
> Dead she was on Thursday,
> Buried she was on Friday,
> Glad I was on Saturday,
> And now I'll buy another.

The ancient cultural belief that woman or a wife was man's property was accepted by many clergymen in the Christian church even though Pope Gregory VII in the eleventh century spoke against the sale of wives as it was practiced, for example, in Scotland.[34] Another example of selling wives that was condoned by the church is found in a baptismal record in Essex. This record lists a baby girl as "by a bought Wife delivered to him [the husband] in a Halter."[35] Sometimes church bells were rung to celebrate the sale of a wife, and on other occasions the church performed the marriage rites after the man had purchased the woman to be his wife.[36]

That church synods and parishes on occasion advocated and tolerated the selling of women may come as a surprise to many. Yet, the religious legitimation of selling human females has an old history. The Hebrews already practiced it in the days of Moses. Exodus 21:7 reads: "When a man sells his daughter as a slave, she shall not go out as the male slaves." A thousand years or so after Moses' time, the rabbis revealed the Hebrew concept of woman as property when they taught that a woman is acquired by one of three means: sexual connection, document, or by purchase with money (*Kiddushin* 1:1).

The Hebrews, like many Christians later, were influenced by patriarchal cultural values and practices that in ancient agrarian times considered

---

[34]Hefele, *Conciliengeschichte*, 5:19.

[35]Menefee, *Wives for Sale*, 56.

[36]Ibid., 140.

woman to be unequal to man. Given the socioeconomic structure of these societies, such beliefs were considered to be natural and right. The social mores, as William Graham Sumner once said, make anything "right." And they did. Once the agrarian mores defining woman as unequal were woven into theological fabric, the cultural shape of sexist theology not only became a reality, but it also made that theology take on the aura of being right and pleasing to God.

CHAPTER 7

LET HER BE VEILED

Almost every twentieth-century person has heard about the ancient cultural practice of veiling women. But very few know why it was done, and even fewer see it as evidence of ancient sexism. In fact, the literature on the veiling of women is sparse and segmental. One has to read and consult many sources in order to put together a meaningful picture. The reason for this probably lies in the fact that it was men who wrote the occasional, brief account of the veiling practice. Given the cultural *Sitz-im-Leben,* it was probably obvious to them why a woman, especially a married one, had to wear a veil. Thus one finds only passing references to the old patriarchal social norm of veiling women.

Veiling women was widespread in many cultures. This fact is well documented in the work of Alfred Jeremias, *Der Schleier Von Sumer Bis Heute* (1931). Jeremias shows the practice of veiling existed among the Sumerians, Assyrians, Babylonians, Egyptians, Greeks, Hebrews, Chinese, and Romans. His work, brief as it is, provides some good photographs of excavated artifacts that reveal what the veil in some instances looked like.

The four sexist characteristics of woman being ''evil,'' ''inferior,'' ''unclean,'' and ''unequal'' need to be recalled if one is to gain a better understanding of the reasons for women having to be veiled. I suggest that these four male-defined characteristics of woman can be subsumed under the broader concept of woman as man's property. What one owns is commonly inferior and unequal to the power and status of the owner. The other two qualities that reportedly characterized woman, namely her being ''evil'' and ''unclean,'' also fit into the property-dimension picture. The required wearing of the veil permitted the property owner, the patriarch, to control these two undesirable female characteristics. The veiled face prevented the ''evil'' desires, seen as present in every woman, from attracting the lustful thoughts of other men, who had no right to what was not their property, that is, another man's wife or concubine. The rabbis taught that the chaste woman only revealed one eye in public (*Shabbath* 80a). The veil also kept the ''unclean'' woman from being seen when she was considered to be the most unclean.

If we keep in mind that woman was man's property, we can obtain a better understanding of why Homer (about 900 B.C.) in *The Odyssey* depicted Penelope, the wife of Odysseus, wearing a veil as she appeared before her male suitors. Like other societies of that era, the Greeks only permitted the husband to see his wife's face. This practice was also true among the Romans.[1] Wilhelm Becker says that the *ricinium* of the Roman female attire was ''a kind of veil.'' He further states: ''But the fact, that they [Roman women] covered the head with a veil, always remained.''[2] Among the Assyrians the husband considered the wife to be his private property, and by veiling her he could keep her facial appearance private as well. Assyrian prostitutes who were public property—for all men to see and use—were forbidden to wear a veil.[3] In fact, G. R. Driver and John Miles show that in ancient Assyria a man's ears were pierced with a cord passed through them and tied behind his head if he failed to report having seen a veiled prostitute.[4] And a prostitute who was caught wearing a veil was flogged, along with having her clothes confiscated and pitch poured over her head, says Wellard.[5] Thus the veil served the function of distinguishing which woman was private or public property.

In some instances a man divorced his wife if she left his house without being attired in a veil. James Donaldson cites the Roman divorce of Sulpicus Gallus as one such case.[6] Among the Greeks, the bride's hair at ''the

---

[1]F. R. Cowell, *Life in Ancient Rome* (New York: Perigee Books, 1961) 73.

[2]Wilhelm A. Becker, *Gallus* (London: Longmans, Green and Company, 1920) 438.

[3]James Wellard, *Babylon* (New York: Schocken Books, 1972) 146.

[4]G. R. Driver and John C. Miles, *The Assyrian Laws* (Oxford: Clarendon Press, 1935) 130.

[5]Wellard, *Babylon,* 147.

[6]James Donaldson, *Woman: Her Position and Influence in Ancient Greece and Rome and among Early Christians* (New York: Longmans, Green and Company, 1907) 88.

marriage ceremony was unbound and unloosed and the *flaneum,* a bright yellow veil placed on her head.''[7] Once the Greek bride was married, she always wore a veil, similar to the wife wearing a wedding ring in Western society today, says Adams.[8]

As already noted, the literature that speaks about veiled women generally provides a rather incomplete picture. This is particularly true of the Old Testament references that mention the practice only a few times, and then without any details. In Genesis 24 we see Rebekah veiling herself before she meets her future husband, Isaac. Genesis 38 shows Tamar posing as a harlot by appearing in a veil, a practice that ordinarily was illegal for Semitic prostitutes.[9] And Isaiah, while he mentions the custom of veiling, gives the impression that he is primarily talking about upper-class women, when he warns that as forthcoming punishment women will be deprived of their veils, along with the loss of perfume, robes, handbags, and so forth (Is. 3:18-23).

While the Old Testament does not shed much light relative to the veiling of Hebrew women, when we come to the rabbinic era, we do find some details. For one, the veil had to cover the woman's entire face. The rabbis also indicate that the veil was worn for chastity purposes. One such reference says: ''It is a godless man who sees his wife go out with her head uncovered. He is duty bound to divorce her'' (*Kethuboth* 2). Thus James Hurley is in error by saying that ''full veiling was not the practice of Talmudic Jews.''[10] Hurley's statement is also at odds with the observation of Strack and Billerbeck, two renowned scholars of rabbinic customs. They say that to the ancient Hebrews an unveiled female head symbolized freedom and therefore such a practice was considered in violation of the man's authority over woman.[11]

---

[7]Q. M. Adams, *Neither Male Nor Female* (Devon, England: Arthur Stockwell, 1973) 192.

[8]Ibid.

[9]Wellard, *Babylon,* 146.

[10]James B. Hurley, *Man and Woman in Biblical Perspective* (Grand Rapids: Zondervan Publishing House, 1981) 67.

[11]H. L. Strack and P. Billerbeck, *Kommentar zum Neuen Testament und Midrash: Die Briefe des Neuen Testaments und die Offenbarung Johannis,* vol. 3 (Muenchen: C. H. Beck'sche Verlagsbuchhandlungen, [1924], 1965) 423-40.

Another rabbinic source states that the Hebrew woman had to be veiled because of her shameful condition. "Why does a man go about bare-headed while a woman goes out with her head covered? She is like the one who has done wrong and is ashamed of people; therefore she goes out with her head covered" (*Genesis Bereshith* 17.18). Here the sexist belief of seeing woman as evil comes to the fore again.

The veiling of woman was not lost in the postapostolic church. Influenced by ancient values and practices of cultural sexism, the church fathers and many councils legalistically required married women to be veiled. Clement of Alexandria (A.D. 150–215) said that when a woman went to church, she was to "be entirely covered. . . . For that style of dress is grave and protects from being gazed at. And she will never fall . . . nor will she invite another to fall into sin by covering her face" (*The Instructor* 8.11). Interestingly, Clement argued that the veiling of women was "the wish of the Word, since it is becoming for her to pray veiled." In support of his belief, he cited pagan evidence. That evidence refers to the wife of Aeneas, who "did not, even in her terror at the capture of Troy, uncover herself; but, though fleeing from the conflagration, remained veiled" (*The Instructor* 3.11).

Clement's contemporary, Tertullian (A.D. 160–220?), who has rightly been called the first real misogynist in the church, told women: "Veil your head: if a mother, for your son's sake; if a sister, for your brethren's sake; if a daughter, for your father's sake. All ages are periled in your person" (*On the Veiling of Virgins* 16). Tertullian scolded women who came to church unveiled. Said he: "Why do you denude [unveil] before God [in church] what you cover before men? Will you be more modest in public than in the church?" (*On Prayer* 22). Almost two centuries after Clement and Tertullian, another church leader, St. Chrysostom (A.D. 347–407), in his *Homilies on 1 Corinthians,* said that woman was to be veiled on a continual basis. And the influential St. Augustine (fourth century) taught that married women were to be veiled if they were to be seen as proper (*Letters* no. 245). He also linked the veiling of women to their lacking the image of God. Here is how he worded it: "Have women not this renewal of the mind in which is the image of God? Who would say this? But in the sex of their body they do not signify this; therefore, they are bidden to be veiled" (*Of the Works of Monks* 32).

Skeptical readers may think that the veiling of women among Christians in the postapostolic church was primarily advocated by one or two chauvinistic church fathers, but this is not so. In addition to a number of church fathers saying that women had to be veiled, the church corporately at various times made canonical statements requiring women to be veiled. *The Apostolic Tradition* (a third-century document of the Christian church) declared: ''And let all women have their heads covered with an opaque cloth, not with a veil of thin linen, for this is not a true covering.''[12] In the latter part of the fourth century the church told women: ''And when thou art in the streets, cover thy head; for by such covering thou wilt avoid being viewed by idle persons'' (*The Apostolic Constitutions* 1.7). Again, it told women: ''If you wish to please him [the bridegroom in heaven], envelop the head when you appear in the street; veil your face to avoid indiscreet glances; and do not rouge that face which God has given you, but walk with lowered eyes, remaining veiled, as decency commands women to do'' (*The Apostolic Constitutions* 1.8). In another context this document defended its position of preventing women from bathing by appealing to its stance on veiling: ''For if she is to veil her face and conceal it with modesty from strange men, how can she bear naked into the bath together with men?'' (*The Apostolic Constitutions* 1.9)

These statements of the church definitely show that it accommodated itself to longstanding pagan culture with regard to veiling women. For example, compare the veiling requirements in *The Apostolic Constitutions* to the words of Dio Chrysostom, the Greek rhetorician. About 300 years earlier, he described the veiling norms of Tarsica, saying ''that women should be so arrayed and should deport themselves when in the street that nobody could see any part of them, neither of the face nor of the rest of the body'' (*First Tarsic Discourse* 45-48).

The human males, including the church fathers, veiled women to a large degree because they were not strong enough to resist what they considered ''sinful'' sexual desires, which among the men of that era were easily aroused by a woman's bare face or even by her unclad forearms. Most men, however, never really saw themselves as weak in regard to their sensual desires. It was always woman's fault, and so she had to be veiled. Raphael Patai's words about ancient Hebrew men also seem very appropriate in describing the church fathers, who required women to be veiled in order to check man's ''concupiscence,'' as they often called it.

---

[12]*The Apostolic Tradition*, trans. & ed. Burton Scott Easton (Cambridge: Cambridge University Press, 1934) 43.

The libido of the ancient Jews was readily aroused. The sight of any exposed part of a woman while she launders, her legs while she crosses a
stream, her hair, or even her little finger. Nor was one supposed to touch
a woman's hand or listen to her singing. Women, when out of doors, had
to wear garments which modestly hid the contours of their bodies, but even
so men were forbidden to walk behind a woman in the street lest they be
aroused to licentious thoughts or acts. At the mere sight of a woman a man
could be overpowered by violent desire for her, which condition, according to the contemporary doctors [rabbis], could only be remedied by enabling him [to] cohabit with her, or, at least, by letting him see her naked.
The rabbis, however, flatly forbade such a man even to talk to her across
the fence; others went so far as to warn against chatting with any woman.[13]

In A.D. 585 the Synod of Auxerre in France demanded in its forty-
second canon that women attending communion had to be veiled.[14] And
in the ninth century (in A.D. 866) Pope Nikolaus I declared ex cathedra in
the fifty-eighth canon: "The women must be veiled in church services."[15]

Henry Alford, the British scholar, believed that the early Christians required women to be veiled as a result of their understanding of 1 Corinthians 11:2-16. Approvingly, he said that this particular chapter in the New
Testament taught "that woman should be veiled in public religious assemblies."[16] Knowingly, or unknowingly, Alford overlooks that *The Apostolic Constitutions* speaks about women having to be veiled on the street,
not just in worship settings. That the veiling of women was not confined
to worship contexts is also given support by the pronouncement of one of
the Irish synods, held by St. Patrick during the decade of A.D. 450. Its fourth
canon said the wife of a priest "must be veiled when she goes out of
doors."[17]

For how long the veiling of women was seen as proper and necessary
behavior by church leaders after Pope Nikolaus issued his canon is diffi-

[13]Raphael Patai, *The Jewish Mind* (New York: Charles Scribner's Sons, 1977) 500.

[14]Carl Joseph von Hefele, *Conciliengeschichte,* vol. 3 (Freiburg: Herder'sche Verlag,
1877) 46.

[15]Hefele, *Conciliengeschichte,* (1879), 4:349.

[16]Henry Alford, *The Greek Testament, with Critically Revised Text: A Digest of Various Readings* (Chicago: Moody Press, 1958) 563.

[17]Carl Joseph von Hefele, *A History of the Councils of the Church* (Edinburgh: T & T
Clark, 1895) 4:9.

cult to say with certainty. Although women still wore veils, for instance, in Ireland in the Middle Ages, my research on this topic has not found church authorities or statements after the ninth century repeating the requirement of veiling woman. Apparently the practice of veiling Christian women slowly disappeared during the Middle Ages.

Why did the church cease to advocate the veiling of women? While there is no unequivocal answer, the ancient cultural forces that once led the human male in agrarian environments to believe woman was his property were affected in time by the processes of social change. By the fourteenth and fifteenth centuries in Western society—especially in Europe, where the Christian church had its base—the agrarian way of life began to shift to an urban ethos. In the urban environment, with its increasing anonymity, heterogeneity, and higher rates of geographic mobility, it is difficult—almost impossible—to enforce agrarian values and life-styles such as the veiling of women. The concept of property, which not only applied to woman and had much to do with her social inequality, became more abstract in the growing urban contexts. Abstract conceptions slowly sensitized men, for example, to see wives more in terms of human relationships rather than in the light of property. This cultural shift began to give women some equality so that even John Knox, a blatantly sexist theologian who railed against women in his *First Blast of the Trumpet against the Monstrous Regiment of Women* (1558), no longer mentions that woman is to be veiled.

As Western societies became more urbanized, the agrarian-patriarchal practice of veiling women slowly disappeared so that woman, while still very much the object of male prejudice, gained a little more freedom and respect. She now could go out in public and not have to hide her face behind a veil. She was free to show men that her face would not lead a man to lustful, sinful thoughts. It was not her unhidden face that tempted the "superior" male, but rather it was the sexist, cultural definitions of women that saw her face triggering "sinful" thoughts.

The urban social forces that in time brought about the removal of the veil presaged a significant change in the direction of freedom and equality for women. Even as the veil made its exit in Western society, other changes—such as the freedom to teach and speak in public—were still unthinkable.

CHAPTER 8

LET HER BE SILENT

That women should be silent was still a vociferous argument in the latter part of the nineteenth century when male chauvinists fought bitterly to keep women from exercising their right at the ballot box. In the United States the advocates of woman's silence finally lost their battle when the Nineteenth Amendment was ratified and became part of the American Constitution in 1920.

Numerous opposing voices can still be heard, especially in some ultraconservative or fundamentalist churches. They argue, almost fanatically, against women's conducting worship services. To many male clergy in these churches it is a matter of "Thus says the Lord." They are particularly quick to cite two New Testament references: "The woman should keep silent in the churches. For they are not permitted to speak" (1 Cor. 14:34). "I permit no woman to teach or to have authority over men; she is to keep silent" (1 Tim. 2:12).

The silencing of women is not something that is confined to sexist theology, however. Greco-Roman culture, before the rabbis and church fathers brought up the subject, had deeply entrenched rules that very effectively silenced women for centuries.

Greek Culture

Ancient Greek literature is replete with references to keeping woman silent. Sophocles (495–406 B.C.) said: "O woman, silence is an adornment to women" (*Ajax* 293). Euripides (480–406 B.C.), a contemporary of Sophocles, has Macaria saying: "Women are to be silent and discrete, remaining within the house" (*The Heracleidae* 476). Aristotle, who apparently paraphrased Sophocles, declared: "Silence gives grace to woman" (*Politics* 1.1260 a:31). And in the fifth century B.C., Democritus, the scientific philosopher and ethicist, is found saying in one of his extant fragments: "Well-mannered is the woman who speaks little."

Long before the days of Euripides, Sophocles, Aristophanes, and Aristotle, Greek culture told women to be silent. Homer portrays Telemachus rebuking his mother, Penelope, for speaking. Dogmatically, he tells her that "speech shall be for men" (*The Odyssey* 1.359). Then in the fourth century B.C., the poet Euripides depicts Achilles telling the wife of King Agamemnon: "Yet shame were this, that I with women talk!" (*Iphigenia at Aulis* 831). Apart from one or two special events—for example, the religious festival of Thesmophoria (an event for women only)—the only time and place that the Athenian woman could speak in public was as a witness in cases of homicide.[1] So stringent was the silencing of women that even the female roles in the famous Greek plays were acted out by men disguised as women. (Even in Shakespeare's day women could not appear or speak on the stage. Disguised as women, men acted out the female roles.)

The silence the Greek woman had to endure was reinforced by a rather strict confinement to her husband's house. A respectable Athenian woman, for example, could only leave the home if she was accompanied by her husband or by a slave escort.[2] When she left home, it was only for special occasions: funerals of relatives, weddings, and religious festivals. Aristophanes notes that husbands were furious when their wives went out of the house without their permission (*Thesmophoriazusae* 792). Evidently there were times that the Greek men were "negligent" in keeping their wives domestically confined. For, as we have seen in chapter 4, Greek husbands, according to Plutarch (A.D. 46–100), kept their "wives under lock and key" (*Lycurgus* 15.8).

Greek women were "expected to prepare the meals, run their households—stay out of sight."[3] When their husbands dined with guests, they had to withdraw to their own quarters on the second floor, known as *gy-*

---

[1]Boaz Cohen, *Jewish and Roman Law* (New York: Jewish Theological Seminary of America, 1923) 128.

[2]James Donaldson, *Woman: Her Position and Influence in Ancient Greece and Rome, and among the Early Christians* (New York: Gordon Press, [1907], 1973) 119.

[3]C. M. Bowra, *Classical Greece* (New York: Time-Life Books, Inc., 1965) 85.

naikeion (woman's room).[4] Only a close, trusted relative could enter the room of a Greek wife. In the words of one scholar: "The life of the Athenian woman was not only exceedingly circumscribed and isolated, but she was actually throughout her life treated as a minor, and under constant tutelage, being subject, at various times, to the authority of her father, brother, grandfather, husband, son or guardian . . . she had practically no authority, except in the sphere of domestic economy."[5]

Thus, it is no surprise to hear Aristophanes in his comedy *Thesmophoriazusae* conveying the thought of woman making speeches and voting as hilarious. He quite accurately reflected the male Grecian view of woman. No wonder the Greeks used the turtle to symbolize woman, for it is a silent and secluded animal.

The rigid restrictions on the Greek woman's freedom applied especially to women who were in the prime of life.[6] Older women, who no longer were attractive to men, were permitted more freedom. (The sexist values are clearly evident here.) Lower-class women also had somewhat more freedom in that they were less confined to their quarters. Aristotle once said: "How is it possible to keep the wives of the poor from going out?" (*Politics* 6.1300 a:7). Aristotle also cited the reason for this difference, namely, "The poor have to use their wives and children as servants since they have no slaves" (*Politics* 6.1323 a:5-7).

As is evident from Greek literature, some of the Greek wives resented their unequal treatment, not only because they were kept silent and confined to their upstairs room, but also because their husbands practiced other discriminatory behavior. "A [Greek] husband always had the right to repudiate his wife, even without showing cause."[7] Greek husbands also spent very little time with their wives, partly because their occupations kept them away from home and partly because they didn't really interact very affectionately with their wives.[8] But what probably caused the greatest resent-

---

[4]Ibid.

[5]Charles Albert Savage, *The Athenian Family: A Sociological and Legal Study* (Baltimore, 1907) 25.

[6]Ibid., 32.

[7]Robert Flaceliere, *Love in Ancient Greece,* trans. James Cleugh (New York: Crown Publishers, 1962) 116.

[8]Savage, *Athenian Family,* 27.

ment among Greek women was the double standard of sexual behavior. The Greek husbands had their mistresses, known as *hetaerae*. "Extra-marital love relationships [with a *hetaera*] were a matter of course for the Greek man." [9]

It was with the *hetaerae* that the men mingled in public, not with their wives who had to remain at home. A virtuous woman (the wife) could not converse with her husband in public social contexts. A *hetaera*, however, could and did. She, as one who was better educated (although scholars debate this point) in comparison to the man's wife, accompanied the man at parties and other social events where the wife was not permitted to go. *Hetaerae* were even permitted to listen to the philosophers in the arcade or to those in the public square, the Areopagus. [10] "The *Symposium* both of Plato and Xenophon make it quite plain that when a gentleman entertained guests the only women present were those who had no reputation to lose." [11] Demosthenes (384–322 B.C.), the great Greek orator, described the situation well: "Mistresses [*hetaerae*] we keep for the sake of pleasure, concubines for the daily care of our persons, but wives to bear us legitimate children and to be faithful guardians of our households" (*Against Neaera* 122).

The pervasive powerlessness of the Greek wives is seen in the words of Calonice, who asks in Aristophanes' play *Lysistrata*, "What can we women do? What brilliant schemes can we, poor souls, accomplish?" (*Lysistrata* 42-43). Again, one reads: "We women can't go out just when we like; we have to wait upon our men, and wake the servants, then we put the children straight; we have to wash and feed them" (*Lysistrata* 16-19). Medea, a wife and the chief character in one of Euripides' tragedies, says: "We women are of all unhappiest. . . . Divorce? 'Tis infamy to us. We may not even reject a suitor" (*Medea* 232, 237).

The low status of the Greek woman went beyond being powerless. Arlene Saxonhouse says: "In the Greek language it was linguistically impossible for a woman to be brave; the term for courage derived from the word meaning 'to be a man.' " [12] Such discriminatory conditions of inequality did not instill

---

[9] Verena Zinserling, *Women in Greece and Rome* (New York: Abner Schramm, 1972) 39.

[10] William H. Sanger, *The History of Prostitution* (New York: Eugenics Publishing Company, 1939) 54.

[11] H. D. F. Kitto, *The Greeks* (Chicago: Aldine Publishing Company, 1964) 219.

[12] Arlene Saxonhouse, *Women in the History of Political Thought* (New York: Praeger Publishers, 1985) 110-11.

confidence or self-respect among the Greek women. In fact, the prevailing social forces socialized women to believe the sexist stereotypes of their oppressors. This is evident from one of Aristophanes' female characters, who doubts woman's ability by asking: "How can the female soul of womankind address the Assembly?" (*Ecclesiazusae* 110.) Medea portrays another example. Representing other Greek women, she seems to accept the prejudiced views of men by saying: "Men say we are impotent for good, but of dark deeds most cunning fashioners" (*Medea* 406-407).

The male chauvinist has on occasion asked: "If women were so oppressed and deprived of rights and freedom in ancient Greece, why then did they figure so prominently in the literature of the Greek poets and philosophers?" This question is sometimes asked by men who are reluctant to believe the sad conditions that were the Greek woman's daily fare. The best response, in my opinion, has been given by Sarah Pomeroy, a competent Greek scholar. She has said that women "returned to haunt men's imagination, dreams, and nightmares."[13] As much as the men despised their wives and used women to their advantage, they could not live without them.

In response to the oppressive cultural attitudes and practices that Greek women were subjected to, F. A. Wright has written a strong indictment. Said he: "The Greek world perished from one main cause, a low ideal of womanhood and a degradation of women which found expression both in literature and in social life. The position of women and the position of slaves—for the two classes went together—were canker spots which, left unhealed, brought about the decay first of Athens and then of Greece."[14] If Wright's analysis is correct, his message ought especially to be heeded by recalcitrant sexists who still are trying to silence women.

Roman Culture

In surveying Roman culture one finds somewhat less discrimination than there was in ancient Greece. Roman women could be present at the meal where men ate; they could in some contexts participate in social conversations with men; and they were permitted to attend public circuses and athletic events, whereas Athenian women were barred from these activi-

---

[13]Sarah B. Pomeroy, *Goddesses, Whores, Wives, and Slaves: Women in Classical Antiquity* (New York: Schocken Books, 1975) 229.

[14]F. A. Wright, *Feminism in Greek Literature: From Homer to Aristotle* (Port Washington: Kennikat Press, 1923) 1.

ties.[15] One even finds rare occasions when the Romans portrayed women as courageous. For example, the Sabine women, who had become Roman wives by the force of rape, entered the fighting between the Romans and Sabines to stop the killing.[16] Yet women were hardly considered equal to men when it came to speaking rights and privileges. One scholar has said that Roman society in the first century of Christendom "required woman's silence nearly or fully as much as the Grecian."[17]

Denying women the right to speak publicly was part of the Roman cultural syndrome. For instance, Roman fathers gave their daughters in marriage at the early age of twelve years. Once she was married, she came under the Roman institution of *cum manus,* which placed her under her husband's authority, preventing her from seriously questioning or repudiating her husband in any way. He, however, had the right to repudiate her in whatever way he wished.[18] The power of *manus* also required her to worship her husband's ancestral gods.[19] Women, although they were permitted to give testimony in Roman courts, could not act as witnesses to a will, according to the law known as *Lex Julia de Adulteriis.* They could not plead in court; they could not leave their children money while they were under the husband's *manus* or *patria potestas.*[20]

Patria potestas is a good illustration, in addition to the institution of *manus,* for recognizing the wife's powerlessness in ancient Rome. As noted in chapter 6, this Roman cultural *mos* or norm gave the husband absolute power over children and also over his wife. For example, if his wife committed adultery, he could put her to death.[21] "A [Roman] woman," said Evan Sage, "was never *sui iuris* and was not a person in the legal sense."[22]

[15]J. P. V. D. Balsdon, *Roman Women: Their History and Habits* (New York: John Day and Company, 1963) 272-79.

[16]Saxonhouse, *Women in the History,* 111.

[17]William Deloss Love, "Women Keeping Silence in Churches," *Bibliotheca Sacra* 35 (January 1878): 1-45.

[18]Jerome Carcopino, *Daily Life in Rome,* trans. E. O. Lorimer (New Haven: Yale University Press, 1940) 95.

[19]Ibid.

[20]O. A. W. Dilke, *The Ancient Romans: How They Lived and How They Worked* (Chester Springs PA: Dufour Editions, Inc., 1975) 49.

[21]Wilhelm A. Becker, *Gallus* (New York: Longmans, Green and Company, 1920) 56.

[22]Evan T. Sage, in Livy's *From the Founding of the City,* vol. 9 (Cambridge: Harvard University Press, 1936) 416.

Charles Merivale highlights the deprivation of rights and lack of meaningful involvement experienced by the Roman woman: "The women were never associated in their husbands' occupations, knew little of their affairs, and were less closely attached to their interests than even their bondmen."[23] Plautus, a Roman comic poet (254?–184 B.C.), portrays the Roman attitude concerning the silence of women quite well by having Trachalio say in one of his plays: "They're [women] silent because a woman's always worth more seen than heard" (*Rudens* 1114). If a Roman woman appeared on a public stage as an actress, which was practically unheard of, the male culture would affix the label of *infamia* to her.[24] Nor was the situation much better if she left her husband's house for religious activities. "Women's journeys from the house for religious purposes were regarded by the elegists and satirists with grave suspicion."[25]

Thus while the Roman woman had perhaps a little more freedom than her Hellenistic counterpart, one nevertheless finds much deprivation and confinement. There is "nothing to suggest that the 'men's club' was not in complete control."[26] Let's not forget, the city councils, the Roman Senate, court cases, and so forth were all run by men. The Roman men, like the Greeks, had no desire to hear women speak in public settings. A number of ancient Roman recordings corroborate this position. Let me cite just one prominent example. In 215 B.C. a group of women assembled in the Roman Forum, which was not open to women. Nevertheless, they protested and asked that the Oppian Law be repealed. This law made it illegal for women to wear multicolored robes, have more than one ounce of gold, and to ride in the carpentum. In response to their having assembled in public to speak against this law, Livy has Cato saying: "Could you not have asked your own husbands the same thing at home?" (*The Founding of the City* 34.10). In other words, women were to be silent in public. If they had anything to say, they were to say it to their husbands at home and then let them take it from there.

---

[23]Charles Merivale, *The Fall of the Roman Empire: A Short History of the Last Century of the Commonwealth* (London, 1853) 226.

[24]William Smith, *A Dictionary of Greek and Roman Antiquities* (New York, 1871) 635.

[25]Balsdon, *Roman Women,* 278.

[26]Robin Scroggs, *The New Testament and Homosexuality* (Philadelphia: Fortress Press, 1983) 23.

The fear of having women make public utterances is also apparent when one reads that self-educated women were dreaded by the men of Rome.[27] Moses Finley has shown that women in ancient Rome were only permitted to say what men wanted them to say. When they failed to conform to the male ideal, they were censured or pictured as female monsters.[28] In short, the Roman woman had no public-speaking rights and privileges.

Hebrew Culture

The sociocultural fear of hearing a woman speak in public was not confined to the Greco-Romans. The Hebrews, especially during the rabbinic era, did not permit women to testify in court (*Yoma* 43b). The gynophobia of the rabbis was equal to or worse than that of the Greek and Roman men. Unlike the Greco-Romans, the Hebrew rabbis placed the prohibition of woman's speaking in the context of religion. To the rabbis, a woman's public speech was an act that offended God.

Josephus, a first-century Pharisee, apparently reflected the Hebrew religious opinion when he said that women were not to speak because the Law of Moses enjoined it (*Antiquities* 4.8.15). The oral law of the rabbis (from about 400 B.C. to A.D. 400), now essentially the Talmud and Mishnah, even warned against heeding a wife's private advice in the home. Said Rabbi Rab: "He who follows his wife's counsel will descend to Gehenna" (*Kiddushin* 59:2). In the context of the synagogue, the rabbis decreed: "Out of respect of the congregation, the woman should not read in the law [Torah]" (*Megillah* 23a). Another rabbinic teaching, as noted in chapter 4, taught that it was "shameful" to hear a woman's voice in public, among men (*Berakhoth* 24a).

In what manner did a woman's voice harm the respect of the congregation or synagogue? How could her voice be seen as shameful? Here we need to remember two things: the entire worship service in the synagogue was conducted by men. Women, if present, were passive listeners, separated from the men by or behind the *michetza* (a partition). As the modern Hebrew scholar Raphael Patai has shown, women in the synagogue were "secluded in an adjoining room or gallery . . . [they] were never supposed to raise their voices."[29] Only the men did the singing or chanting. The Jew

---

[27]Becker, *Gallus,* 177.

[28]Moses Finley, "The Silent Women of Rome," *Horizon* 7 (1965): 55-64.

[29]Raphael Patai, *The Jewish Mind* (New York: Charles Scribner's Sons, 1977) 365.

never spoke to God; he always sang or chanted to God.[30] Patai says that Jewish women were not permitted to sing in a synagogue service until the Enlightenment era and then only in the Reformed synagogues or temples.[31] Thus for a woman to chant or sing the law (Torah) would have violated the socioreligious norms of the Hebrew male. It would have shown lack of respect to the entire male contingent present at the service.

A woman's voice would also have produced shame among the men because it would have given the impression that the men were not able to read and thereby have embarrassed the men.[32] It would have shown that the "superior" man was not really superior. Such an impression would have indicated that woman was equal or even in a particular instance superior to man. That would have been intolerable to a Jewish male who prided himself on his superiority vis-à-vis woman.

There was still another reason that explained the "shame" of a woman reading in the synagogue. The rabbis taught: "A woman's voice is a sexual excitement . . . for sweet is thy voice and thy countenance is comely" (*Berakhoth* 24a). Her voice, like her hair, was a sexual stimulant to the Hebrew male of that cultural era, similar to what a low-cut dress or a bikini bathing suit is to men in today's Western culture. Her voice would have distracted the men from worship to sexual thoughts, and that would have been shameful, especially if another man would have noticed his associate's sexual interest. Perhaps this is why the rabbis also taught: "A woman is a tube full of garbage with her mouth full of blood" (*Shabbath* 152a). Still another rabbinic teaching said: "The voice of a woman is filthy [uncovered] nakedness."

Given their theologically sexist view of woman, the rabbis prohibited girls or women from learning the Torah, the Law of Moses. As stated in chapter 4, one rabbinic norm demanded:"Let the words of the Law, be burned rather than committed to women. . . . If a man teaches his daughter the Law, it is as though he taught her lechery" (*Sotah* 3:4). The rabbis derived this belief from their interpretation of Deuteronomy 11:19, which says only sons are to be taught the Torah. In fact, *Sotah* specifically says "but not your daughters."

---

[30]Ibid., 366.

[31]Ibid.

[32]Samuel Krauss, *Synagogae Altertuemer* (Berlin: B. Harz, 1922) 174. See also Sally Priesand, *Judaism and the New Women* (New York: Behrman House, 1975) 56.

Before the rabbinic era of Hebrew history, it seems there was less opposition to women's speaking in public. Evidently, the Hebrews during the rabbinic era were strongly influenced by the Greco-Roman attitudes and practices toward woman. During the days of Moses we read about a rather prominent woman, Miriam. She is favorably mentioned in Exodus, Numbers, Deuteronomy, 1 Chronicles, and also by Micah. Miriam publicly sang praises to God (Exod. 15:21). (This act of hers is significant because from at least the rabbinic period on, Judaism no longer permitted women to chant or sing in worship settings; and as we have seen above, it was not until the eighteenth century that Jewish women were allowed to sing among men, and then only in Reformed Judaism.) The prophet Micah gave equal honor to Miriam, along with Aaron and Moses (Mic. 6:4). He has God saying that Miriam was one of the three leaders sent to free Israel from bondage in Egypt. She is not portrayed as subordinate to man.

Another outstanding woman in Hebrew history was Deborah. When Israel was ruled by judges (twelfth century B.C.), women evidently were permitted to engage in public speaking, for instance, making religious statements before men. This is apparent from Deborah's behavior. She said: "The Lord, the God of Israel commands you" (Jud. 4:8). Deborah said these words after she summoned Barak and then told him to lead a military expedition against Sisera's army.

The biblical record of Deborah's day does not indicate that she violated any socioreligious mores. In fact, Barak not only willingly obeyed her, but he requested that she accompany him on his assignment. Deborah was neither silent nor submissive, and she acted as God's mouthpiece. These three activities have been conveniently overlooked by many theologians.

Huldah was still another Hebrew woman who served as God's spokesperson. During the seventh century B.C. she, as a prophet, spoke to several men, one of them a priest, Hilkiah (2 Kings 22:14-15). In the presence of the men, whom she told to give her message to King Josiah, Huldah said: "Thus says the Lord" (2 Kings 22:15). In addition to her saying this, her message also contained what some theologians called "law-gospel" words.

Deborah and Huldah were not uppity women who rebelled; rather, they exercised their God-given talents by speaking and leading. As prophets (or "prophetesses," as men have been prone to say), they participated in a prominent Hebrew religious institution, a fact all but forgotten by the rabbis and the church fathers many years later. Over time the culture of sexism shaped a theology significantly different from that which employed the talents and resources of Miriam, Huldah, and Deborah. By the time of the Jewish oral law (from c. 250 B.C. to c. A.D. 400), it was considered more noble to burn the Torah than to teach it to a woman.

By citing the above three women and their respective roles, I do not intend to say that there was an essential equality between the sexes among the Hebrews of the Old Testament period. Rather, these examples seem to illustrate that there was considerably more freedom for women among the earlier Hebrews than there was later during the rabbinic era or at the time of Jesus.

The Postapostolic Church

When one looks to the writings of the influential church fathers, in addition to what we have noted about them in previous chapters, it is quite apparent that they were as sexist in their beliefs and practices as were their cultural predecessors of ancient Greece and Rome. The church fathers and their long train of successors did their utmost to keep women from teaching, preaching, and, as we shall see, also from singing in the church. In doing so they unwittingly—and contrary to Christ and the apostles—wove the ancient pagan cultural views of women into the church's theology, which was (and still *is* in many quarters of the church) heralded as the plan and will of God.

The Greco-Roman philosophers and poets simply said women were to be silent in the presence of men. They rarely, if ever, gave any reason. They didn't have to give any. It was a cultural norm, a *mos,* a way of life. The church fathers and later theologians, however, went one step farther. By arguing that women had to be silent among men because that was God's will, they not only blinded themselves from seeing centuries of sexist discrimination, but they also gave to the ancient pagan cultural beliefs and practices a theological legitimation that they never had among the Greeks and Romans. Keeping women silent, especially in churches, was now a matter of "Thus says the Lord." It never occurred to the theologians that God might have been shocked or even angered to be credited with something that was not issued from the heavenly mansions. The powerful force of ancient culture did not permit that kind of introspection.

Two New Testament passages, 1 Corinthians 14:34-35 and 1 Timothy 2:11-12, were favorite references used to silence Christian women. The Corinthian reference reads: "As in all the churches of the saints, the women should keep silent in the churches. For they are not permitted to speak, but should be subordinate, as even the law says. If there is anything they desire to know, let them ask their husbands at home. For it is shameful for a woman to speak in church." The passage in Timothy reads: "Let a woman learn in silence with all submissiveness. I permit no woman to teach or to have authority over men; she is to keep silent."

The first church father to use 1 Corinthians 14 to silence women was the misogynist, Tertullian (A.D.160–220?). He said that women could not baptize or teach (*On Baptism* 17). Origen (A.D.185–254), the Greek church father who castrated himself, declared: "It is not proper to a woman to speak in church, however admirable or holy what she says, merely because it comes from female lips."[33] Cyprian (A.D. 200–258), bishop of Carthage, said women were to be silent in church, and he referred to 1 Corinthians 14 and 1 Timothy 2 to make his argument (*The Treatise of Cyprian*). St. Chrysostom (A.D. 347–407), whose sexist views of woman were noted in chapter 3, not only cited 1 Corinthians 14, but he linked this reference to Genesis 3:16 (*Homily on First Corinthians* 37). He believed women were to be silent in the Corinthian church because by nature they were "easily carried away and light minded." Cyril of Jerusalem (A.D. 315–368), a bishop, taught that women were to pray in church by moving their lips without making any audible sounds. Said he: "Let the married woman imitate them [the virgins]; let her pray, and her lips move, but let not her voice be heard" (*The Procatechesis* 14). To support his opinion, he cited 1 Corinthians 14:34.

The synods and councils also tried to silence and exclude women from equal participation with men. The *Didascalia Apostolorum,* an early-fourth-century document that sets forth church rules, stated: "It is neither right nor necessary therefore that women should be teachers, and especially concerning the name of Christ and the redemption of his passion. For you have not been appointed to this O woman, and especially widows, that you should teach. . . . For if it were required that women should teach, our Master himself would have commanded these to give instruction with us" (chap. 15). But perhaps the most astounding act of silencing and depriving women was the edict issued by the Synod of Elvira in A.D. 306. It denied women the right to communicate in writing. Canon 81 proclaimed:

---

[33]Cited in George H. Tavard, *Woman in Christian Tradition* (Notre Dame: Notre Dame University Press, 1973) 68.

"Women shall not presume on their own, without their husbands' signatures, to write to lay women who are baptized, nor shall they accept anyone's letters of peace addressed only to themselves."

Following the church fathers and some of the councils, theologians and parish priests for more than 1,000 years have cited 1 Corinthians 14 and 1 Timothy 2 in support of their efforts to silence and exclude women from meaningful participation with men. For the most part, the clergy tried to keep women silent in terms of teaching and preaching. But as we have seen, there were other serious attempts to silence women, namely, not letting them pray aloud, prohibiting them from writing, and not allowing them to sing audibly in church services.

The theology of silencing women in the postapostolic church was beginning to become institutionalized in the latter part of the second century. Two factors, very compatible with the agrarian culture, prompted this discriminatory action. One reason was that the church fathers forgot, or perhaps didn't want to remember, that the first silencing of women in the late second and early third century in large measure began because most women at that time were uneducated and therefore not really competent to address the skeptical unbelievers. The Syriac *Didascalia* (early third century) makes this reason very clear:

> But no widow is obliged to speak about the destruction of idols, about the fact that God is one, about the kingdom of the name of Christ and about his leadership. For in so far as they speak *without knowledge* [my emphasis] of the teaching, they bring contempt upon the Word. For if the educated heathen hear the Word of God but it is not proclaimed to them in an orderly and suitable fashion for the production of life, especially because it is a woman who is telling about how the Lord assumed a body and how he suffered, they will laugh and mock instead of praising the teachings (*Didascalia* 3.5).

The *Didascalia* knows nothing of woman having to be silent because of some "order of creation" (an argument that later became popular with some who tried to silence women) or because she was a woman per se. Woman didn't teach because she lacked competency; the culture of that era prevented her from having an education equivalent to man. It is also interesting to note that the *Didascalia* does not base its argument on 1 Corinthians 14 or 1 Timothy 2.

Another factor that led to the silencing of women was the church fathers' overreaction to the Montanists and the Gnostics. These groups who permitted women to teach—in conformity with the teachings of Jesus and the apostles—were seen as heretical by the church fathers. That these groups treated women equally to men was soon added to their list of despised qualities, which led the church fathers and some of the synods not just to reject their teachings but also to reject their practice of feminine equality. From this it was but a small step to bar women from teaching, speaking, and even singing. This overreaction was noted by the famous German scholar Adolph von Harnack in his *Expansion of Christianity in the First Three Centuries* (1905).

The male clergy of the fourth and fifth centuries also overreacted to the Spanish Priscillianists, another group that—among other teachings—gave women rights unknown to the Greco-Roman or rabbinic culture. Thus in A.D. 380 the Council of Saragossa declared that women be separated from men for reading and other gatherings in the church. It said: "Let them not come together with those who read to others, nor to study, either teaching or learning. For the apostle [Paul] taught this."[34] Here we see that over-reaction not only led to women's being silenced but also to their being segregated from men in worship services, a practice very similar to that of the Hebrew synagogues. Apparently in trying to guard itself from certain errors that impinged on some basic Christian tenets, the church unwittingly accepted beliefs and practices of the Judaizing contingent within its midst.

The silencing of women in the church gained momentum with St. Jerome, the influential ascetic who gave the church the Latin Vulgate and popularized belief in Mary's perpetual virginity (a conviction still held by Roman Catholicism and some scattered Lutherans). Jerome was unequivocally opposed to hearing a woman's voice in public. This monk once studied under the rabbis, who would not let women be heard in the synagogues, and apparently he was considerably influenced by them. "And you are not content with having given your cohort a knowledge of Scripture, but you must delight yourself with their [women's] songs and canticles, for you have a heading to the effect that 'Women also should sing unto God.' Who does not know that women should sing in the privacy of their rooms, away from the company of men and the crowded congregations? But you allow what is not lawful" (*Against the Pelagians* 1.25).

---

[34]Joannes Dominicus Mansi, *Sacorum Conciliorum Nova et Amplissima Collectio,* vol. 3 (Leipzig and Paris: H. Welter, 1901) 638.

Jerome's words clearly indicate that the so-called orthodox churches barred women from singing in worship services where men were present. The followers of Pelagius (a contemporary of Jerome), who was considered heretical, evidently gave women the right to sing and chant. Jerome, and others of like mind, followed the rabbinic and Greco-Roman tradition of keeping women silent in the presence of men.

Opposed as Jerome was to hearing the voice of women in the church, he once admitted that two learned women were coauthors with him when the Latin Vulgate was produced. Apparently what was repugnant to him was women's speech, rather than the mere work or influence of women. Nevertheless, later theologians in the church erased the names of these women and substituted the words "venerable brothers."

Not permitting women to sing in church services evidently existed for centuries following St. Jerome. Some 450 years after Jerome we find Pope Leo IV, who reigned from 847–855, issuing a canon that continued to bar women from singing in church (*Leonis Papae Homilia* 34). And in the thirteenth century we hear Thomas Aquinas, the revered Catholic theologian, saying: "The voice of a woman is an invitation to lust, and therefore must not be heard in the church" (*Summa Theologica* 14.89). While Aquinas does not specifically mention singing, he undoubtedly had singing in mind because the prohibition against women's preaching or teaching in the presence of men had by then become socially and theologically ironclad, so singing is the only thing that he could have meant. The second Lateran Council in A.D. 1139 forbade nuns to sing with monks. Yet, the matter of women singing or speaking could not be completely squelched; it kept coming up time and again.

By the time of the Protestant Reformation, women were permitted to sing in some Protestant churches. But they were not permitted publicly to pray aloud. Martin Luther tells us: "Now they [women] read and sing but they do not pray."[35] Some Protestant churches followed this practice well into the nineteenth century. For example, the Ohio Synod of the Reformed Church still prohibited women from praying out loud as late as 1842, according to one report.[36] And in 1873 a Presbyterian clergyman wrote in the

---

[35]Martin Luther, "Lectures on 1 Timothy," in *Luther's Works*, vol. 28, ed. Hilton C. Oswald (St. Louis: Concordia Publishing House, 1973) 271.

[36]Cyrus Cort, "Women Preaching Viewed in the Light of God's Word and Church History," *Reformed Quarterly Review* 29 (January 1882): 123-30.

Presbyterian Quarterly and Princeton Review, advocating that women were not to pray audibly in church assemblies. He based his argument on 1 Corinthians 11:3-16.[37]

Luther was no great advocate of women's speaking, not even in private settings. He once said: "I wish that women would repeat the Lord's Prayer before opening their mouths."[38] Another time he mumbled: "But eloquence is not to be praised in women; it becomes them better to stammer and lisp."[39]

Luther's remarks relative to women being allowed to sing was, however, not true of all Protestant churches in his day, or even 350 years later. For instance, the Southern Presbyterian Synod of Virginia did not permit women to sing in a worship service until the latter 1890s.[40]

That women today are publicly permitted to pray audibly with men even in ultraconservative churches indicates that the cultural forces now have changed. For at least 1,000 years in the Christian church—from Tertullian to Thomas Aquinas—the passages in 1 Corinthians 14 and 1 Timothy 2 meant that women could not sing or pray audibly among men. Today, the silence of women is no longer seen as applying to singing or praying. In fact, even ultraconservative clergy, who commonly lack a historical or cultural understanding of women's imposed silence, find it difficult to believe that the church once outlawed women from singing or praying aloud. And even if some zealous, misguided clergymen were to try to silence women relative to singing, praying, or asking questions in a Bible class, their efforts would fail. The urban cultural milieu of the twentieth century would not allow that practice again.

Enforced Silence Outside of Church-Worship Contexts

Silencing women for centuries in the Western world was not just confined to worship or ecclesiastical settings. Women were not permitted to speak formally in secular gatherings when men were present. It is only since

[37]J. M. Stevenson, "Woman's Place in Assemblies for Public Worship," *Presbyterian Quarterly and Princeton Review* 2 (January 1873): 42-59.

[38]Roland Bainton, *Here I Stand* (New York: Abingdon-Cokesbury Press, 1950) 301.

[39]Preserved Smith, *The Life and Letters of Martin Luther* (Boston: Houghton Mifflin Company, 1911) 180.

[40]*Lutheran Witness,* 21 January 1900, 126.

the early 1920s, after the ratification of the Nineteenth Amendment to the Constitution, that the clergy have been saying the silence of women applies only to formal worship. Prior to the 1920s 1 Corinthians 14 and 1 Timothy 2 were commonly applied to prohibiting women from engaging in any type of formal, public speaking. In 1837 a pastoral letter was issued in Massachusetts against Angelina and Sarah Grimke, who were known to engage in public speaking.[41]

In 1837 Oberlin College, a one-time missionary- and clergy-training school in Ohio, was the first American college to enroll women as students. It did so in order "to provide ministers with intelligent and cultivated wives."[42] While the college enrolled women, it did not permit them to read their graduation essays aloud. Men had to read them for the women. Nor were women permitted to take courses in public speaking.[43]

In the 1840s Catherine Beecher toured the northeastern United States to promote female education. In her appearances she was not allowed to read her speeches. Her accompanying brother read them while she sat behind him.[44] And it was not until 1853 that a woman, Susan B. Anthony, was allowed to address the New York State Teachers Convention, and as she did, she shocked the women teachers, who made up about two-thirds of the delegates.[45]

In the 1880s Heinrich A. W. Meyer, a theologian in Germany, in his popular commentary said that the silence of women in 1 Corinthians 14 directed "*against public speaking of women.*"[46] Meyer said nothing about this reference applying only to women's speaking in public worship settings. To him, as to others of his time, it was wrong to have a woman speak in any public forum. As I said earlier, the so-called public worship argument made its appearance as a result of the sexist clergy's having to regroup to fight on a different front. It was a last-ditch attempt to keep woman

[41]Una Stannard, *Mrs. Man* (San Francisco: Germaine Press, 1977) 57.

[42]Ann Oakley, *Subject Women* (New York: Pantheon Books, 1981) 117.

[43]Stannard, *Mrs. Man,* 57.

[44]Ibid.

[45]Ibid., 58.

[46]Heinrich A. W. Meyer, *Critical and Exegetical Handbook to the Epistles of the Corinthians,* vol. 6 (New York: Funk and Wagnalls, 1884) 332.

silent, if no longer in public secular settings, then at least in public worship gatherings.

The Antisuffrage Movement

Prior to the time women were given the right to vote in national or regional elections—whether in North America or Great Britain—the arguments that theologians used to keep women from speaking publicly were also used by them to keep women from voting at the ballot box. What the theologians had said for centuries with regard to women's silence was seen as having secular relevance as well. Moreover, many laymen were not slow picking up this line of argument. For example, on 12 January 1915, Congressman Frank Clark of Florida spoke against woman suffrage in the House of Representatives in Washington: "Ah, Mr. Speaker, if it is shameful for a woman to speak out in public in the service of the Master, what is it in the sight of God for her to stand upon a goods box on the corner and appeal to the gaping crowd for votes?"[47] Clark also cited biblical references—not surprisingly, 1 Corinthians 14 and 1 Timothy 2. He did not just refer to these passages obliquely; he quoted them verbatim. He also made much of believing "every word" of the Bible, such that the efforts made to give woman the right to vote was "an attempt to take woman from the sphere in which God intended she should move and place her in direct antagonism to the teachings of the Scriptures."[48]

To keep women voiceless at the ballot box, opponents readily found biblical support. Here it is interesting, almost amusing, to see the logic that was employed. For instance, Orestes Brownson, writing in a Catholic periodical, contended that woman suffrage in the United States would be wrong because it would violate 1 Corinthians 11:9, which said woman was made for man and not man for woman.[49] Analogous to this argument was the contention that woman suffrage conflicted with such biblical statements as "wives submit yourselves to your husbands" and "the head of every woman is the man."[50] Ernest Eckhardt, a Missouri Synod Lutheran clergyman, argued that woman suffrage in society was "a right that could

---

[47]See his speech in the *Congressional Record*, 1915, 1413-14.

[48]Ibid.

[49]Orestes Brownson, "The Woman Question," *Catholic World* (May 1869): 147.

[50]Conway Sams, *Shall Women Vote?* (New York: Neale, 1913) 15-17.

not be granted to Christian women." He asked: "Is that not an example of women ruling over men?"[51]

Horace Bushnell, a prominent clergyman in the Congregational Church during the latter half of the nineteenth century, said women were not to vote because "they are put under authority by their nature."[52] To Bushnell, woman suffrage was a reform against nature. In fact, the subtitle of his book opposing woman suffrage was *The Reform against Nature.* Thus woman suffrage was a violation of the order of nature, an idea that goes back to St. Jerome in the fifth century. Jerome said, "It is contrary to the order of nature and of the law that women should speak in a gathering of men" (*In Primam Epistolam Ad Corinthios* 14). And in 1915 an editorial, in one of the official publications of the Missouri Synod Lutheran Church, argued that giving women the right to vote in society would be a violation of the "order of creation."[53]

Other arguments against woman's right to vote proliferated, as men fought the suffrage movement. One argument, which had great appeal, asserted that woman suffrage would destroy marriage and the family. For instance, James M. Allan, a British opponent of woman's right to vote, made bold to say: "Anticipate the social revolution, disruption of domestic ties, desecration of marriage . . . dissolution of the family—which would result from the political enfranchisement of married women."[54] Orestes Brownson said that woman's right to vote would "weaken and finally break up and destroy the Christian family."[55]

Many clergy argued in the same vein. The Reverend John Milton Williams wrote in the 1890s that giving the vote to women would be a "revolt against marriage."[56] Williams further asserted: "Woman has no call to the ballot box. . . . She is the divinely appointed guardian of the home."[57] He

---

[51]Ernest Eckhardt, *Frauenstimmenrecht* (Battle Creek NE, 1915) 14.

[52]Horace Bushnell, *Women's Suffrage: Reform against Nature* (New York: Charles Scribner's Sons, 1869) 56.

[53]Editorial, *Der Lutheraner* 71 (8 June 1915): 226.

[54]James McGrigor Allan, *Woman Suffrage Wrong in Principle and Practice* (London: Remington and Company, 1890) 269.

[55]Brownson, "The Woman Question," 150.

[56]John Milton Williams, "Woman Suffrage," *Bibliotheca Sacra* 50 (April 1893): 335.

[57]Ibid., 343.

also believed that "the influence of woman suffrage on the home cannot but be divisive."[58] In 1913 the then mostly German-speaking Missouri Synod Lutheran Church, in one of its official periodicals, approvingly cited an antisuffrage statement made by a woman, who said woman suffrage would result in empty homes and racial suicide.[59] Louis Sieck, a Lutheran clergyman, contended: "Neither God nor nature ever intended her for politics. And whatever aims to take woman out of her proper sphere and place her on the same level with man is a blow at the home upon which the welfare of Church and State rests."[60] Having in mind those states that already had given women the right to vote before the Nineteenth Amendment was ratified, Sieck blamed them for causing women to become "masculinized in their dress and habits of speech."[61] Joseph V. McKee, writing in the journal *Catholic World,* maintained that woman suffrage would lead to easy divorce laws.[62] And some Catholic bishops proclaimed that to give woman the vote would be equivalent to having her become a "fallen woman."[63]

After the Nineteenth Amendment had become law, another clergyman, J. Frederic Wenchel, said: "The home and children . . . and American mothers and children, like Christian charity, will be a rarity."[64] He also predicted: "Many women will be so busy about voting and political office that the home and children will have no attraction for them."[65] Still another clergyman, A. L. Graebner, wrote that the push for woman's suffrage was a sign that the end of the world was approaching. Women who desired the right to vote forfeited their crown for a foolscap. He also said that Christians were the salt of the earth; therefore, they were not to sup-

---

[58]Ibid., 336.

[59]Editorial, "Zur Kirchlichen Chronik," *Der Lutheraner* 64 (1 April 1913): 109.

[60]Louis Sieck, "Attitude Lutherans Should Take towards Woman's Suffrage," *Lutheran Witness* 38:13 (May 1919): 179.

[61]Ibid., 180.

[62]John V. McKee, "Shall Women Vote?" *Catholic World* 102 (October 1915): 52.

[63]Cited by Rosemary Ruether, *New Woman, New Earth* (New York: Seabury Press, 1975) 22.

[64]J. Frederic Wenchel, "Washington Letter," *Lutheran Witness* 39:12 (October 1920): 330.

[65]Ibid.

port the woman's movement. To support his antisuffrage argument, he cited passages from the Old and New Testaments.[66]

The rather strange logic or reasoning that was employed by the opponents of woman suffrage, many of whom were clergy, did not end with predicting the demise of the family. Centuries of cultural discrimination against women led these clergy and others to make predictions that when heard today bring incredulous smiles even to the faces of schoolchildren. The Reverend Horace Bushnell maintained that if women were to vote, they would develop heavier brains, lose their feminine features, and endanger their purity and morality.[67] Louis Sieck argued against woman suffrage on the basis of woman being the "weaker vessel." Woman's "frailer form, the more delicate organs, the more sensitive and timid nature" made her unfit for voting.[68]

Today when one tells certain opponents of woman's ordination that the same biblical references that they presently cite to keep women from becoming clergy were once widely employed to oppose woman's right to vote, they find it difficult to believe this piece of history—probably because it points out a real irony to them. After all, they and their friends take their wives with them to vote for conservative candidates in state or national elections. These modern-day sexists have never had a second thought about their wives' voting. They have no twinge of conscience with regard to such behavior, which their ultraconservative predecessors once saw as violating God's will, as well as going against the "order of creation." Once again one sees how culture has shaped and reshaped their theology regarding women.

Arguments since the Enactment of the Nineteenth Amendment

After the modern sociocultural forces in Western societies had slowly overcome the sexists' arguments against woman's suffrage, the clergy in many denominations took a new tack. They reluctantly began to accept woman's right to vote as one way that her voice could be heard and exercised. The biblical references that were cited to keep women silent now were seen as *only* keeping women from leading or conducting ecclesias-

---

[66]A. L. Graebner, "Frauenrechte," *Der Lutheraner* 50 (April 1894): 72.

[67]Bushnell, *Women's Suffrage,* 136.

[68]Sieck, "Woman's Suffrage," 38.

tical services. Modern cultural forces had led theologians to reinterpret the biblical passages that were once used against all manner of public speaking, including the right to vote.

Male theologians, like other human beings, often have a number of vested interests that frequently produce a variety of defense mechanisms to keep those interests intact. So now that the battle against woman suffrage was lost, they moved their verbal artillery from the double front of keeping woman silent in ecclesiastical and secular contexts to the single front of keeping woman silent only in the church. But this single front soon brought new problems. Some said that "let the woman be silent" (1 Cor. 14:34) meant woman could neither preach nor vote in congregational assemblies. Others said it only prevented women from preaching but not from voting in church meetings.

After 1920 much of the arguing over woman's silence revolved around whether women should be allowed to vote in congregational matters. One theologian, S. B. Goodenow, firmly and resolutely declared that according to 1 Timothy 2 and 1 Corinthians 14, "Voting [in the church] is certainly more questionable than any other mode of expression, for this carries 'authority' rather than 'subjection' in it. And if the actual majority vote of all men composing a church be over ruled by votes of women turning the scale, it may be hard to see why this is not the very using of 'authority over the man' which Paul forbids."[69] Similarly, Frederich P. Mayser, a Lutheran pastor, contended that the Bible banned women from voting in the church. "Voting," he said, "is one of the strongest and most effective ways of speaking and governing (ruling) in the church, and if done by women, it is clearly in violation of the original fundamental order established at creation and continued in the New Testament dispensation."[70] In a 1908 editorial the official organ of the Missouri Synod Lutheran Church proclaimed that granting women the right to vote in the church was "unlutheran and unbiblical."[71] J. H. C. Fritz, a prominent member of this church body and a seminary professor, in 1932 spoke against women's voting in the church. He said: "It will be admitted without dispute, we believe, that

[69]S. B. Goodenow, "Woman's Voice in the Church," *New Englander* 36 (January 1877): 120.

[70]Frederick P. Mayser, "Shall Women Vote in the Church?" *Lutheran Church Review* 18 (July 1899): 482.

[71]Editorial, *Der Lutheraner* 64 (8 September 1908): 287.

the right to vote is the right to rule or govern.''[72] And for women to rule and govern was "unthinkable" and "unbiblical."

The words of men like Goodenow, Mayser, and Fritz eventually became idle talk. The old position of woman's silence was now being changed by new cultural forces. Now the culture was shaping a theology that was more responsive to the needs and talents of women, rather than against them.

There were, however, some obstinate resisters, even as the culture had already prompted many clergy and their denominations to approve woman suffrage in the church. One notable opponent to woman's voting in the church was the Lutheran Church–Missouri Synod. This denomination did not allow its women members to vote in congregational meetings until 1969. And even then many of its clergymen and theological professors saw this act on the part of the synod as unbiblical and liberal. Some still do.

The Wisconsin Lutheran Synod, which even prohibits its boys from joining the Boy Scouts of America, has thus far not even considered the possibility of woman's voting in its parishes. The officialdom would never permit the question to be brought to a vote on the convention floor, even if some pastor or congregation were to muster enough courage to raise the issue. Ancient sexist cultural values, disguised as biblical theology, have barred Christian liberty from having any meaningful function in this denomination relative to women.

The above historical illustrations clearly indicate that countless clergy, for centuries, unknowingly have been espousing ancient, agrarian cultural views of woman's role as "Thus says the Lord." They are unaware that the public silencing of women was practiced by the Greeks, Romans, Hebrews, and others. There is nothing godly or Christian about silencing women. The practice is virtually as old as paganism itself. If the advocates of woman's silence were to examine the origins of this old, discriminatory position, many would probably see their error and help promote the cause of women's rights.

---

[72]J. H. C. Fritz, "Shall Women Vote in the Churches?" *Lutheran Witness* 51:26 (April 1932): 161.

CHAPTER 9

JESUS BREAKS THE SILENCE BARRIER

G. K. Chesterton once said it is not that the teachings of Christ have been tried and failed, but rather that they have never really been tried. This is especially true when one notes how the followers of Jesus, only 100 years or so after his time, increasingly began to view and treat women in sexist, un-Christian ways. The church's leaders unwittingly reverted back to the agrarian culture's patriarchal practices regarding women.

Theologians, beginning with men like Tertullian and Origen, were more influenced by pagan culture than by Christ, whose name they ritualistically confessed. The theology of women in the postapostolic church was largely based on a couple of New Testament passages (1 Cor. 11:8-9, 1 Cor. 14:34-35, and 1 Tim. 2:11-15, discussed in the previous chapter). Influenced by centuries of patriarchal values from an agrarian era, theologians saw these passages as having timeless, universal application. Their culture did not permit them to ask whether these references perhaps were only addressed to a temporal or particular problem that existed in a given congregation in the apostolic church.

These passages were seen (and still are), especially by men who are opposed to women's teaching or preaching, as prescriptively binding. Yet other references that were equally as prescriptive soon lost their authority. For instance, 1 Corinthians 7:20 says: "Everyone should remain in the state in which he was called." Yet, the theologians in the early church did not condemn Christians who changed occupations. Had they done so, many would not have been able to enter the monasteries to become monks. Paul told Christians: "Greet one another with a holy kiss" (1 Cor. 16:20; 1 Cor. 13:12; Rom. 16:16). At first these references were taken seriously and literally, but not for very long. Clement of Alexandria (A.D. 160–215) already indicates that the kiss of peace was perhaps not to be followed in a literal sense, evidently because the practice was causing problems (*The Instructor* 3.11). In Matthew 10:5-14 Jesus sent out the disciples and told them not to take any money, extra clothing, or food. Each of these references, as well as many others, were interpreted as having temporal or particularistic application. But not so with the passages that said women were to be silent or submissive to men. Those were seen as having a timeless, universal application. Why the difference?

The fairest explanation is that the cultural values of sexism, unrecognized by clergymen, were too powerful to permit any other interpretation. So strongly ignored were Jesus' teachings with respect to women that one can easily find hundreds of lengthy treatises citing biblical references about woman's supposed subordinate roles and functions, but to find a single citation of Jesus' numerous liberating and equality-giving acts to women is about as rare as finding a hen's tooth.

In the discussion that follows, I wish to credit Leopold Zscharnack, who in 1902 drew attention to the liberating acts of Jesus with respect to women.[1] I am also indebted to some of Leonard Swidler's observations.[2] His article "Jesus Was a Feminist" has shocked and angered many sexist males. After all, they have certainly read the four Gospels, and they didn't see Jesus as a feminist. Moreover, not being cognizant of how badly culture treated women in Jesus' day, they don't even see any significance in his treatment of women.

Soon after the apostolic age, and for almost 2,000 years after, agrarian culture with its patriarchal accents prevented most of the church fathers and other clergy from even noticing women's oppressed position. The roles assigned to women were seen as morally right. After all, several references in the New Testament epistles said women were to be silent, veiled, and subordinate to men. So typically when the four Gospels were read in the early *post*apostolic church, Jesus' revolutionary interactions with women had little or no effect. When male theologians read the words and acts rel-

---

[1]Leonard Zscharnack, *Der Dienst der Frau in den Ersten Jahrhunderten der christlichen Kirche* (Göttingen, 1902).

[2]Leonard Swidler, "Jesus Was a Feminist," *Catholic World* 212 (January 1971):177-83; idem, *Biblical Affirmations of Woman* (Philadelphia: Westminster Press, 1979). Also helpful was Alicia Craig Faxon's *Women and Jesus* (Philadelphia: United Church Press, 1973).

ative to Jesus' contacts with women, they went in one ear and out the other. In their having failed to see his revolutionary, nonsexist treatment of women, one is reminded of the words that he spoke on one occasion: "Seeing they do not see, and hearing they do not hear, nor do they understand" (Matt. 13:13).

Today, countless male clergy commonly fail to see Jesus' contacts with women as liberating because Western culture has for some time freed women from many of the ancient patriarchal oppressions. Thus Jesus' interactions with women were not—and still are not—seen as unusual by many ultraconservative clergy. Their ignorance of ancient culture, and what women had to endure in that culture, before and during Jesus' day, has prevented them from seeing that Jesus broke the silence barrier that had kept women silent for centuries.

Jesus Taught Women Theology

The socioreligious definition that for hundreds of years defined woman as intellectually, biologically, socially, and spiritually inferior was solidly entrenched and institutionalized in Jesus' day. But he went against this age-old, patriarchal definition. It made no difference to him that this definition was espoused by those who were considered to be the theological elite (priests, scribes, or Pharisees). He questioned, in word and deed, the taken-for-granted positions that treated women as subordinate and inferior beings in every context of human life. Jesus was true to his own words: "I came that you might have life, and have it more abundantly" (John 10:10). If any group of human beings was in need of a more abundant life, spiritually or socially, it was the women in his male-dominated culture.

The Samaritan Woman Encounter. The way Jesus treated and responded to the Samaritan woman, for instance, may not appear unusual to the reader in today's Western culture. Yet what he did was extremely radical in his day.

First, he ignored the Jewish prejudices that considered Samaritans to be inferior on religious and ethnic grounds. The Samaritans were not permitted to worship in Jerusalem. They acknowledged only the five books of Moses as God's inspired word. Their having "gentile blood" was yet another reason why the Jews saw them as inferior. The Samaritan woman was very much aware of these prejudices the Jews had against the Samaritans. She was also aware of living in a sexist culture, because when Jesus approached her for a drink, she asked him: "How is it that you, a Jew, ask a drink of me, a woman of Samaria?" (John 4:9).

Second, he ignored the fact that the Samaritan was a woman. Jesus confronted not only the Jewish bigotry against the Samaritans, but he also attacked the prejudices against women by his actions. Note that the woman could merely have said, "How is it that you, a Jew, ask a drink of me, a Samaritan?" But instead she said "a woman of Samaria."

To speak to a Samaritan was bad enough, but Jesus also spoke to a woman in public. Such an act was to trample underfoot the highly revered religious values of the Hebraic community. Remember, the rabbis, who reflected the agrarian-patriarchal values of Jesus' day, taught: "He who talks with woman [in public] brings evil upon himself" (*Aboth* 1:5). Another rabbinic teaching declared: "One is not so much as to greet a woman" (*Berakhoth* 43b).

Not only did Jesus speak to a woman in public and thereby openly violate one of the rabbinic religious doctrines, but he also did more than just talk; he taught her theology. He told her: "God is spirit, and those who worship him must worship him in spirit and truth" (John 4:24). This was an unthinkable act to a faithful Jewish male. Again, we need to recall that the oral law (cited in chap. 4) taught: "Let the words of the Law [Torah] be burned rather than taught to women. . . . If a man teaches his daughter the Law, it is as though he taught her lechery" (*Sotah* 3:4). The disciples, as faithful Jews, were surprised and puzzled that he was carrying on conversation with a woman. The text says: "They marveled that he was talking with a woman" (John 4:27). They were not amazed because he was talking with a *Samaritan* woman, but rather that he was interacting with any *woman*.

The fact that Jesus taught the Samaritan woman theology has, with very few exceptions, not been noticed by the church's male theologians. The few that have taken note were too culture-bound to help the church learn and benefit from Jesus' precedent-setting behavior. For instance, Origen saw the Samaritan woman as an apostle (*Commentariorum in Evangelium Joannis* 14.417). Similarly, Theophylactus (died after 1071) said that Jesus made an apostle out of the Samaritan woman (*Ennarratio in Evangelium Joannis* 4.1241). Yet, neither Origen nor Theophylactus urged the church to make use of women to teach publicly the words and deeds of Jesus Christ.

These two theologians, like countless others, failed to see that Jesus responded to the Samaritan woman just as he did to men. They also failed to note that when he and the woman parted, he did not say: "Woman be silent." Nor did he say that she could not teach. In fact, John says this woman did speak to others publicly about what she experienced in her encounter with the carpenter of Nazareth. Moreover, she must have been quite effective in her public speaking, for we read: "Many Samaritans . . . believed in him because of the woman's testimony" (John 4:39).

The Mary-Martha Incident. Jesus saw woman as a full-fledged human being, rather than subordinate, submissive property. In the Mary-Martha incident Martha is the sociocultural conformist. Apparently, she had deeply internalized the patriarchal idea that woman's place was in the kitchen. She busied herself preparing a meal for Jesus, her guest. Mary, her sister, did what only men did, namely sit down and learn theology. No woman in her right mind, according to the Hebraic-rabbinic teachings, would think of doing what Mary did. Luke says that Mary "sat at Jesus' feet and listened to his teaching" (Luke 10:39). But what is even more significant in this account is that Jesus was the greater deviant. He, after all, taught Mary. Such behavior was a flagrant violation of the established theology. We also need to remember that it was not just rabbinic law that kept women from becoming informed theologically. In Deuteronomy the Israelites were told to teach God's commandments to the sons only. (See Deut. 6:7; 11:19; 12:28; 29:22; 29:29; 32:46.)

The translators (Luther, Cranmer, Tyndale, and others since the Protestant Reformation) have rendered the Hebrew word *benim* as "children." The Hebrew text, however, does not say "children"; it says "sons." The Old Testament made no provision for females to be educated formally, much less for them to be educated theologically. Perhaps this helps explain why Mary was so eager to have Jesus teach her.

Translating *benim* as "children" is another example of culture's having shaped theology. In this case it was the culture of the early postpatriarchal era. Ironically, to render the Hebrew word "sons" as "children" seems to be the first desexing of the Bible.

Jesus did more than flaunt the established religious view of women. He praised and defended Mary for her deviant behavior, saying: "Mary has chosen the good portion, which shall not be taken away from her" (Luke 10:42). Martha was in no way praised for her domestic, kitchen concerns.

Not knowing the ancient cultural restrictions that were imposed on women, nor the rabbinic theology, many modern Christians read the Mary-Martha account and miss much of the significance of what Jesus and Mary really did. Since today even sexist theologians permit women to learn some theology, for example, in a Bible class, they erroneously assume that Mary merely irritated Martha by not helping her in the kitchen. While it is true that Martha was irked by Mary's behavior, it is an oversimplification to focus only on the concerns of Martha. The account teaches something very different from what most theologians of the past perceived. It teaches that Jesus and Mary violated the sexist theology of the Hebraic religious establishment. It also reveals the blindness of countless theologians who since Jesus' day have failed to see that the actions of Jesus and Mary were diametrically opposed to the sexist religious practices that kept women veiled and silent.

One wonders whether Jesus' laudatory words to Martha might not be applied to all women today who, like Mary, are assuming the traditional religious roles assigned to men. It is quite possible that Jesus would say to those who, like Martha, complain about the new roles and positions of women in today's church: "[These women have] chosen the good portion which shall not be taken away."

Teaching Martha. On another occasion Jesus told Martha: "I am the resurrection and the life, he who believes in me, though he die, yet shall he live, and whoever lives and believes in me shall never die. Do you believe this?" (John 11:25-26). These words, which contain the heart of the Christian gospel, are only spoken once in the four Gospels. And to whom were they spoken? To a woman. To teach a woman was bad enough, but he did more than that. He called for a verbal response from Martha by asking, "Do you believe this?" It was another incident of Jesus' breaking the silence barrier for women.

Jesus Rejects the Baby-Machine Image. For hundreds of years male-dominated values have created the belief that woman's only lasting contribution to life is being a mother. Some modern critics of this view, such as Swidler, have called this the "baby-machine" image of woman.

As Swidler noted, Jesus was not impressed by this ancient view of woman. One day while he was preaching, a woman came to him, apparently wishing she had given birth to a man like Jesus. She said: "Blessed is the womb that bore you, and the breasts that sucked you" (Luke 11:27). The woman undoubtedly meant well when she spoke. Yet, Jesus, who was no male chauvinist, said in response: "Blessed rather are those who hear the word of God and keep it" (Luke 11:28).

Jesus' words again, as in other instances, flew in the face of the extant socioreligious values. For one, he did not blindly accept the belief that woman's worth lay primarily in being a "baby machine." Here one needs to recall the great emphasis that the Hebrews made in the Old Testament about many children being a blessing *to the man*. For instance, the Psalmist said: "Happy is the man who has his quiver full of them [children]" (Psalm 127:5). Second, Jesus' words indicate that hearing God's words was also meant for women. Here too Jesus was going against the grain of his Hebrew ancestors, who made no formal provision for a woman to learn religious doctrines. Thus, by implication Jesus was telling the woman— who really valued the "baby-machine" image—that not only men, but also women, were to become theologically conversant. To learn and study religious tenets was not just for men who bore no babies, centuries of male-dominated beliefs notwithstanding.

Jesus refused to legitimate the socioeconomic values of the agrarian-patriarchal system of his era, which is what he would have done had he agreed with the woman's statement. The patriarchy in many ways needed an abundance of children. Without large numbers of children, the agrarian-patriarchal system would have atrophied.[3] However, Jesus was interested in having people establish proper relationships with God and human beings. This is abundantly evident throughout the four Gospels. He once proclaimed: "You shall love the Lord your God with all your heart, and with all your soul, and with all your mind, and with all your strength. The second [commandment] is this: You shall love your neighbor as yourself" (Mark 12:30-31). In conclusion, he said: "There is no other commandment greater than this" (Mark 12:31b). Jesus never said anything about the blessedness of having many children, a notion this woman wanted him to underscore and support.

The Woman with a Menstrual Problem. Another revolutionary act on Jesus' part was how he ignored or spurned the ancient taboo regarding contact with menstruating women. In culture upon culture, for centuries upon centuries, a woman's menses were reason enough for men to reject and isolate her. Now note what Jesus did when "a woman who had a flow of blood for twelve years" touched him (Mark 5:25). Contrary to Hebrew religious values of his time, he not only permitted the "unclean" woman to touch him, but he also registered no shock or surprise at her behavior, which

[3]Fustel de Coulanges, *The Ancient City* (Boston: Lee and Shepherd, 1882) 91-94.

a faithful Jewish male would commonly have done. Ritualistically and religiously speaking, according to Leviticus 15, he was now unclean. He should have gone through a purification ritual to make himself clean again. Leviticus 15:22 demanded: "Whoever touches her [the menstruating woman] . . . shall wash his clothes, and bathe himself in water and be unclean until the evening."

After the woman had touched Jesus, she came to him in "fear and trembling" (Mark 5:33). Jesus had asked: "Who touched my garments?" (Mark 5:30). Any woman in her right mind would have been fear stricken. After all, she violated an ancient religious law that told woman in no uncertain terms that she was not to touch another person, especially not a male, in her menstrual state. So when Jesus asked who touched him, she not only was overwhelmed by fear, but she also fell down before him (Mark 5:33). And what was Jesus' response to this woman's fear? He told her: "Your faith has made you well" (Mark 5:34). Surely, it is not difficult to imagine what went through the minds of the sexist men—priests and others—as Jesus flaunted two religious laws, namely ignoring the menstrual taboo and speaking to a woman in public.

Jesus and a Prostitute. One day as Jesus was attending a dinner invitation in the home of Simon, a prostitute lavishly anointed his feet with ointment. She evidently felt remorseful, because she shed tears as she wiped his feet with her hair.

Simon, a socially and religiously "proper" Pharisee, could not let this woman's behavior go by uncriticized. Nor could he let Jesus alone. So he said: "If this man were a prophet, he would have known who and what sort of woman this is who is touching him" (Luke 7:39). In reality, Simon saw no harm in using this woman for sexual gratification or, as Swidler has said, a "sex object."[4] But one had dare not extend human decencies to her, as Jesus did. Jesus, however, was impressed by what she did now, rather than who she was. What mattered was that she showed great love.

Before the incident in Simon's house was over, Jesus told the woman that her sins were forgiven. Again, he not only spoke to a woman in public, but he also spoke to her theologically.

Jesus Teaches Women about His Resurrection. Jesus' continued bent toward according women equal rights, and sometimes even exclusively selecting women, is especially evident in how he related to the several women

---

[4]Swidler, "Jesus Was a Feminist."

who came to his open tomb. He picked the women to tell his disciples that he had risen from the dead. Said he: "Do not be afraid, go and tell my brethren to go to Galilee, and there they will see me" (Matt. 28:10). This act is noteworthy because John, the Gospel writer, says that Peter and John came to the open tomb before the women did, but he did not reveal himself to Peter and John.

It is difficult not to see something very different here. Why did Jesus not tell Peter and John to go and tell the other disciples, their companions? Why did he have the women tell the men? The answer is not too hard to see, especially when one remembers that based on his own hardships, he always came to the defense and assistance of the deprived and oppressed. In choosing the women to tell the disciples, he favored the socially and religiously oppressed. In fact, his action here brings to mind words that he spoke on another occasion: "Some who are last will be first, and some who are first will be last" (Luke 13:30).

The significance of Jesus' choosing the women—one of whom was Mary Magdalene—to tell the disciples was overlooked in the church of the postapostolic age. One finds only one or two minor exceptions to this tragic oversight. For instance, Bernard of Clairvaux (1091–1153) saw this incident as one that made these women "apostles to the apostles" (*Sermones in Canticorum* 183:1148). Bernard's observation, however, had no effect on the already established views and practices of the church's theology pertaining to women. Nor did George Fox's observation in the seventeenth century make any impact on the sexist theology of the church at large. On the basis of the women's telling the disciples about Christ's resurrection and the Acts 18 account of Priscilla's having taught Apollos, Fox said women were not to be silenced in the church.

Very few modern readers take notice that Jesus had women tell the disciples about his resurrection. They fail to grant that in the first century such a directive was revolutionary. Not to recognize this fact is to let modern, urban-technological culture of the Western world—which permits women to speak in public—prevent one from seeing and understanding that the agrarian culture of the first century did not permit women to talk to men in public about religious matters or really about anything else, for that matter.

Women Followed Jesus

All three writers of the Synoptic Gospels mention a very unusual occurrence in the life of Jesus, namely that women followed him. Matthew

27:55-56 says: "There were also women there, looking from afar, who had followed Jesus from Galilee . . . among whom were Mary Magdalene, and Mary the mother of James and Joseph, and the mother of the sons of Zebedee." Mark says there were "many other women who came up with him to Jerusalem" (Mark 40:41).

Most Christians, when they read or hear about these female followers of Jesus, completely miss the significance of it. Their present-day culture, which allows women to talk and interact with men in public, has prevented them from seeing that such behavior was not engaged in by decent, religiously respectable women. But in the Greco-Roman era and in Jesus' day, only prostitutes or women of very low social status would be found going from one town to another without a male escort, who would be either the husband or the father or someone designated by him.[5]

This brief reminder of how women's freedom of movement was virtually nonexistent shows that the women who followed Jesus ran counter to the ancient male values and practices. Jesus himself condoned the breakup of the patriarchal stranglehold that the culture had on women. He placed those who followed him on a higher level than those who adhered to discriminatory cultural practices. Spiritual ties were more important to him than patriarchal family bonds. Evidently that is why he once said: "Everyone who has left houses, brothers, sisters, father, mother, children or lands, for my name's sake will receive a hundred-fold, and inherit eternal life" (Matt. 19:29).

Nor was Jesus oblivious to what his teaching and actions would produce. He said: "Do not suppose that I have come to bring peace on earth; I have not come to bring peace, but a sword. For I have come to set a man against his father, and a daughter against her mother, and a daughter-in-law against her mother-in-law, and a man's foes will be those of his own household" (Matt. 10:34-36). In the light of these words and his egalitarian acts vis-à-vis women, one gets a better understanding why the Gospel of Luke (23:2) has an early variant reading in which some of Jesus' contemporaries accused him of "misleading women and children." This accusation was one of those made at Jesus' trial before Pontius Pilate.

Jesus' requirements for worship were not tied to cultural or institutionalized symbols, such as worshiping with the right sex in the right temple.

---

[5]J. P. V. D. Balsdon, *Roman Women: Their History and Habits* (New York: John Day and Company, 1963) 278.

To the Samaritan woman, he said that correct worship conduct was to revere God "in spirit and truth" (John 4:24); it didn't matter whether one worshiped in Jerusalem or on Mount Gerizim. The latter place is where the Samaritans worshiped.

Nor was one's worship life to be dictated by ancient family structures. For instance, in first-century Roman life the father, as absolute head of the family, determined which god his wife and children worshiped. Plutarch, in the first century, summed it up well: "It is becoming for a wife to worship and know only the gods that her husband believes in, and to shut the door upon queer rituals and outlandish superstitions" (*Congiugalia Praecepta* 140 D). This practice Plutarch mentions was the logical outgrowth of the Roman institution of *patria potestas* and *manus*. As explained in chapters 4 and 7, these two institutions gave the father absolute power, such that he could even command the death of his family members.

Given the ancient Greco-Roman and Hebrew cultural institution of the father being in total control of the family, including its religious practices, the words and actions of Jesus vis-à-vis women went beyond the mere call for a mental or spiritual allegiance to him. What he said and did was not trivial or superficial. When basic, longstanding cultural institutional practices are threatened, such as how one relates to women and how one worships, serious conflict is inevitable.

The Adulterous Woman

Given that Jesus had so often revealed unconventional attitudes and practices toward women, it is quite likely that the scribes and Pharisees saw an excellent opportunity there to trap Jesus by dragging a woman before him who reportedly was caught in adultery. They could test his loyalty to the laws of Moses, which said: "If a man commits adultery with the wife of his neighbor, both the adulterer and the adulteress shall be put to death" (Lev. 20:10). So they asked him: "Teacher, this woman has been caught in the act of adultery. Now in the law Moses commanded us to stone such. What do you say about her?" (John 8:5).

Had Jesus possessed the mind-set of the scribes and Pharisees, who loved splitting hairs theologically and prided themselves on following Moses' law, he might have asked them at least two legal questions. One, he could have asked why the woman's accomplice was not present to be stoned with the woman. After all, Leviticus 20:10 called for the man to be stoned with the woman, since he had had sex with someone else's wife.

That the man was not arraigned along with the woman really shows the sexist disposition of the scribes and Pharisees. They were more interested in using a defenseless woman to entrap Jesus than in attaining justice. Two, Jesus could have inquired whether they had two eyewitnesses, as called for in Deuteronomy 19:15. But Jesus, who was never interested in legalistic questions, instead voiced a spiritual concern. Said he: "Let him who is without sin among you be the first to throw a stone at her" (John 8:7). This response was too much and too unexpected. So the self-righteous, sexist scribes and Pharisees departed.

When everyone was gone except the woman, Jesus asked her: "Has no one condemned you?" She replied: "No one, Lord." To this response he declared: "Neither do I condemn you; go and do not sin again" (John 8:10-11).

"A Daughter of Abraham"

Luke 13:10-16 tells us that one particular Sabbath day Jesus broke the law by healing a woman who had had an infirmity for eighteen years. This deviant act ended with his calling the woman "a daughter of Abraham," a most unusual expression to be applied to a Hebrew woman. Jesus undoubtedly meant it to be the theological equivalent of the common expression "son of Abraham," which to the Jews symbolized an intimate faith relationship with God. Jewish men took great pride in being the spiritual heirs of Abraham; however, the Hebrews in the Old Testament made no reference to their women being spiritual heirs of either God or Abraham. For example, one reads about the "God of Abraham, of Isaac, and of Jacob" (Exod. 3:16), but never about the God of Sarah, Rebekah, or Rachel. A woman had no spiritual heritage, in life or death, that was linked to God or Abraham. Yet, that is precisely what Jesus did when he called the woman in the Lukan account "a daughter of Abraham."

Undoubtedly, Jesus' attitude and responses to women contributed to people's thinking that he had taken leave of his senses. In Mark 3:21 his friends are cited saying: "He is beside himself." These accounts, as well as others in the Gospels, portray a very radical posture on Jesus' part. Unlike people of his day or our time, he never spoke derogatorily to or about woman. He saw every woman as a person, not as a sex object or subordinate entity that existed for man's benefit. In his eyes, women were to be equal to men. Jesus ignored—deliberately so—the material, economic bases and values of his agrarian cultural era. He also knew that if others were to follow him in defying basic cultural practices, this amounted to taking up "the cross." He not only invited the socially, spiritually, and economically oppressed—in this case, women—to come to him, but he also went *to them* as well.

Few people, including scholars, really notice that this man of Nazareth was a feminist in the best sense of the word. For centuries Jesus' revolutionary views and acts pertaining to women were unwittingly disguised by the chauvinistic theology of male clergy and church leaders. They saw and presented Jesus' deeds through a prism of cultural sexism that often hid woman's best friend for almost 2,000 years. Even today, with new awareness of women's rights, there are few who recognize that the church frequently acted contrary to the teachings of its founder.

CHAPTER 10

WOMEN IN THE APOSTOLIC CHURCH

Given that Jesus broke with the agrarian culture in which the patriarchal tradition kept women veiled and silent, one is compelled to ask whether the apostles continued his pathbreaking behavior or whether they found it more comfortable to stay with the old cultural practices that kept woman in her "place." This chapter contends that for the most part the apostolic church (from about A.D. 30 to 150) continued the precedent set by Jesus, whom it called "Lord."

Women Taught Theology

Priscilla. In Acts, which briefly traces the growth and development of the church from Jerusalem to Rome, we learn of a woman named Priscilla. She apparently grew up in a wealthy and influential family in Rome. This background seems to explain her better-than-average knowledge and sophistication, which Paul used to advance the Christian mission. Some scholars, such as Elsie Thomas Culver, believe Priscilla "had the responsibility for sending copies of various Pauline letters to house churches . . . when their reading was one of the most important parts of the Christian gatherings."[1] Culver thinks Priscilla also did editorial work for Paul and even polished his letter to the Romans, one of his most famous epistles.

---

[1]Elsie Thomas Culver, *Women in the World of Religion* (New York: Doubleday and Company, 1967) 60.

Priscilla seems to have understood the role and function that Jesus assigned to women, when he at the time of his resurrection told them to tell (teach) the disciples. Acts 18 notes that Priscilla and her husband, Aquila, heard Apollos, an eloquent speaker, expounding on the teaching of Christ. According to Acts 18:26, Priscilla and Aquila felt that Apollos needed to present Christ's teaching more accurately, so they took it upon themselves to correct his understanding of Christianity.

How long Apollos was taught by Priscilla and Aquila is not known. But that Priscilla was the primary teacher, as well as the one who assumed a leading role in the church, is evident for several reasons. First, it appears that her husband served as her assistant, rather than she as his. For instance, the New Testament mentions Priscilla and Aquila six times, and four of these times her name is cited before his. The order of names in ancient times indicated priority of role and importance. The practice is corroborated by St. Chrysostom (A.D. 347–407), who was no feminist, to be sure. He wrote: "It is good to look at Paul's motive, when he greets them, for placing Priscilla before her husband. . . . He did not do so without reason: the wife must have had, I believe, greater piety than her husband . . . this woman took him [Apollos], instructed him in the way of God, and made him an excellent teacher" (*In Illud, Salutate Priscillam et Aquilam* 191-92).

Fifteen hundred years after Chrysostom, the famous scholar Adolph von Harnack said: "Plainly the woman [Priscilla] was the leading figure of the two."[2] Harnack also saw Priscilla's being listed before Aquila as significant. In fact, he argued that she may be claimed as "an apostle."[3] Even if one were to yield to the dissenters that Priscilla was not the primary teacher of Apollos, it is still very significant that she taught at all, even with her husband. In Greco-Roman or Hebrew socioreligious culture, women were not even permitted to read before or to men, much less teach one of them.

Second, Paul in his epistle to the Christians in Rome says she and Aquila were thanked and well known by the Gentile churches (Rom. 16:4). Would the churches have known her well had she assumed the traditional wom-

---

[2]Adolph von Harnack, *The Expansion of Christianity in the First Three Centuries*, vol. 2, trans. James Moffat (G. P. Putnam's Sons, 1905) 219.

[3]Ibid., 209.

an's role of being veiled and silent? Moreover, in the previous verse Paul said Priscilla was one of his fellow workers (*synergos*), a term that he also used relative to Timothy and Titus, both teachers and preachers. She could hardly have been a "fellow worker" if she had been silent and passive, as women in Jewish religious contexts commonly were.

Third, Priscilla's role and influence in the apostolic church must have been highly significant. One of the oldest, and the largest, catacombs in Rome (*Coemeterium Priscilla*) was named in her honor. A church on the Aventine in Rome bears her name. In addition, a number of monuments in Rome carry the name of Priscilla. Thus it is not surprising to read that a renowned scholar in the nineteenth century said that Priscilla "occupied a peculiar relation to the church of Corinth."[4] This scholar, Carl von Weizsäcker, said that Paul's calling her one of his "fellow workers" shows that "Priscilla and Aquila occupied a different position from that of Paul's other co-workers. The apostle distinctively set them side by side with himself."[5]

Fourth, some scholars have argued that Priscilla wrote the Epistle to the Hebrews in the New Testament. This observation was first made in 1905 by Adolph von Harnack. In addition to Harnack, other scholars have suggested that Priscilla may very well have written the Book of Hebrews, whose authorship, according to Origen, was known only to God.

Several arguments have been cited for Priscilla's authorship of Hebrews: (a) the letter may purposely have been kept anonymous in order not to prejudice its acceptance; (b) she may not have written it anonymously, but some male removed her name from the epistle's prescript; (c) sometimes the author's voice is plural, perhaps suggesting reference to her husband, Aquila; (d) nautical terms are mentioned, probably because she took part in sea trips (Acts 18:18); (e) she certainly was capable of authoring the epistle, given her well-known teaching talent and the fact that Paul called her his "fellow worker." Ruth Hoppin has cited additional arguments for Priscilla's authorship.[6]

---

[4]Carl von Weizsäcker, *The Apostolic Age of the Christian Church*, vol. 1, trans. James Miller (New York: G. P. Putnam's Sons, 1899) 309.

[5]Ibid., 1:394.

[6]Ruth Hoppin, *Priscilla: Author of the Epistle to the Hebrews* (New York: Exposition Press, 1969).

Phoebe. In Romans 16:1-2 Paul says Phoebe, in the church at Cenchreae, was a *diakonos* (deacon), not "deaconess" as male theologians have mistranslated this work in many Bible versions. (The feminine form of *diakonos* did not appear in the literature until about 300 years after St. Paul addressed Phoebe in the Epistle to the Romans. *The Apostolic Constitutions* [a Syriac document of about A.D. 375] is the first known Christian writing to use the feminine form of *diakonos*.) The word *diakonos* appears many times in the New Testament. In the King James Version (KJV) it is most often translated as "minister" when it speaks about a man holding this office. Three times the KJV translates the word as "deacon." Only in one place does it use the word *servant,* and that occurs in Romans 16:1, where Phoebe is mentioned.

Evidently, beginning with the KJV, English translators were overwhelmed by sexist values because the Miles Coverdale edition, about seventy years earlier (1535), still translated *diakonos* in Romans 16:1 as "minister." Closer to our time, the Revised Standard Version renders *diakonos* as "deaconess," while the New International Version, like the KJV, has "servant."

Paul's calling Phoebe a *diakonos* indicates several things of note. First, Paul does not distinguish this office or position relative to sex. In fact, he used the term *diakonos* of himself in 1 Corinthians 3:5 and of Timothy in Acts 19:22. Second, Paul used the word *diakonos* together with *coworker* (*synergos*) in 1 Corinthians 3:5, 9 and also in 2 Corinthians 6:1, 4. And in 1 Corinthians 16:15-16 he said the coworkers "have devoted themselves to the diakonia of the saints." Third, being a *diakonos,* Phoebe in all likelihood taught theology to men and women, and perhaps even in different churches. A. Lemaire has shown that the function of *diakonos* commonly meant teaching and preaching in the first two centuries of the church's existence.[7] According to Elizabeth Schuessler Fiorenza, "In NT Greek the title of *diakonos* means not primarily 'servant' or 'deacon' but 'herald' or official messenger."[8] Having been a *diakonos* would indicate that Phoebe

---

[7]A. Lemaire, "From Services to Ministries: Diakonia in the First Two Centuries," *Concilium* 14 (1972): 35-46.

[8]Elizabeth Schuessler Fiorenza, "The Apostleship of Women in Early Christianity," in Leonard Swidler and Arlene Swidler, eds., *Women Priests* (New York: Paulist Press, 1977) 137.

held a "position of authority in the churches."[9] Fourth, why was there no feminine word for *diakonos* in the Greek language? There likely was none because in the Greek culture only males performed the important religious functions as *diakonoi*. Yet Paul did not hesitate to address Phoebe by a well-known Greek religious term used only for male functionaries. He probably did so because she performed religious activities that were commonly performed by males in his day and age.

Paul not only called Phoebe a *diakonos,* but he also said she was a *prostatis* (Rom. 16:2). This title meant "leading officer" in the literature at the time the New Testament was written, similar to what today in the English language would be called "superintendent." The Epistle of Clement of Rome uses *prostatis* in reference to Christ. According to Fiorenza, in 1 Thessalonians 5:12 the word *diakonos* "characterizes persons of authority in the community, and in 1 Timothy 3:4-5 and 5:17 it designates the functions of the bishop, deacon or elder."[10] Wayne Meeks contends that Phoebe probably held a position similar to the one mentioned in Philippians 1:1, where *diakonos* is used in a complementary sense to the position of *episkopos*.[11] In ancient Greek literature the word *prostatis* meant "to preside in the sense of to lead, conduct, direct, govern," according to Bo Reicke.[12] When one realizes that Phoebe carried the Epistle to the Romans a distance of 400 miles to Rome from Corinth, it becomes all the more plausible that she was an important leader in the church.

The high value placed on Phoebe's church activities is not just a reflection of modern ("liberal") theologians. Origen (A.D. 185–254), who can hardly be accused of being a feminist, saw Phoebe's having apostolic

---

[9]E. A. Judge, "Early Christians as Scholastic Community," *Journal of Religious History* 1 (1960–1961): 128-29.

[10]Elizabeth Schuessler Fiorenza, "Word, Spirit and Power: Women in Early Christian Communities," in Rosemary Ruether and Eleanor McLaughlin, eds., *Women of Spirit: Female Leadership in the Jewish and Christian Traditions* (New York: Simon & Schuster, 1979) 36.

[11]Wayne Meeks, "The Image of the Androgyne: Some Uses of a Symbol in Earliest Christianity," *History of Religions* 13 (1973–1974): 198.

[12]Bo Reicke, "Proistemi," in Geoffrey Bromiley, ed. and trans., *Theological Dictionary of the New Testament,* vol. 6 (Grand Rapids: Eerdmans, 1968) 700.

authority on the basis of Romans 16:1-2 (*Comentariorum in Epistolam B. Pauli Ad Romans* 10, 1278).

Junia. The King James and the Revised Standard Version translate Paul's words in Romans 16:7 as: "Greet Andronicus and Junias, my kinsmen and fellow contenders, who are of note among the apostles." Here it is important to note that for the first 1300 years of Christendom, the companion of Andronicus was seen as a woman, not a male as the name "Junias" indicates. Biased male translators have assumed, a priori, that a woman could not be someone of "note among the apostles." So they concluded this person's name, found in the accusative form in the Greek text of Romans 16:7, had to be masculine, even though grammatically the word can also be translated as "Junia," a common Roman name for a woman.

That Andronicus's companion was a woman—probably his wife—is almost beyond doubt, in spite of what various translations have led readers to believe. St. Chrysostom said the person in question here was a woman. Commenting on Romans 16:7, he declared: "Oh, how great is the devotion [*philosophia*] of this woman, that she should be even counted worthy of the appellation of apostle" (*Epistle to the Romans,* Homily 31). St. Jerome said Junia was a woman, as did Peter Abelard in the twelfth century. In fact, until Aegidius of Rome (1245–1316) no one saw the name as referring to a man. The name "Junias" is not to be found in the Greek and Roman literature, according to Bernadette Brooten.[13]

Junia, a woman, certainly could have been an apostle, as Chrysostom said, because Paul did not restrict the term to the twelve disciples and himself. For instance, he called James, the brother of Jesus, an apostle (Gal. 1:19; 1 Cor. 15:7). He also used the word *apostle* interchangeably with *diakonos* in 2 Corinthians 11:13.

In the first half of the second century, Origen said that Romans 16, with its reference to Phoebe as *diakonos* and to Junia as a notable apostle, shows that women had "apostolic authority" (*apostolica auctoritate*) in the church. These citations indicate that the involvement of women in the apostolic church evidently was so widespread and pronounced that the church

---

[13]Bernadette Brooten, "Feminist Perspectives on New Testament Exegesis," in Hans Küng and Jürgen Moltmann, eds., *Conflicting Ways of Interpreting the Bible* (New York: Sundbury Press, 1980) 55-61.

fathers could not deny this culture-shocking, religious behavior, even if they would have wanted to do so. But the in-depth participation of women in the apostolic church was soon to be forgotten as the church aged. Woman, as in pagan cultures, was again veiled and silenced. By the fourth century, given the influence of St. Jerome and others like him, it was wrong and contrary to God's word for a woman audibly to sing, pray, or speak, much less to teach. Even Mary Magdalene was not exempt. Once called an "apostle to the apostles" by Bernard of Clairvaux (preacher of the second Crusade), "in later ecclesiastical consciousness she [had become] the 'prostitute' and 'sinner.' "[14]

Women in the House Churches

Today when people hear the word *church*, they think of a building with a steeple. That, however, was not the meaning of the word Paul used when he spoke about the "church" in his writings. The word commonly used for "church" in the New Testament was the Greek word *ecclesia*. This word was also used with reference to small gatherings of Christians, as for instance in Galatians 1:2, 22; 1 Corinthians 16:1, 19; 2 Corinthians 8:1. These small groups had no formal building of their own in which they could worship. They either worshiped in a synagogue or in private houses, known as house churches today. It was not until the third century that Christians began building structures for *ecclesia* gatherings.[15]

In these house churches women played a prominent role.[16] Evidently the existence of house churches during the apostolic era was a custom borrowed from some well-to-do Roman women who, prior to the time of Christ, practiced religious activities in their homes.[17] Thus it is not surprising that the house churches of the New Testament frequently met in the

---

[14]Elizabeth Schuessler Fiorenza, "You Are Not to Be Called Father," *Cross Currents* (Fall 1979): 316.

[15]Robert Banks, *Paul's Idea of Community: The Early House Churches in Their Historical Setting* (Grand Rapids: Eerdmans, 1980) 41.

[16]F. V. Filson, "The Significance of the Early House Churches," *Journal of Biblical Literature* 58 (1939): 105-12.

[17]M. F. Lefkowitz and M. Fant, *Women in Greece and Rome* (Toronto: Samuel-Stevens, 1977) 86.

homes of women. One such church met in Mary's (the mother of John Mark) house. Nympha in the town of Laodicea had a "church in her house" (Col. 4:15). Priscilla and Aquila, mentioned above, had a "church in their house" (1 Cor. 16:19). And Apphia, whom Paul called "our sister," evidently was a leader in a house church in the city of Colossae (Philem. 2). Especially noteworthy is that in these house churches there was preaching and teaching (Acts 5:42). The Lord's Supper was also celebrated in these homes.

Since it is evident from the New Testament, as well as from research on house churches, that women played a prominent role in establishing house churches, it is difficult to believe that women were not also teaching and preaching in these small gatherings. Most likely Priscilla taught Apollos in such a setting. In these churches it is difficult to see women conforming to the Hebrew custom of worship that required them to be silent. Moreover, since women outnumbered men in the apostolic church, it is very improbable that they did not assume active roles in leading and conducting the teaching and worship activities. One also needs to remember, as Robert Banks has shown, that the rules of the synagogue were not operative in the house churches.[18] Women had a freedom in the apostolic church that not only was encouraged by Jesus and Paul, but also by the fact that early Christians had no formally established physical structures of their own for worship.

The phenomenon of house churches in part reflects a crumbling of the Greco-Roman institutions of *patria potestas* and paterfamilias. These two sociolegal institutions once held women in firm subjection. Whenever women, who in theory were under paterfamilias, converted to Christianity and practiced a religion that was different than their husbands'—not to mention that they often worshiped with other Christians in their husbands' houses—such actions indicated "a potential political offense against the patriarchal order. It [was] an infringement of the political order, for the patriarchal order of the house was considered the paradigm for the state. Since the patriarchal *familia* was the nucleus of the state, conversion of the

---

[18]Banks, *Paul's Idea of Community.*

subordinated members of the house, who were supposed to share in the religion of the *paterfamilias* constituted a subversive act.''[19]

Women in the Book of Acts

Luke recorded that women, one of them Jesus' mother, prayed with the men in an upper room in Jerusalem (Acts 1:14). Again, we need to remember that such behavior was highly irregular. Women were to be silent in the Judaic tradition.

This event of women praying with men was followed by the outpouring of the Holy Spirit at Pentecost. Women along with men received the Holy Spirit, according to Acts 1 and 2. The women, as well as the men, spoke in foreign languages. At this time Peter tells the astonished audience that they should not be surprised by what was happening. Undoubtedly the people were not only surprised to hear Jesus' followers speak in foreign tongues, but also to hear women speaking religious messages. So Peter in Acts 2:17 cites the Old Testament prophet Joel, showing that an ancient prophecy was being fulfilled: ''I will pour out my Spirit upon all flesh, and your sons and *daughters shall prophesy*'' (emphasis added).

The prominence of women promoting apostolic Christianity, a phenomenon that was begun and encouraged by Jesus, did not sit well with Paul before he became a Christian. As is known, Paul (Saul) was a zealous persecutor of the early Christians. Acts 8:3 says that he went from house to house (remember the house churches) dragging ''off men and *women* and committed them to prison'' (emphasis added). Acts 9:1-2 and 22:4-5 are two additional references that mention Paul's persecuting women. These references, of course, prompt a very significant question: would he have persecuted women along with men if they had been veiled and silent? To ask the question is to answer it. He persecuted women because they assumed and exercised roles equal to men in spreading the message of Christianity.

Not only were women assuming roles equal to men in promoting Christianity, but there is some evidence that they were more zealous in doing so than men often were. St. Chrysostom (late fourth century) said: ''The women of those days [early apostolic church] were more spirited than

---

[19]Elizabeth Schuessler Fiorenza, *Bread Not Stone: The Challenge of Feminist Biblical Interpretation* (Boston: Beacon Press, 1984) 76-77.

lions." Luke in the Book of Acts refers to Tabitha, a seamstress in Joppa, as a "disciple." She probably played a spirited role in the embryonic church because many wept when she died. Yet, as Constance Parvey has noted, Tabitha has virtually been ignored by male theologians.[20] As proof of her obscurity, one need only ask, Did I know that a woman was called a "disciple" in the New Testament? The answer is undoubtedly negative.

Women in the Corinthian Church

Any discussion of the regnant involvement and leadership of women in the apostolic church would be woefully incomplete if it did not consider the passages in 1 Corinthians 11:5 and 14:34-35. The latter reference, already discussed in earlier chapters, has been (and still is) typically employed by many theologians to silence women in the church.

In 1 Corinthians 11:5 Paul tells the Corinthian Christians that a woman may pray and prophesy, provided she has her head covered. By saying this Paul obviously made a break from the Jewish practice, where women were by no means permitted to speak or read out of respect to the men in the congregation or synagogue.

Males with a sexist orientation have tried to minimize the role of women's prophesying by saying that Paul had in mind women's prophesying in the privacy of their home rather than in the public context of the church. So says R. C. H. Lenski.[21] This argument is faulty because in 1 Corinthians 14:4 Paul states that prophesying is to edify the church. If that is the objective, then obviously it must occur publicly in the presence of assembled church members. Thus the prophesying done by women must also fall into this category. This conclusion is corroborated by 1 Corinthians 14:24, where Paul speaks about everyone ("all") prophesying. In 1 Corinthians 14:31 he says: "For you can *all prophesy,* one by one, so that all may learn and all be encouraged" (emphasis added). In light of these references, can one really say that "all" means only men and not also women?

---

[20]Constance Parvey, "The Theology and Leadership of Women in the New Testament," in Rosemary Radford Ruether, ed., *Religion and Sexism: Images of Woman in the Jewish and Christian Traditions* (New York: Simon & Schuster, 1974) 145.

[21]R. C. H. Lenski, *The Interpretation of St. Paul's First of Second Corinthians* (Minneapolis: Augsburg Publishing House, 1963) 436.

It is highly unlikely that Paul wanted women to prophesy only in private, since prophesying was a very important activity to him. Its importance is evident in 1 Corinthians 14:1-5, 20-25, 31, and 39. The latter verse reads: "So my brethren [men and women] earnestly desire to prophesy." And in 1 Thessalonians 5:20 he urged: "Do not despise prophesying."

Prophesying was also very important to the church after Paul's sojourn. The *Didache* (a second-century Christian document) likens those who prophesy to high priests saying the eucharistic prayers. When prophets or apostles could not be present, local deacons and presbyters would take their place, according to the *Didache*.

If women prophesied, which obviously meant speaking, then how does one explain the expected silence of women 1 Corinthians 14:34-35? That text reads: "The women should keep silent in the churches. For they are not permitted to speak, but should be subordinate, as even the law says. If there is anything they desire to know, let them ask their husbands at home. For it is shameful for a woman to speak in church." Some theologians resolve the conflict between the prophesying of women (Acts 2:17; 1 Cor. 11:5) and the silence of women (1 Cor. 14:34-35) by saying that these references are contradictory.[22] Those who do not see these references as contradictory attempt to resolve the problem by saying that the prophesying in Acts 2:17 and 1 Corinthians 11:5 refers to a private context, whereas 1 Corinthians 14:34-35 talks about a public context. This argument, given that Paul wanted Christians to be publicly edified by prophesying, is not very convincing.

There is a third alternative, namely that Paul indeed wanted women to prophesy and teach. This view is supported by his words in 1 Corinthians 11:5 and also by the reference in Romans 16, where he speaks about Phoebe being a *diakonos* and *prostatis* (superintendent) and Junia being "of note among the apostles." What does one then do with 1 Corinthians 14:34-35? This reference seems to be a quotation from the Judaizers in Corinth, who in the letter Paul received from that congregation cited the rabbinic oral law in their efforts to silence women and keep them from practicing their newly found freedom. That oral law, noted earlier in this chapter, made it disrespectful to read in the presence of men.

[22]Meeks, "The Image of Androgyne," 203.

These words from the oral law are very similar to those in 1 Corinthians 14:34-35. The Judaizers in Corinth, following a longstanding rabbinic religious tradition, were upset by the speaking and teaching roles that women assumed in the work of the church. Just as the Judaizers tried to tie rabbinic legalism to Christianity with regard to circumcision in the Galatian congregation (Gal. 20), so now also in Corinth they tried to impose their rabbinic legalism on the Corinthians by not permitting women to speak in the church among men.

The quoted words in 1 Corinthians 14:34-35 are from the letter that Paul received from Corinth and to which he, in part, responds in 1 Corinthians. Verses 34 and 35 are a preface to what Paul says in verse 36, where he strongly asserts: "What! Did the word of God originate with you, or are you the only ones it has reached?" In other words, Paul is rejecting the Judaizing efforts to silence women. In fact, he shows his anger by asking them whether they are the only ones who know what is pleasing to God. He further subdues the Judaizers by saying, "What I am writing to you is a command of the Lord" (1 Cor. 14:37).

Parenthetically, it is interesting to note that the women in Corinth were only asking questions, because verse 35 reads: "If there is anything they desire to know, let them ask their husbands at home." That fact, of course, made no difference to the Judaizers, who apparently took the words of the Jewish oral law very seriously.

To say that the words in 1 Corinthians 14:34-35 are quoted from the oral law of the rabbis is not a new argument. Already in 1829 Johann Friedrich Schleusner, a renowned lexicographer, alluded to this possibility when he discussed various usages of the Greek word *nomos* (law) in his *Novum Lexicon Graeco-Latinum in Novum Testamentum*. He saw the words "as even the law [*nomos*] says [v. 34]" as a citation from the oral law of the Jews.[23] In the early 1920s Katherine C. Bushnell, a conservative biblical exegete who believed in the inerrancy of the Bible, also contended that the words in verses 34 and 35 were not Paul's, but rather a quote from the oral law of his time. She buttressed her argument by saying that it was not like Paul to use the laws and traditions of the Jews "as a final authority on a matter of controversy in

---

[23]Johann Friedrich Schleusner, *Novum Lexicon Graeco-Latinum in Novum Testamentum* (London: Jacobi Duncan, 1829) 168.

the church. He spent a large share of energy battling against these very 'traditions' of the Jews, as did his Master, Jesus Christ.''[24] Bushnell continues her contention by citing Titus 1:14: "Paul warns against 'giving heed to Jewish fables and commandments of me, that turn from the truth.' ''[25] Similarly, James Crouch, a respected New Testament scholar, says the word "law" (*nomos*) in 1 Corinthians 14:34 likely refers to the "Hellenistic Jewish version of the 'Law' which emphasized the inferiority of woman and her submission to her husband.''[26]

More recently a Catholic scholar, Neal Flanagan, has also argued that 1 Corinthians 14:34-35 is a quotation from the Jewish oral law. He believes that this reference, which has been used as God's will to silence women, ''is an indication, not of Paul's antifeminism, but of his opposition to a male-dominated group in Corinth.''[27] Flanagan also thinks that if the quotation hypothesis is true, then 1 Corinthians 14:34-35 is not in conflict with 1 Corinthians 11:5 and Galatians 3:28, but rather an extension of these latter two passages.

Why has the quotation argument not really been noted? After all, it involves no "higher critical" assumptions, which conservative theologians strenuously seek to avoid. In fact, the quotation explanation is simply an example of what often is called "lower textual criticism." So two answers come to mind in terms of the question just asked. First, conservative books and articles in the area of hermeneutics fail to mention that the New Testament, especially 1 Corinthians, has numerous quotations. A number of New Testament scholars have shown that in many places 1 Corinthians cannot be correctly interpreted without this knowledge. John Hurd's *Origin of 1 Corinthians* cites at least twenty-four scholars who show that Paul's

[24]Katherine Bushnell, *God's Word to Women* (Oakland CA: published by the author, 1923 [?]) 201.

[25]Ibid.

[26]James E. Crouch, *The Origin and Interpretation of the Colossian Haustafel* (Göttingen: Vandenhoeck and Ruprecht, 1972) 110-11.

[27]Neal M. Flanagan, "Did Paul Put Down Women in 1 Corinthians 14:34-36?" *Biblical Theology Bulletin* 11 (January 1981): 12.

letter to the Corinthians is interlaced with various quotations.[28] It is too bad
that writers of ancient literature, like St. Paul, did not use quotation marks
or footnotes. Somehow the absence of these modern techniques has led all
too many theologians to not even think about the possibility of Paul's quot-
ing from the letter he received from Corinth. Second, male theologians,
not very sensitive to the pervasive sexism in the cultural era of Jesus and
Paul, have overlooked that the legalism of the Judaizers in Christian circles was very much concerned with having women conform to the principles of the oral law. An overabundance of clergy hear the word *Judaizers*
and think only about the situation in Jerusalem or Galatia where the Judaizers argued that every man had to become circumcised in order to be a
Christian. This understanding is woefully incomplete.

Judaistic legalism was not just confined to the issue of circumcision; it
also concerned itself with having women conform to the rabbinic law. Nor
were the Judaizers confined to Jerusalem or Galatia; although they were a
minority in Corinth, they nevertheless had a strong hold on the Christians
there.[29] Professing to be Christian, they still clung to the patriarchal culture
and theology of the rabbis. They were irritated by the freedom Christianity
gave to women. They wanted the "liberal" practice of women's speaking
and teaching stopped. So they appealed to the oral law of the rabbis, which
did not allow a woman to read aloud in the presence of worshiping men.

An alternative explanation, which ignores the quotation argument, says
the words of 1 Corinthians 14:34-35 are not Paul's but an interpolation. In
a number of Greek and Old Latin manuscripts, these words appear at the
end of the chapter.[30] Some scholars believe that when a certain portion(s)
of a text is found in different places in given manuscripts, this provides
good reason to believe that such references are scribal insertions or inter-
polations that eventually became part of the text. The original writer, in
this case Paul, therefore never wrote the words in question.

---

[28]John C. Hurd, *The Origin of 1 Corinthians* (London: SPCK, 1965).

[29]William J. Conybeare and J. S. Howson, *The Life and Epistles of the Apostle Paul*
(New York: Thomas Crowell, n.d.) 474.

[30]A. Merk, *Novum Testamentum Graece et Latinae* (Rome: Scripta Pontifici Biblici,
1933).

Finally, an important question or two must be asked of those who see 1 Corinthians 14:34-35 as Paul's own words. The reference says that if women desire to know anything that goes on in the church, they are to ask their husbands at home. This poses a real problem. It is a known fact of history that in the days of Paul women greatly outnumbered men in the church. So was Paul telling the Christian women to go home and ask their non-Christian husbands about the life and functions of the church?

Women in the Ephesian Church

Another reference frequently cited by male theologians to silence women has been 1 Timothy 2:11-12. Timothy, a young pastor among the Christians in Ephesus, was advised by Paul in this letter: "Let a woman learn silence with all submissiveness. I permit no woman to teach or to have authority over men; she is to keep silent."

Several questions come to mind upon closely reading these two verses. First, why do some theologians continue to cite these passages as timeless and prescriptive, while the preceding two verses (1 Tim. 2:9-10) are interpreted as descriptive of a bygone era and thus not applicable to the twentieth-century life of women in the church? Verses 9 and 10 read: "Women should adorn themselves modestly and sensibly in seemly apparel, not with braided hair or gold or pearls or costly attire, but by good deeds, as befits women who profess religion." If it is wrong or "unbiblical" for women to teach or to have authority over men, then why is it not also wrong for women to come to church with fancy hair styles, gold earrings, and shining necklaces? Elementary logic compels one to see both sets of verses as either prescriptive and timeless—as, for example, the Amish do—or to see both as descriptive of a particular situation in the congregation in Ephesus. Both sets of references, after all, are from the same context addressing woman's worship conduct. To interpret verses 11 and 12 as prescriptive for all time and yet declare 9 and 10 as essentially descriptive of a past era is to practice "cafeteria theology."

Male theologians have tried to reinforce their argument that 1 Timothy 2:11-12 bars women from speaking or teaching in the presence of worshiping men by appealing to the next two verses, 13 and 14. These two references speak about Adam having been created before Eve. Furthermore, because Eve sinned before Adam did, the content of verses 11 and

12 is as permanent in meaning as is the "order of creation." Again, one must ask: If the so-called order of creation compels one to interpret verses 11 and 12 literally and prescriptively, then why does it not also apply to verses 9 and 10?

Nor is it very convincing to argue, as many ultraconservative clergy do, that verses 9 and 10 today teach the principle of modesty. This argument, in effect, says that in our culture men are no longer offended by seeing women wear costly jewelry or exotic styles. Today they would instead be offended by some other type of unacceptable dress or appearance. If this type of logic is acceptable here, it must also be applied in understanding verses 11 and 12. In Timothy's day most men were intensely disturbed by a woman's teaching a man or exercising authority over him; such behavior was contrary to the patriarchal ethic. Today, however, very few secure men are bothered by such behavior. Hundreds and thousands of men are under the authority of women in colleges, universities, radio, television, and even in many churches. Women serve as prime ministers, state governors, mayors, members of parliament, cabinet officers, and as executives in government and business. In each of these positions they exercise authority over men. Thus if verses 9 and 10 can be seen as teaching a principle, then verses 11 and 12 also teach a principle—namely that when men and women assemble in worship, they are to maintain peace and harmony *within* the congregation. The latter seems to have been the primary goal of Paul's advice to Timothy. Given the culture of that time, most men could not tolerate women's speaking in public. Men became agitated and upset, causing group unrest. So for this reason and for *only this group of Christians in Ephesus,* Paul asked women not to teach.

Another possible explanation of the words in 1 Timothy 2:8-12 is that Paul wrote what he did in order to help Timothy preserve the congregation's peace and harmony from the *outside.* This argument gains plausibility when one notes that some church historians have shown that at the time of Nero, many Christians were persecuted rather intensely between A.D. 60–64, especially in certain areas. Ephesus, according to Paul's own experience, was one such region (Acts 19:23-41; 20:17-19). If persecution problems faced Paul, it should not surprise us that he would urge Timothy to have the women temporarily learn in "quietness" (1 Tim. 2:11), not in "silence," as so many translations have erroneously been rendered.

WOMEN IN THE APOSTOLIC CHURCH   193

To have women learn and speak as they did in the apostolic church was a religious, cultural shock. With Christian women assuming roles not previously condoned in male-dominated societies, they became targets of persecution. If they had been veiled and silent, there would have been no need to persecute them. "The Christians," as Sir William Ramsay said, "were enemies to civilized man and to the customs and laws which regulated society."[31] It is also known from the Roman historian Tacitus (A.D. 55–120) that Christians were a "people detested for their evil practices." One such "evil practice" was that of Christian women's speaking and teaching. That practice made many men feel inferior, when for centuries their socioreligious culture told them they were superior to women. Here the words of William H. Lecky come to mind:

> The general superiority of [Christian] women to men in the strength of their religious emotions, and their natural attraction to a religion which made personal attachment to its Founder its central duty and which imparted an unprecedented dignity and afforded an unprecedented scope to their characteristic virtues, account for the very conspicuous position that female influence assumed in the great conversion of the Roman empire. In no other movement of thought was it so powerful or so acknowledged. In the ages of persecution female figures occupy many of the foremost places and ranks of martyrdom.[32]

Christian women were also despised because the freedom that Christianity had given them was seen as a domestic peril, especially with regard to the influence they exercised "over the male members of their families."[33] Tertullian describes the anger of one Roman husband whose wife became a Christian (*Ad Nationes* 1, 4). The Roman family, says J. Vogt, was held together by ancestral religious rites and beliefs.[34] Christianity, by

---

[31]William Ramsay, *The Church in the Roman Empire before the Year A.D. 170* (New York: G. P. Putnam's Sons, 1893) 236.

[32]William H. Lecky, *History of European Morals from Augustine to Charlemagne*, vol. 1 (New York: D. Appleton, 1870) 385.

[33]Ibid.

[34]J. Vogt, "Pagans and Christians in the Family of Constantine the Greek," in A. Momigliano, ed., *The Conflict between Paganism and Christianity in the Fourth Century* (Oxford: Oxford University Press, 1963).

allowing and advocating women to take up their own religion, broke up the Roman family. This disruptive social phenomenon was no trivial matter, and Christian women were the chief perpetrators.

Leopold Zscharnack, the German church historian, underscores that the apostolic church gave previously unknown freedom to women. Said he: "Women, like other oppressed individuals of that era, saw liberation and salvation in Christianity that drew them to it."[35] Woman's newly found freedom was not just a mental construct; it had dramatic social effects. Christianity grew and spread, and to a large degree this growth was the result of women's being equally and totally involved with men in all facets of the church's life. Sir William Ramsay caught the full impact of woman's involvement when he said: "Gradually people began to realize that Christianity meant a social revolution."[36]

To protect the church from the outside, Paul told Timothy not to allow women to be openly engaged in teaching and speaking, but rather to let them learn in quietness while the persecution was in progress. His advice was primarily restricted to this particular problem, so he expressed his personal concern. This is quite clear in his statement: "*I permit* no woman to teach" (1 Tim. 2:12, emphasis added). His advice is not stated in the imperative form, but it seems to be similar to what he said to the Corinthians regarding marriage. To them he said: "I wish that all were [single] as I myself am" (1 Cor. 7:7). Yet a few passages later he remarked, "But if you marry, you do not sin" (1 Cor. 7:28). Sir William Ramsay understood Paul as having given Timothy personal, not God-directed, advice. He said: "The advice given by St. Paul as to the relations of Christians to society in which they are placed, is always in accordance with situation . . . as occupied by them under Nero."[37]

Advising Timothy to have the women not teach was not the only time Paul gave personal advice. In the fifth chapter he told Timothy to take a little wine for his stomach's sake. Few, if any, have seen Paul's advice

---

[35]Leopold Zscharnack, *Der Dienst der Frau in den ersten Jahrhunderten der christlichen Kirche* (Göttingen: Vandenhoeck and Ruprecht, 1902) 19.

[36]Ramsay, *Church in the Roman Empire,* 130.

[37]Ibid., 246.

here as having timeless, prescriptive value. Yet, ironically and inconsistently, the personal advice he gave regarding women has been given a timeless, universal interpretation and application by many men.

The "Order of Creation" Argument

Unyielding, chauvinistic theologians insist that the words of Paul to Timothy do carry a prescriptive force. To tell them that they are practicing cafeteria theology is useless. Often they invoke the "order of creation" argument thought to underly Paul's words in 1 Timothy 2:14. This reference says: "Adam was formed first, then Eve, and Adam was not deceived, but the woman was deceived and became a transgressor." Thus just as God's created order cannot be changed, so likewise the words about woman not teaching and having authority over men are unchangeable and timeless. So goes their reasoning.

Across the centuries, some clergy have used the order-of-creation idea in various ways to limit women's roles in the church. *The Apostolic Constitution* (late fourth century) argued that women were not to baptize because "it is not just to abrogate the order of creation" (Book 3.9). About 100 years later, St. Jerome said,"It is contrary to the order of nature and of the law that women should speak in an assembly of men" (*In Primam Epistolam Ad Corinthios* 14). A thousand years after Jerome, John Knox, in opposing the rule and influence of Mary Tudor, Mary Stuart, and Elizabeth I, wrote: "For God first by the order of creation . . . hath pronounced the contrarie [namely, for her not to rule or have authority]."[38]

In the latter part of the nineteenth century Stephen Knowlton, a Congregationalist clergyman, contended that if women were permitted in any matter to speak in church, they would be violating the "order of creation."[39] Frederick Mayser, a Lutheran who opposed woman suffrage in the church, similarly declared: "It is clearly in violation of the original and fundamental order established at creation and continued in the New Tes-

---

[38]John Knox, *The First Blast of the Trumpet against the Monstrous Regiment of Women* (New York: Da Capo Press, [1558], 1972) 13.

[39]Stephen Knowlton, "The Silence of Women in the Churches," *Congregational Quarterly* 9 (1867): 329-34.

tament dispensation.''[40] Still others used the order-of-creation idea to keep women from voting at the secular ballot box. (See chap. 8.)

Today, many sexist clergy are unaware of how cultural forces have narrowed their interpretation of the order-of-creation concept as they apply it primarily to keeping women out of the ranks of clergy. Will history repeat itself in fifty years, so that by the year 2039 chauvinistic theologians will have forgotten what was said in the 1980s regarding woman's role in the church and the order of creation? Such an outcome is a strong probability, for culture through the centuries has shaped and reshaped the theology of woman's place in the church. There is thus every reason to believe that in fifty years culture will have shaped a very different theology of women, namely one giving her greater equality than she has today, if not full equality.

The order-of-creation concept—or its synonym, ''order of nature''—has been frequently used but rarely defined. One definition says it is ''that which designates the particular position which by the will of the Creator any created object occupies in relation to others.''[41] This definition is fraught with difficulties. Does ''particular position'' refer to sequence or priority in time? Does it refer to function? To strength? To intelligence? Furthermore, how can these different relationships be discovered? If this definition is taken seriously, then these questions cannot be ignored.

Not so long ago the order-of-creation argument was used by some to justify slavery. The Reverend R. Harris in his *Scriptural Researchers on the Licitness of the Slave Trade, Shewing Its Conformity with the Principles of Natural and Revealed Religion Delineated in the Sacred Writings of the Word of God* (1788) argued that slavery was ''against the order of things, which the Divine government established.''[42] Another clergyman, Bishop Mead of Virginia, said: ''Almighty God hath been pleased to make you [the blacks] slaves, and to give you nothing but labor and poverty in

---

[40]Frederick Peter Mayser, ''Shall Women Vote in the Church?'' *Lutheran Church Review* 18 (July 1899): 482.

[41]The Lutheran Church–Missouri Synod, ''Report of the Committee on Woman's Suffrage,'' *Convention Proceedings* (1956): 555.

[42]Cited in H. Shelton Smith, Robert T. Handy, and Lefferts Loetscher, *American Christianity,* vol. 2 (New York: Scribner's, 1963) 204.

this world.''[43] Slavery was designed by God, said Methodist Alexander McCaine.[44] The black person too was to be submissive on the basis of the order of creation. Today, of course, the order-of-creation argument is no longer applied relative to slavery. Now the cultural forces in Western society are so strongly opposed to slavery that even highly prejudiced clergy, or those who interpret the Bible literally, do not argue that slavery is compatible with Christianity. But with regard to keeping woman in subjection, the "divine design" argument still holds sway with many clergy in ultra-conservative churches.

Another difficulty with the order-of-creation concept (as some understand it) is that it posits a biological determinism that goes beyond the realm of the biological aspects of human life. True, only women can have babies; that function is biologically programmed. But to say that biology determines social roles—that only women are to rear children or that women are not to teach men religious concepts—is to argue that biology determines the nonbiological realm of life. Such a position is simply contrary to fact.

Some theologians see the order-of-creation concept as referring to a sequential or progressive process—that is, "God in creating, progressed from the simple and inorganic to the organic, or from the imperfect to the perfect.''[45] If this is so, then one is hard pressed to see why woman should be submissive to man and silent. If Adam was superior to the animals because of his having been created after them, then following this idea, Eve (woman) is superior to Adam (man); thus man ought to be submissive to woman and silent. If, on the other hand, the order of creation is understood in the sense that woman is to be submissive and silent because Adam (man) was formed *before* Eve (woman), then other questions arise. Was Adam subordinate to the animals that were created ahead of him? Is a son subordinate to his mother because she was born before he entered the world?

---

[43]Cited by Trevor Bowen, *Divine White Right* (New York: Harper and Brothers, 1934) 110.

[44]James O. Buswell, *Slavery, Segregation and Scripture* (Grand Rapids: Eerdmans, 1964) 17-18.

[45]Francis Pieper, *Christian Dogmatics,* vol. 1 (St. Louis: Concordia Publishing House, 1950) 469.

The order-of-creation argument is largely a theological attempt to say that biology is destiny. It confuses biological functions with sociocultural roles in that it makes certain roles ipso facto follow from biology, an ancient belief that has been made obsolete in the urban-technological culture. In a technological environment there is hardly any sociocultural role that woman cannot perform as well as a man. That certain social roles are often seen as the result of sex difference does not come from biology but from culture. It is culture, not biology, that says woman is inferior to man. This latter fact is completely overlooked by the order-of-creation advocates.

Finally, with regard to order of creation, it needs to be noted that it has been the mark of human beings to amend and improve the created order rather than be slaves to it. In fact, it can be argued that this human propensity is quite compatible with the command in Genesis 1:28 that enjoined humans to ''subdue'' the earth, God's creation.

Galatians 3:28

Theologians who have made much of the order of creation have commonly been confronted by Galatians 3:28. This passage reads: ''There is neither Jew nor Greek; there is neither slave nor free; there is neither male nor female; for you are all one in Christ Jesus.''

This Galatian reference, which has been called the Magna Charta of Christianity, has obviously caused some theologians some difficulty. But given their reluctance to see these words as setting forth a complete equality of socioreligious roles for men and women, they instead speak of an ''order of redemption.''[46] This concept says that men and women are equal spiritually by having been redeemed for eternal life in the world to come; however, in the present world, where socioreligious roles have to be exercised, women are not equal. Thus the order of creation is not annulled by the order of redemption.

At first blush this argument sounds almost persuasive, especially if one has not been encouraged to question the institutionalized sexism so widespread in the church and society. One of the first major difficulties that the order of redemption poses is that the Hebrews did not teach that people

---

[46]Peter Brunner, ''Das Hirtenamt und die Frau,'' *Lutherische Rundshau* 9 (1959).

were redeemed on the basis of being born a Jew, a nonslave, or a male, even though the rabbis and many Jewish men prayed: "Blessed be he that did not make me a gentile; blessed be he that did not make me a poor [ignorant slave]; blessed be he that did not create me a woman." This prayer (seen as a blessing by sexist men) was uttered daily by rabbis and Jewish men in Paul's day. It was a prayer that the Hebrews apparently borrowed from the Greeks. Diogenes Laertius in his *Lives of Eminent Philosophers* credits the philosopher Thales (sixth century B.C.) for having coined this prayer, while Plutarch believes Plato (fourth century B.C.) was the first to formulate this prayer (*Marius* 46:1). Lactantius in his *Divine Institutes* also attributes it to Plato.

In this daily prayer the Jewish man thanked God for sparing him the inferior socioreligious roles that slaves, Gentiles, and women were assigned in the Hebrew culture. The prayer referred to daily life experiences, not to being spiritually redeemed or saved, as the proponents of the order of redemption would have it. In the words of C. G. Montefiore: "It is quite true that the wife and mother played a very important part in Rabbinic life; it is true the Rabbis were almost always monogamists; it is true they honored and cared for their wives. But that is only one side of the story. 'Women, children and slaves': that familiar and frequent collection means and reveals a great deal. Women were, on the whole, regarded as inferior to man in mind, in function and status."[47]

Evidently, Paul in Galatians 3:28 meant to counteract this Jewish male prayer that probably was used by the Judaizers in Galatia. The Jewish scholar Raphael Loewe says: "All three [components of the prayer] are controverted by St. Paul."[48] More than fifty years ago H. L. Strack and P. Billerbeck published a multivolume work that commented on the New Testament in the light of Talmudic (rabbinic) literature. They overlooked "the obvious parallel to Galatians 3:28," says Loewe.[49] Hans Kosmala has also noted this obvious omission on the part of Strack and Billerbeck.[50] Again one sees the powerful

---

[47]C. G. Montefiore, *A Rabbinic Anthology* (Philadelphia, 1939) xviii.

[48]Raphael Loewe, *The Position of Women in Judaism* (London: SPCK, 1966) 43.

[49]Ibid.

[50]Hans Kosmala, "Gedanken zur Kontroverse Farbstein-Hoch," *Judaica* 4 (1948): 229.

role cultural forces played in preventing many male scholars of the New Testament from seeing this obvious parallel.

While Galatians 3:28 has spiritual significance, one cannot limit the meaning of this reference to the order of redemption, as has been (and still is being) done. Spiritual messages in the New Testament have practical implications in Christianity. The gospel of Jesus Christ was never intended to console people only spiritually, but also to motivate them to imitate and follow him with acts of love, justice, and mercy. Now and then Christians have understood Galatians 3:28 in this twofold sense. James Crouch has shown that the Galatian reference did cause unrest among Christian slaves and women who longed for emancipation in the era of early Christendom.[51] During the Protestant Reformation one Katherine Zell in Strasbourg, France, said Galatians 3:28 gave her the right to speak in favor of priests' having the right to marry, in spite of church leaders telling her to be silent as a woman.[52]

Those who argue that Galatians 3:28 speaks only of a spiritual equality vis-à-vis men and women must then logically also say the same about slaves vis-à-vis nonslaves: slaves are only equal to nonslaves spiritually and not equal otherwise. Those who hold only to the order of redemption relative to Galatians 3:28 cannot have it both ways. Yet, since slavery is no longer fashionable politically and theologically—as it once was for centuries—one no longer hears anything about the order of creation relative to slavery, an argument that went back to Aristotle, at least.

Another erroneous interpretation of Galatians 3:28 goes back to some early, misguided Christians, the Gnostics, who believed that this passage meant that human sexual (biological) differences disappeared. For instance, Vibia Perpetua (third century A.D.), a young married woman and prophet, said just before being martyred that she saw herself having become a man while still a woman (*Acts of the Christian Martyrs* 8:10). The belief that female believers in Christ became men was not just confined to the Gnostics. One can also find it in the writings of the "orthodox" St.

---

[51]James E. Crouch, *The Origin of the Colossian Haustafel* (Göttingen: Vandenhoeck and Ruprecht, 1972) 126.

[52]Roland Bainton, *Women of the Reformation* (Minneapolis: Augsburg Publishing House, 1977) 55.

Ambrose and St. Jerome. Said Ambrose: ''She who does not have faith is a woman and should be called by the name of her sex, but she who believes progresses to perfect manhood. . . . She then does away with the name of her sex'' (*Evangelius Secundum Lucum* 10.161). Very similar are the words of Jerome: ''[As] long as woman is for birth and children, she is different from man as body is from soul. But when she wished to serve Christ more than the world, then she will cease to be a woman and will be called a man'' (*Commentarius in Epistolam and Ephesios* 3).

Both St. Ambrose and St. Jerome evidently were influenced by the *Gospel of Thomas,* which in one of its sayings indicates: ''Every woman who makes herself a man will enter the kingdom of heaven'' (Saying 114). The beliefs of Ambrose and Jerome, as well as those of Gnosticism, bear little or no real resemblance to the efforts that are being made today to bring about sexual equality in the church. While the Gnostics essentially permitted women to serve in traditional male roles, they were still bound to a sexist mentality in that they believed a woman had to become a male in order to realize the true spiritual benefits of Christianity. This is very different from the modern advocacy of equal rights in the church, where the stress is on equality of roles, not biological functions. Thus the present-day effort to bring about sexual equality in the church is by no means a Gnostic heresy. It is a gross oversimplification to make this equation, as some have tried to do.[53] Gnosticism in the early church, as Elaine Pagels has shown, was by no means unanimous in affirming the role of women. In fact, many Gnostic works were quite sexist, reflecting ''a higher status for men than for women.''[54]

Ephesians 5:21-33

Another New Testament reference that men have used to keep women from exercising their God-given talents in the church is Ephesians 5:21-33. This portion speaks only about husband-wife relationships in family life. To apply this reference to what role(s) women should or should not

---

[53]Louis Brighton, ''The Ordination of Women: A Twentieth-Century Gnostic Heresy?'' *Concordia Journal* 8 (January 1982): 12-18.

[54]Elaine Pagels, *The Gnostic Gospels* (New York: Vintage Books, 1981) 77-83.

exercise in the church is quite inappropriate. The words of this text have no relevance for activities within the church's formal organizational life. Nevertheless, chauvinistic theologians have frequently ignored this section's context and invoked it to keep women silent and submissive in the church.

Ephesians 5:22-23 says: "Wives be subject to your husbands, as to the Lord. For the husband is the head of the wife as Christ is the head of the church." What is noteworthy about these words is that they are preceded by verse 21, which reads: "Be subject to one another out of reverence for Christ." This latter reference is commonly overlooked by men who have their minds made up with regard to woman's role in life. For example, already in the latter part of the fourth century St. Chrysostom ignored verse 21 and began his homilies with verse 22 (*Homilies on Ephesians* 20).

Why did Paul write this section of Ephesians 5? Here we must try to understand the culture of Roman family life in which Christians in the apostolic era found themselves. Although in Paul's day paterfamilias had lost some of its harshness and rigidity, it still had a significant effect on the life of a married woman. The paterfamilias was the absolute head of the family, which included slaves and even the children of his sons. This power and control commonly stayed intact until the father (pater) died. Then the sons became paterfamilias over their family members.

The Roman *familia* was not a biological unit like the Western family of today; it was an economic unit. The paterfamilias, in exercising his *patria potestas*, "alone was competent, in charge against the domestic order. He could inflict the death penalty, sell into slavery, or banish, as he saw fit."[55] Andrew Stephenson says the Roman man "alone could be head of the family and as such was recognized as a member of the community or state. The woman necessarily belonged to the household [*familias*] and not to the community."[56] In short, the paterfamilias was the only full person recognized by Roman law.[57] Those in his *potestas* (power) were *in man-*

---

[55]Andrew Stephenson, *A History of Roman Law* (Boston: Little, Brown & Co., 1912) 94.

[56]Ibid., 27.

[57]Barry Nicholas, *An Introduction to Roman Law* (Oxford: Clarendon Press, 1962) 65.

cipio (subjection) and were called *aliene iuris* (in the power of another), according to Barry Nicholas.[58]

Cato the Elder of Rome described the Roman father this way: "The *pater* is the judge of his wife; his power has no limit; he can do what he wishes. If she has committed a fault, he punishes her; if she has drunk wine, he condemns her; if she has been guilty of adultery, he kills her."[59] In the words of Fustel de Coulanges: "Justice for his [the pater's] wife and son was not in the city, because it was in the house. The chief of the family was their judge."[60] The wife was only accountable to the pater, not to the state or the city.

The paterfamilias alone had the right to recognize a child at birth or to reject it (*Herodotus* 1.59). He could divorce his wife; his wife could not divorce him. In a divorce only he received the children. The mother had no voice in the marriage of her daughter. It was the pater who gave his daughter in marriage; the perpetuity of the *familias* was his concern. Only he could emancipate his son(s) or exclude a son from the household hearth (place of worship). It was his uncontested right to name a guardian for his wife and children.[61]

While these customs had lost some of their power in the days of the apostolic church, many of the old features were still in vogue. For example, a wife in no way was equal to her husband. She had little or no formal education, was commonly married at age fourteen, and pregnant as often as nature would allow. If a husband left or divorced her, she was economically and socially destitute because she had no education or skills. Given this kind of family life, it is not too surprising for Paul to tell husbands to love their wives as "Christ loved the church" (Eph. 5:25). Knowing the ordinary wives would not be able to survive on their own, Paul urged them

---

[58]Ibid., 68.

[59]Cited in Numa Denis Fustel de Coulanges, *The Ancient City* (Boston: Lee and Shepherd, 1882) 90.

[60]Ibid., 90ff.

[61]W. K. Lacey, *The Family in Classical Greece* (New York: Cornell University Press, 1968) 24.

to "be subject to your husbands" (Eph. 5:22). It would have been fool-hardy and an invitation to harm for a wife not to be subject to her husband.

Urging wives to be subject to their husbands at first blush appears as though Paul is giving left-handed approval to the existing culture of family life. Such approval might have been evident had he not begun his words on family life with Ephesians 5:21, where he told husbands and wives to "be subject to one another out of reverence for Christ." This advice was quite revolutionary in that it placed husband and wife on equal terms, something that was totally out of sync with the paterfamilias and the *patria potestas.*

Lydia

According to Acts 16, in the city of Philippi lived Lydia, a business-woman who sold and traded purple goods, commodities highly sought after by individuals of relatively high socioeconomic status. She and her entire household (family and employees) became Christians, most likely as a re-sult of her directly teaching the members of her household. She obviously was no veiled and silent figure, conforming to Greco-Roman or Hebrew sexist stereotypes. The very fact that she is mentioned as being head of a household indicates that she was no ordinary woman.

Women in that day were not heads of households. Even when a wom-an's husband died, she could not legally become his replacement as head. *Lex Voconia,* a law issued by emperor Quintus Voconius Saxa in 169 B.C., even severely limited the amount of property a wife could inherit. Cato the Elder, who was a strong advocate of the Voconian law, said that a woman did not even have the right to tell her husband's slaves what to do (*Aulus Gellius Noctium Gellius* 8.6.10). The Voconian law was still in effect at the time of St. Augustine (fifth century A.D.), who at one time opposed it. Nor was the situation any better among the Greeks. "Women did not in the fullest sense own landed property at any stage in Greek history (except Sparta)."[62] Greco-Roman mores also did not support the idea of women in business.

Thus it is quite apparent that Lydia was a cultural deviant whose "de-viancy" did not deter Paul from befriending her for the purposes of pro-

---

[62]H. D. F. Kitto, *The Greeks* (Chicago: Aldine Publishing Company, 1964) 221.

moting Christianity. Was Paul practicing the principle of the end justifying the means? No, he simply ignored the age-old agrarian discriminations that barred women from equal participation in religious activities. Where and whenever female teaching and other activities did not cause conflict or dissension, Paul gave women the same rights and privileges that men had in the church. In the words of Robin Scroggs, "Paul esteemed women as his peers. They helped gather and lead the church; they prayed and prophesied in public assemblies. There is not the slightest shred of evidence that Paul withheld any activity in the church from women. What evidence we have suggests precisely the opposite."[63] Lydia is but one of many examples that in the apostolic church women held prominent leadership roles.

Euodia and Syntyche

In his letter to the Philippians, Paul says Euodia and Syntyche "labored side by side with me in the gospel together with Clement and the rest of my fellow workers" (Phil. 4:2-3). Two significant facts reveal themselves in this citation. First, Paul says that Euodia and Syntyche "contended" (as one would in an athletic event) with him in spreading the gospel. Second, Paul says that these two women were his "fellow workers." One New Testament scholar states that Paul would not have used this expression "if they [Euodia and Syntyche] had merely 'assisted him with material help and hospitality,' while remaining in the background."[64]

Paul's saying that Euodia and Syntyche were his "fellow workers" is remarkably similar to calling Priscilla and Aquila his coworkers in Romans 16:3. In the Philippians reference, along with Euodia and Syntyche there is another fellow worker—Clement, a male. Thus Paul is clearly showing that he treated women and men as equals in promoting and spreading Christianity. In this context it is difficult not to hear echoes of Galatians 3:28, where Paul declared "there is neither male nor female" in terms of Christian rights and privileges.

---

[63]Robin Scroggs, "Paul: Chauvinist or Liberationist?" *Christian Century* (15 March 1972): 308.

[64]W. Derck Thomas, "The Place of Women in the Church at Philippe," *Expository Times* 83 (January 1972): 119.

The Elect Lady

John's second epistle begins: "The presbyter to the Elect Lady and her children, whom I love in the truth" (2 John 1). Some theologians, such as the translators of the Revised Standard Version of the Bible, say in a footnote that the Elect Lady "probably refers to a local congregation, whose members John calls 'children.' " More recently some scholars believe that the Elect Lady of this epistle was a woman overseer, similar to a bishop. This observation is not entirely new. Cassiodorus, in the sixth century, said John's second letter was written to a "Babylonian Lady, by the name Electa, and indicates the election of the Holy Church" (*Fragments of Clemens Alexandrinus* 4). The Greek term *electa* (elect), according to Joan Morris, "was sometimes used to denote a clerically ordained person."[65] To buttress her observation, she cites one of Clement of Alexandria's writings that uses *electa* in this sense. Leonard Swidler supports Morris's exegesis of this term.[66]

Thus Elect Lady does not seem to mean one specific congregation or church group, as some theologians have understood the term. The words of Aida Besancon Spencer are pertinent here. She asks: "If 'elect lady' stands for a church, then who are 'her children'?" Spencer also notes: "A church would have to be called *either* elect lady *or* children in John's language scheme, not both."[67] In all likelihood, the epistle was addressed to a female leader in the apostolic church, just as the opening verse of 3 John is addressed to a male leader.

Women Presbyters

Two passages in 1 Timothy, namely 4:14 and 5:17-19, speak about male presbyters. In 1 Timothy 5:1-2, where female presbyters are also mentioned, the male form of *presbytero* is translated in the Revised Standard

---

[65]Joan Morris, *The Lady Was a Bishop: The Hidden History of Women with Clerical Ordination and the Jurisdiction of Bishops* (New York: Macmillan, 1973) 2.

[66]Leonard Swidler, *Biblical Affirmations of Woman* (Philadelphia: Westminster Press, 1979) 316.

[67]Aida Besancon Spencer, *Beyond the Curse: Women Called to Ministry* (New York: Thomas Nelson Publishers, 1985) 110.

Version as "older man," and the female form of *presbyteras* is rendered as "older woman." These two instances are more accurately translated as "male presbyter" and "female presbyters," so the entire reference would read: "Do not rebuke a male presbyter, but exhort him as you would a father; treat younger men like brethren, women presbyters like mothers, younger women like sisters."

First Timothy 4:14 states that Timothy was ordained by the presbyterate. This reference prompts an interesting question: did women presbyters, together with male presbyters, participate in the laying on of hands as Timothy was ordained? After all, as we have seen in 1 Timothy 5:2, women were presbyters. The question may be inconceivable to those whose cultural theology for centuries has been dominated by male interpretations.

Even though the New Testament clearly speaks about women presbyters, the forces of cultural sexism soon gained the upper hand. Thus by A.D. 381 the Council of Laodicea outlawed women presbyters. It also barred women from approaching the altar, apparently because as presbyters they performed liturgical functions. In this latter action the church reverted to the old menstrual taboo laws of Leviticus.

A Concluding Thought or Two

This chapter has tried to show that qualified women in the apostolic church engaged in speaking and teaching activities that for centuries were off-limits to women. What women did in the apostolic church was contrary to the Judaic oral law at the time of Christ and the apostles. Their widespread involvement was also contrary to the Roman culture with its accent on *patria potestas,* which in the first century A.D., according to Elizabeth Schuessler Fiorenza, was losing its grip and "often amounted to little more than legal fiction."[68] Well-to-do women, as mentioned in Acts 17:4 and 12, as well as Phoebe, Priscilla, Lydia, and others, evidently no longer could be bound by the agrarian institution of *patria potestas.*

For women to speak and teach—along with singing, and perhaps even preaching—was revolutionary. The apostles, and Jesus before them, not only tolerated such activities, but they actually encouraged them. Only in

[68]Schuessler Fiorenza, *Bread Not Stone,* 77.

situations where persecution made these revolutionary acts unwise did Paul tell women not to teach, but temporarily to learn in quietness. Nor did Paul wish to see the temporary situations such as that in Ephesus become a universal, timeless practice. Such a wish would have contradicted what he said regarding Phoebe in Romans 16:1, where he commended her work as a deacon in the congregation in Cenchreae. It would have contradicted what he said elsewhere regarding the work of Priscilla, Junia, Euodi, Syntyche, and others.

During the apostolic era women were given full equality in the church, not only spiritually but also socially in terms of roles and functions. A number of women "were apostles and ministers like Paul, and some were his coworkers."[69] That women were able to exercise equal rights and privileges vis-à-vis qualified men is very significant. Condoning such behavior went against the cultural grain. The agrarian-patriarchal culture did not give women the opportunity to attain educations equal to men's so naturally they were seen as unqualified. For instance, St. Chrysostom saw women in his day as "untutored in doctrine, careless in piety."[70] Chrysostom, like many other sexist church fathers who evidently had forgotten or never known the freedom that women had in the apostolic era, did not recognize that his male-dominated culture had created a self-fulfilling prophecy. The patriarchal-agrarian culture defined women as unworthy of education and then later used their lack of education against them in barring them from equal participation in religious roles with men.

The unusual equality offered women in the apostolic church was so noteworthy that even some of the antifeminine church fathers could not help but make reference to it. For instance, Origen and Chrysostom referred to some of the women in the New Testament as "apostles." The apostolic church, when it came to spreading the gospel, according to Charles Rishell, "knew no distinctions of sex."[71] Rishell, a nineteenth-century scholar,

[69]Elizabeth Schuessler, *In Memory of Her: A Feminist Theological Reconstruction of Christian Origins* (New York: Crossroads Publishing, 1983) 183.

[70]Donald F. Winslow, "Priesthood and Sexuality in the Post-Nicene Fathers," *St. Luke's Journal of Theology* 18 (1975): 217.

[71]Charles W. Rishell, *The Official Recognition of Women in the Church* (Cincinnati: Cranston Stowe, 1892) 32.

even argues that women in the apostolic church were ordained as well as men and claims that they performed the same tasks. Ordination (the laying on of hands) in the apostolic church had not yet become the formal ritualistic ceremony that it became by the third and fourth century. So the evidence indicates that women were even treated equally with regard to ordination, given its incipient status. Quite similar are the words of another nineteenth-century historian, who said: "Originally deaconesses were looked upon as the female part of the clerus; and ordination was given them for purposes of consecrating them in their office, in the same sense as it was given to other clergy."[72] But not too long after the apostles were gone, the church reverted to the sexism once practiced by the Greeks, Romans, and the rabbis before the days of Jesus and the apostles.

---

[72]August Neander, *General History of the Christian Religion and Church,* trans. Joseph Torrey (Boston: Houghton Mifflin, 1871) 156.

CHAPTER 11

THE POSTAPOSTOLIC CHURCH
AND THE GREAT REVERSAL

The unheard-of freedom, equality, and responsibilities that Jesus, Paul, and the apostolic church gave and assigned to women continued in the early years of the postapostolic church, but not for very long. After the apostolic period, the church through the influence of its leaders (church fathers, bishops, priests, popes, and others) increasingly reverted to the sexist practices of the agrarian-patriarchal cultures that preceded Jesus and the apostles. Max Weber, the famous European sociologist, noted in his analysis of early Christianity that as church functions became routinized and regimented, it excluded women from leadership roles.[1] Katherine Bushnell observed that "woman's only century in the Christian church was during the apostolic days and a little while thereafter."[2] Two other scholars, Alfred Brittain and Mitchell Carroll, describe the rise and fall of woman's freedom and equality in the church as follows: "In the community of the Jerusalem Christians [woman] was neither slave nor subordinate. The burden of the daily provisions, which still falls so heavily on the vast majority of women, was here rendered extremely light, for all helped each and each helped all. Equal fellowship also in the great spiritual possessions caused all marks of woman's inferiority to vanish, and the sexes freely mingled

---

[1]Max Weber, *Sociology of Religion* (Boston: Beacon Press, 1957) 104.

[2]Katherine Bushnell, *God's Word to Women* (Oakland CA: published by the author, 1923[?]) 362.

in a pure and noble companionship. But this perfect society was not destined long to endure.''[3]

The cultural forces of ancient sexism increasingly gained the upper hand after the apostolic era. Indeed, ''The church of the second century objected to the prominent position of women in the Apostolic age.''[4] Then in the third, fourth, and fifth centuries the antifeminine views of the Babylonians, Sumerians, Greeks, Romans, and Hebrews came back in full force, causing the church fathers and others to formulate theological pronouncements that were highly sexist in theory and practice.

In spite of mounting resistance that came from the church fathers, woman's equality in church roles and functions, however, was not squelched overnight. There were many courageous women who were not easily veiled and silenced again. They remembered the words of Paul to the women who had churches in their houses: Chloe in 1 Corinthians 10:11; Mark's mother in Acts 12:12; Nympha in Colossians 4:15; Lydia in Acts 16:14-15; and Priscilla in Romans 16:3-4. They were aware of how Paul treated women as his equals—''fellow workers,'' as he called them (Rom. 16:3)—and how he let the church know that Euodia and Syntyche ''contended'' with him side by side (Phil. 4:2). They must have known that Greek women of relatively high social status were among the believers in Thessalonica (Acts 17:12). And surely they knew about the many women who, like the men, were active in promoting the gospel of Christianity, behavior that for many led to persecution. William H. Lecky, the nineteenth-century historian, has shown that women occupied ''many of the foremost places in the ranks of martyrdom.''[5]

The Story of Thekla

Since Thekla was a companion of St. Paul, her brave and amazing missionary work in Asia Minor (Galatic Phrygia) might have been discussed in the previous chapter. However, I did not discuss her church activities

---

[3]Alfred Brittain and Mitchell Carroll, *Women in All Ages and in All Countries: Women of Early Christianity* (Philadelphia: Rittenhouse Press, 1907–1908) 38.

[4]A. C. Headlam, ''Prisca or Priscilla,'' *Dictionary of the Bible,* vol. 4 (New York: Charles Scribner's Sons, 1911) 102-103.

[5]William H. Lecky, *History of European Morals from Augustine to Charlemagne,* vol. 2 (New York: Appleton, 1870) 385.

there because that chapter confined itself to the role of women mentioned only in the New Testament.

The moving story of Thekla in the apostolic church is portrayed in the second-century document *The Acts of Paul and Thekla*. Thekla, who was reportedly converted by Paul, was twice sentenced to die, once for abandoning her fiancé and once for defending herself against rape. According to *The Acts* she was miraculously rescued from these life-threatening events. She had an unusual admiration for Paul, and apparently he had great confidence in her. *The Acts* has Paul telling her "Go teach the word of God" (chap. 41), as she told him that she was about to go to Iconium. She not only taught new converts, but also baptized them. In the ninth century Nicetas of Paphlagonia said Thekla also baptized people in the town of Isauria.[6]

Thekla's active, unveiled, and nonsilent role in the early church irritated Tertullian (A.D. 160-220?). With regard to Thekla, he wrote: "The brashness of this woman who took upon herself the right to teach . . ." (*On Baptism* 17.4). Tertullian did his best to discredit the authenticity of the accounts mentioned in *The Acts*, even calling *The Acts* a work "falsely so named." Yet, competent scholars consider the book's account historically reliable. Leopold Zscharnack in 1902 approvingly cited *The Acts* as one proof of the active roles that women assumed in the early church. William Ramsay in his *Church in the Roman Empire before the Year A.D. 170* also considers *The Acts* a reliable document.

Not long after Tertullian, a sexist segment of the church was so upset with the account of Thekla's role in the church that a search was made to determine the authorship of *The Acts*. Its authorship was traced to someone who was a presbyter in one of the Eastern churches. He acknowledged having written *The Acts*, saying that he wrote the work to honor St. Paul. This presbyter was tried, convicted, and deposed from the ministry.[7]

Antifeminist acts such as these did not immediately thwart all Christminded females from emulating the women of the apostolic church. Stalwart women, here and there, though their number declined, still continued to assume roles in the church that were increasingly being defined as only for men. Although the number of sexist theologians in the early life of the

---

[6]William A. Ramsay, *The Church in the Roman Empire before the Year A.D. 170* (New York: G. P. Putnam's Sons, 1893) 375.

[7]C. B. Waite, *History of the Christian Religion to the Year Two Hundred* (Chicago: C. V. Waite and Company, 1900) 25.

postapostolic church was growing and setting the role of women back in the church, one can still find the odd male theologian who supported woman's equality. In the third century Firmilian (d. 269), the bishop of Caesarea, wrote a letter to Cyprian, the bishop of Carthage, in which he spoke approvingly of a woman's celebrating the Eucharist and baptizing "using the accustomed and lawful form of questioning, so that she seemed in no respect to differ from the ecclesiastical rule." And even as late as A.D. 500, there were some men in the Breton church in Armorica who did not bar women from distributing wine at the Lord's Supper, according to Zscharnack.[8] Not only did women serve as teachers and perform other ecclesiastical activities in spite of the growing discontent of the church fathers, but some evidently even served as bishops.

Women Bishops

In recent years some scholars have found evidence that women served as bishops in the early era of the postapostolic church. Joan Morris says: "An *episcopa Terni* is mentioned in canon 20 of the Council of Tours which is reproduced in the *corpus inscriptionis* of Le Blant and also referred to by Gross-Grondi in his book on Christian epigraphs."[9] Morris also draws attention to a mosaic portrait in the Zeno chapel of St. Praxidis, a basilica in Rome. (St. Praxidis is one of the earliest titular churches, where bishops presided.) This mosaic depicts four female heads. To the left of three women (Saint Praxidis, Virgin Mary, and Saint Pudentiam), who are each pictured with circular halos, is a woman with a square halo. Her square halo indicated that she was still alive at the time the mosaic was constructed, most likely in the fifth century. But more significant is the fact that in a right-angular form, above and beside this woman's head, is the inscription "Episcopa Theodora." This inscription and the woman's picture provide empirical evidence that women in some places served as bishops in the early church.

Sexist theologians, of course, have tried their best to squelch the historical fact of Theodora's having been a bishop. In the present mosaic the

---

[8]Leonard Zscharnack, *Der Dienst der Frau in den ersten Jahrhunderten der christliche Kirche* (Göttingen, 1902).

[9]Joan Morris, *The Lady Was a Bishop: The Hidden History of Women with Clerical Ordination and the Jurisdiction of Bishops* (New York: Macmillan and Company, 1973) 6.

letters "ra" in the name of Theodora have been removed. The removal of these two letters was verified by J. B. de Rossi, a mosaic expert who in 1899 admitted that "the mosaic cubes [of the entire portrait] were old with a few modern ones put under the name of Theodo, where the 'ra' had been eliminated."[10] The tampering is even evident to the untrained eye, as I can vouch for, having seen it myself in June 1985. That the original mosaic in all probability read "Episcopa Theodora" is further supported by the fact that the words "Theodora Episcopa" are also found on a marble slab column outside the Zeno chapel.

Altering the inscription "Episcopa Theodora" to "Episcopa Theodo" so that readers would see her as the wife of a male bishop named Theodo can only deceive the uninformed because "the coif of her habit [dress] makes it clear that she is not married."[11] Morris believes that Theodora was the episcopa (bishop or overseer) of St. Praxidis church and that this church was named after Praxidis, who was the "elect lady," a position similar to the "elect lady" addressed by the writer of 2 John 1 in the New Testament.[12]

Women Deacons

Earlier in chapter 10 I noted that the feminine form of the word "deacon" did not come into existence until the latter part of the fourth century. Thus when Paul in Romans 16:1 addressed Phoebe, he called her a "deacon," not a "deaconness," which is the form favored by many translators.

The differentiation of terms came later as the church adopted the sexist posture of the ancient, pagan cultures that preceded and still surrounded it.

The position of deacon in Acts 6:4 is used in reference to "even the highest Christian office [activity], the preaching of the Gospel."[13] Hamilton Hess believes that the diaconate was the first universally established formal ministry by A.D. 70, and that deacons performed several functions,

---

[10]Ibid., 5.

[11]Dorothy Irvin, "The Ministry of Women in the Early Church: The Archaeological Evidence," *Duke Divinity School Review* 45 (Spring 1980): 81.

[12] Morris, *Lady Was a Bishop,* 5.

[13]Hermann W. Beyer, "Diakoneo, Diakonia, Diakonos," ed. Gerhard Kittel, trans. Geoffrey W. Bromiley, *Theological Dictionary of the New Testament* (Grand Rapids: Eerdmans Publishing Company, 1964) 2:87.

including liturgical performances.[14] Zscharnack shows that around A.D. 500 the Breton church in Armorica still used women deacons to distribute wine at the Lord's Supper.[15] And the *Didascalia* (an early-fourth-century A.D. document) depicts women deacons as religious teachers (Book 3.12).

Even though many leaders in the postapostolic church greatly curtailed the activities of female deacons and even coined a new word—*deaconess*— to make their biased theology creditable, many women deaconesses were still ordained. As late as A.D. 692 the Synod of Trullo in its fourteenth canon approved of the ordination of women deaconesses by the laying on of hands, similar to the rite of ordaining male priests. This synod required women to be at least forty years old in order to be ordained.

The action of Trullo was preceded by differing, even conflicting, canons of other church councils. The Council of Nicaea (A.D. 325) considered deaconesses as clergy. The Council of Nimes in France (A.D. 394) annulled the orders of deaconesses, apparently in reaction to the Priscillianists. The Council of Orange in A.D. 441 declared in its twenty-sixth canon: "Deaconesses shall no longer be ordained and they shall receive the benediction only in common with the laity." The second Council of Orange in A.D. 533 reissued its previous ban of A.D. 441. But it also said that if deaconesses were unmarried they could continue in that position. The second Synod of Orleans (A.D. 535) in its eighteenth canon also outlawed ordination of deaconesses, primarily because women were the weaker sex.

These decisions of the church councils and synods clearly demonstrate that the church in time became more and more sexist in its theology. The New Testament, which considered the position of deacon appropriate for male and female, was ignored. Thus, by the fourth and fifth centuries the ancient, pagan view regarding women not only had made great inroads into the church, but it had in fact become victorious. The influence and actions of Jesus and the apostles had lost their impact and effectiveness.

Convents and Monasteries

The existence of convents and monasteries, in which women sometimes played active roles in the Middle Ages, has led some to think that

---

[14]Hamilton Hess, "Changing Forms of Ministry in the Early Church," in James A. Coriden, ed., *Sexism and Church Law: Equal Rights and Affirmative Action* (New York: Paulist Press, 1977) 49.

[15]Zscharnack, *Der Dienst der Frau*, 18-22.

this was a context where women had essential equality with men. For instance, Eleanor Commo McLaughlin claims, "There seems to be found in Anglo-Saxon monasticism an effective equality between the sexes which belies the closeness of those centuries to the deeply misogynist patristic tradition."[16] To be sure, Chaucer (1340-1400), in the prologue to *The Canterbury Tales,* mentions a nun (prioress) having a female chaplain with her on the trip to Canterbury. But as Lina Eckenstein has shown in her book *Women under Monasticism,* the few women chaplains that did exist during the Middle Ages were far from equal to monks or priests. She says that nun chaplains apparently only "recited the inferior services in the chapel of the nunnery."[17] And Albert Baugh thinks the female chaplain cited by Chaucer was merely an administrative assistant to the prioress.[18]

The belief that women had an essential equality in some of the monasteries of the Middle Ages is the result of an erroneous understanding of the "double monasteries." These institutions have on occasion been portrayed as having practiced sexual equality. But as Penny Schine Gold has shown, such equality did not exist, not even at Fontevrault in France, whose double monasteries have been cited as an example of egalitarianism. Gold says monks and nuns were not even sexually integrated, much less equal. Although the Order of Fontevrault (founded in 1160) had a female head (abbess) and men were to serve women, the women were still dependent on the men, especially with regard to formal religious services. Nuns were not permitted to preach, nor were they allowed to give themselves the Lord's Supper.[19] Moreover, a nun could not even go outside the cloister unless she was accompanied by at least two men, one religious and one secular.[20]

---

[16]Eleanor Commo McLaughlin, "Equality of Souls, Inequality of Sexes: Woman in Medieval Theology," in Rosemary Radford Ruether, ed., *Religion and Sexism* (New York: Simon & Schuster, 1974) 237.

[17]Lina Eckenstein, *Women under Monasticism* (London: Cambridge University Press, 1894) 377.

[18]Albert C. Baugh, ed., *Chaucer's Major Poetry* (New York: Appleton-Century-Crofts, 1963) 241.

[19]Penny Schine Gold, *The Lady and the Virgin* (Chicago: University of Chicago Press, 1985) 101.

[20]Ibid.

Nor did women have any greater freedom or equality in monasticism several centuries earlier. Eckenstein notes that women in convents under St. Boniface's (eighth century) direction "remained throughout in a state of dependence, while the men . . . maintained the independence of their monasteries."[21]

Why the Great Reversal?

Given that women in the church at the time of Jesus and the apostles were free to participate in all activities that previously were only open to men, why did the postapostolic church revert to the sexism of the ancient cultures? Here it is appropriate to note that when behavior does not become institutionalized, as in the case of woman's equality in the apostolic church, it eventually dies or it is taken over by previously existing behavior.

Why then did the freedom and equality of women in the apostolic church not become institutionalized? First, centuries of entrenched cultural beliefs and practices are never easily set aside or replaced. The antifeminine, in some instances even misogynistic, stance of the church fathers, who fashioned the church's theology, had been much influenced by the sexist philosophers and poets of the Greco-Roman culture. As one astute observer said some fifty years ago: "To read the early church fathers is to feel sometimes that they never heard of the Nazarene, except as a peg on which to hang their tortured diabolism—as a blank scroll upon which to indite [sic] their furious misogyny."[22] They were also in part influenced by the rabbinic view of women: for example, Irenaeus and Jerome studied under the rabbis. So they forgot—or never really noticed—what role women played in Christ's activities and in the apostolic church.

The church fathers, and their successors for hundreds of years after them, seemed to have forgotten the truth so well expressed by Leopold Zscharnack in 1902: "Christendom dare not forget that it was primarily the female sex that for the greater part brought about its rapid growth. It was the evangelistic zeal of women in the early years of the church, and later, which won the weak and the mighty. Women, like other oppressed individuals of that era, saw liberation and salvation in Christianity that drew

---

[21]Eckenstein, *Women under Monasticism,* 138.

[22]John Langdon-Davis, *A Short History of Women* (New York: Literary Guild of America, 1927) 202.

them to it.''[23] Women were prominent leaders of the new faith. Zscharnack says that even the pagans noted this unusual phenomenon.[24] The pervasive involvement of women in the apostolic church brings to mind the observation that a religion flourishes when it is relevant, and it dies when it becomes irrelevant. The apostolic church was very relevant to the women in that it gave them unparalleled freedom and released them from centuries of cultural oppression. That is why women were so extensively and intensively involved in the life of the apostolic church.

Second, the equal participation of women in the apostolic church did not become institutionalized because soon after the apostolic era the church lost much of its urban ethos. Scholars ranging from Max Weber to Wayne Meeks have noted the apostolic church's strong urban qualities.[25] It was so urban that it called non-Christians "pagans," meaning rural dwellers or rustics in Latin. In an urban environment agrarian-sexist role distinctions are relatively difficult to maintain. They are, in fact, often detrimental socially and economically. Christianity, however, did not remain an urban phenomenon. It spread to the nonurban areas of Africa and Europe, where agrarian cultural values of sexism held sway. Moreover, many of the church fathers were not "metropolitan Romans but provincials whose thinking reflected their own social milieux and Jewish accents on the religious and legal incapacity of women. Texts from Roman Law, many obsolete, were used to justify the Greco-Jewish bent for keeping women away from public functions."[26]

A third factor that barred the egalitarian role of women in the apostolic church from becoming institutionalized has to do with Emperor Constantine's legalizing Christianity. Soon after Christianity became legal the leaders of the church wanted it to be seen as respectable, as supportive of Roman culture. There were, of course, exceptions to this desire, but for the most part the church leaders and the church councils conformed to many prominent Roman values. One need only recall how soon the church legitimated Christian participation in war (see chap. 2). The publication of

---

[23]Zscharnack, *Der Dienst der Frau,* 19.

[24]Ibid., 21.

[25]Weber, *Sociology of Religion,* 83. See also Wayne Meeks, *The First Urban Christians: The Social World of the Apostle Paul* (New Haven: Yale University Press, 1983).

[26]Julia O'Faolain and Lawro Martines, eds., *Not in God's Image* (New York: Harper Torchbooks, 1973) 128.

St. Augustine's *City of God* was still another attempt to show how Christianity really was not a threat to Roman culture, as it once definitely was. Thus it is not too difficult to see how the ancient cultural values and practices of sexism would also be retained in the life of the church. If the church could so readily relinquish its early antiwar posture, it could certainly also let go of its early prowomen practices. Both changes made the church more acceptable to the agrarian orientation of the culture at large.

Fourth, the church fathers' cultural and educational experiences also led to the return of sexist theology. Irenaeus and St. Jerome, who both had negative views regarding women, were influenced by rabbinic thinking. Irenaeus, in particular, was affected by Jesus Ben Sirach's *Ecclesiasticus*. Chapter 26 of *Ecclesiasticus* has a number of negative remarks about women. One passage reads: "A wife's harlotry shows in her lustful eyes, and she is known by her eyelids."

Clement of Alexandria, Origen, Tertullian, Dionysius of Alexandria, St. Ambrose, St. Chrysostom, St. Augustine, and others were all influenced by Greco-Roman philosophy and literature that often complemented Judaic thinking with regard to women. Frequently these men quoted from the ancient poets and philosophers, along with references from the Old and New Testament, in trying to make their theological positions acceptable. Thomas Boslooper has said it well: "The Church Fathers, instead of carrying on the ideals of Jesus and Paul which would include women along with men as equal in importance for bringing about moral and ethical and spiritual change throughout the world, began to talk more like Aristotle and Xenophon than like Jesus or Paul."[27]

A fifth reason has to do with the agrarian-patriarchal view of woman. The agrarian culture liked woman to be pregnant as frequently as possible, gave her little or no formal education, and prevented her from realizing meaningful participation in society. Moreover, because physical strength was highly valued in the agrarian context, the church fathers, like other men of that time, concluded that women were inferior to men. This age-old perception led them to ignore the rights and privileges that Jesus and Paul gave to women. The church fathers, according to Donald Winslow, argued "that only the most able could be worthy of or aspire to the [priestly]

---

[27]Thomas Boslooper, *The Image of Women* (New York: Rose Sharon Press, 1980) 146-47.

office.''[28] Winslow continues: "Since women, therefore, were naturally perceived in the patristic period to be less able than men, the thought of their being ordained would have struck [them] as preposterous.''[29] To the church fathers, being a priest was a difficult task, not one for uneducated and untutored people, such as women. Thus women, who were also defined as biologically inferior, were not seen as fit for the role of clergy in the church. This being the case, women in some instances were barred from the priesthood on nontheological grounds.[30]

---

[28]Donald Winslow, ''Priesthood and Sexuality in Post-Nicene Fathers,'' *St. Luke's Journal of Theology* 18 (1975): 216.

[29]Ibid.

[30]Ibid., 215.

CHAPTER 12

URBAN-TECHNOLOGICAL CULTURE: WOMAN'S FRIEND AND ALLY

With the exception of the brief interlude during the time of Jesus and the apostolic age, when the ancient sexist values and practices were ignored by Jesus and his apostles, culture over the centuries has been exceedingly unfair and even cruel to women. Consistent with its agrarian bases, it not only influenced theologians to shape sexist opinions and perceptions that portrayed women as evil, inferior, unclean, and unequal, but it also prompted men to construct social institutions that actualized those agrarian opinions and perceptions. Those institutions not only enforced the various sexist values, but they also socialized countless women to accept and internalize those opinions. The agrarian-based culture in effect had created a self-fulfilling prophecy, which convinced male chauvinists that their perceptions and opinions were morally right, even reflecting the will of God.

Knowing the powerful role that culture played in depriving women of their inalienable dignity, freedom, and rights, a sympathetic observer might wish to condemn culture forever. While such a response would be understandable, it would be untimely in the sense that culture now is losing the agrarian bases that once prompted the many sexist values and practices in the church and society at large. Modern culture, with its urban-technological bases, is slowly initiating and even institutionalizing many nonsexist values and practices. It is even making a few ultraconservative theologians recognize that many biblical practices were cultural and hence need not be followed today. The disappearance of veils—which once were prescribed in 1 Corinthians 11—is one such example.

Such progress is not yet widespread because many chauvinistically oriented clergy still obstinately resist the thought that culture shaped the past
theological definitions of women to which they hold so tenaciously. They
quickly forget 1 Corinthians 11 and their admission of cultural influence.
Against this admission, they believe that culture only recently has begun
to influence theology, which, of course, makes it "liberal." Somehow they
are unable to see that culture had its powerful effect on the thinking and
writings of Jerome, Augustine, Luther, Calvin, and many others.

A New Culture

So frequently has reference been made in this book to culture's shaping
theology that some may raise the issue of cultural determinism. In other
words, my argument must be that culture alone shapes events; events can
never shape culture. But that would be a faulty conclusion. Early in the
book (chapter 1) I noted that culture itself is often subject to change and
that cultural change often occurs through some prominent act(s) of highly
innovative individuals deviating from some of their culture's institutionalized values and practices.

New or revolutionary acts on the part of such deviant individuals commonly occur on a subcultural level. In order for culture to change, however, social innovations must move beyond the subcultural realm by
becoming accepted and institutionalized by the culture at large. If this does
not occur, the culture will not change. This process helps explain why the
subcultural behavior of Jesus and the apostles, which gave women equality, soon disappeared.

The liberating acts of Jesus and the apostolic church failed to become
institutionalized because they were too incompatible with the agrarian bases
underlying the culture of that time. Their egalitarian acts did not mesh with
the imbedded components of agrarianism, which required physically ac-
complished men to till the soil or herd the livestock, and required women
to bear many children for labor, productivity, and parental security. Frequent pregnancies also occurred in an attempt to offset the infant mortality
rates so that some offspring would survive to maintain the agrarian way of
life. If women were literally to follow Jesus and his apostles, as they did,
they would not have been able to bear many children, and men would have
lost their authority over those women. Indeed, the teachings of Jesus and
the apostles were diametrically opposed to the cultural norms of the established socioeconomic structure of their era.

One needs to remember the culturally shocking words Jesus spoke in Matthew 10:34-38, where he said: "I have come to set a man against his father, and a daughter against her mother, and a daughter-in-law against her mother-in-law; and a man's foes will be those of his own household; He who loves father and mother more than me is not worthy of me; and he who loves son or daughter more than me is not worthy of me; and he who does take his cross and follow men is not worthy of me." To have family members follow an itinerant teacher was bad enough, not to mention what effect it would have on the agrarian way of life. Jesus' words called for more than mere lip-service or intellectual loyalty. He wanted actions that would convey this greater love. Jesus called for those who would literally follow him down highways and byways as he taught people his message.

Now in the latter part of the twentieth century, a period of history in which the agrarian culture of the past is being replaced by urban-techno-logical needs and values, a new culture is beginning to make it possible for women to be treated as equal to men. It is no mere accident of history that woman's rights and opportunities are most advanced in urban-industrial societies, where neither men nor women are tied to the soil. In an urban society women no longer need to bear numerous children. In fact, in urban society many children in a family are an economic liability, not an asset as they were in agrarian societies. Moreover, women now are also able to practice birth control owing to technological advances. Woman no longer has to be pregnant every year during her child-bearing years. She now has time to become educated and compete with men for the same occupations. Technology has essentially erased the agrarian distinctions with respect to male or female jobs. What position is there in modern technological so-ciety that a woman cannot perform so well as a man?

In societies with urban-technological cultures, women have the op-portunity to attain an education equal to men and even to teach them pub-licly. In the early stages of the urban-technological era, women were only allowed to teach children in Sunday schools, and then eventually they even were permitted to teach men in college. But this freedom did not come eas-ily or quickly. As noted in chapter 8, when Oberlin College in Ohio be-came the first American institution of higher education to open its doors to women in 1837, it only allowed them to take courses in homemaking. Courses in public speaking were off-limits to them, and they were not per-mitted to read their graduation essays. Oberlin was a church school, so 1 Corinthians 14:34—"let the woman be silent"—was interpreted literally. In England, Queen's College was founded to educate women "in all branches of female knowledge."[1] Nevertheless, in time the urban-technological forces removed the sexist education restrictions that had their origins in agrarian cultures of the past. So today women in many contexts may study or teach any subject open to men. There are, of course, still some obstacles to overcome. In many denominations women still are barred from studying and teaching theology or religion courses. These change-resistant denominations are still clinging to agrarian-patriarchal values of ancient culture, which have led them to equate those values with the will of God.

Having attained the right to acquire higher education, the right to vote was woman's next battle. Here too the old agrarian values were not easily overcome. But by the late 1920s woman's suffrage was legal and well established in most Western countries. Again, the church, reflecting the culture at large, held out longer than most other institutions in resisting woman's right to vote. Eventually, however, even most churches—except the sectlike denominations—granted women the right to vote in congregational meetings. The urban-technological culture was becoming too strong and too pervasive. In time it even convinced many reluctant theologians that it was not against God's will for women to vote. Modern culture, unlike its ancient predecessor, had become woman's friend and ally.

Urban-technological culture, which is even making inroads into many Third World countries, has abolished the distinction between male and female occupations. Cultural awareness and empirical data show that women perform as competently in so-called "male" jobs as men. Thus it is only logical that this knowledge would challenge the old agrarian belief that only men may be clergy; and indeed, more and more women are entering that oldest and most exclusive male "club," the ministry or priesthood. In effect, modern culture has turned 180 degrees from its ancient agrarian bases to where it now has become an ally of women's rights, slowly promoting their equality in terms of image and reality. Just as culture shaped the sexist theology of the past era, it is now shaping a theology that in many religious denominations is slowly losing its sexist character.

Some Ironies

As one observes the new egalitarian treatment—theological or otherwise—of women, several ironies come to the surface. First, Jesus' non-

---

[1] R. Strachey, *The Cause: A Short History of the Women's Movement in Great Britain* (G. Bell and Sons, 1928) 61.

sexist views and treatment of women, which were too deviant and too radical for the agrarian culture of his day, now are being incorporated into the social fabric of everyday life even though his many other teachings are no more eagerly accepted than they were 2,000 years ago. Thus the equality of women that is being promoted by today's urban-technological culture is not the result of greater respect for the carpenter of Nazareth, but because some of his views and practices now complement the basic values of the modern industrial era. Perhaps this is what is meant by saying, "It is not only necessary to be right but also to be right at the right time." One can argue that Jesus' teachings were always morally and ontologically right, but they did not conform to the agrarian culture of his day.

It is useful to ponder the age-old resistance that Christian theologians since the first century have displayed toward Judaizing tendencies within the church. In Galatians and Acts 15, one reads about the Judaizers who argued that circumcision was necessary to be a Christian. Acts 15:1 expresses this position: "Unless you are circumcised according to the custom of Moses you cannot be saved." The remainder of Acts 15, and much of Galatians, shows how Paul and his supporters rejected the Judaic position of combining legalism with the Christian gospel. Paul, for instance, did not require that Titus be circumcised. In Galatians 2 Paul opposed Peter, who had given in to the circumcision (Judaizing) position. According to Paul in Romans 6:15, Christians were saved by grace; they no longer were under the law.

The irony is that not too long after the church rejected Jewish legalism in one context, it unwittingly accepted it in another by excluding women from teaching and preaching roles. Although Jesus and the apostolic church rejected rabbinic (Judaic) legalism, the postapostolic church (through the influence of Tertullian, Irenaeus, Clement of Alexandria, and others following them) developed a theology of women that would have pleased the most sexist male among the Judaizers. The church fathers and their successors, many of whom were influenced by the rabbis, forgot that Paul called women "fellow workers" (Rom. 16:3) and "contenders" in the faith who "labored side by side with me [Paul] in the gospel" (Phil. 4:2-3). This latter Pauline expression, according to *The New Schaff-Herzog Encyclopedia of Religious Knowledge* (1912), "can mean nothing else than the 'preaching of the Gospel.' "[2] The leaders of the apostolic church forgot

---

[2]Louise Seymour Houghton, "Women's Work in the Church," in Samuel Macauley Jackson, ed., *The New Schaff-Herzog Encyclopedia of Religious Knowledge* (Grand Rapids: Baker Book House, [1912], 1950) 414.

how Paul lauded the teaching of Priscilla. And they overlooked the words
he wrote to Titus, whom he warned about Christians' "giving heed to Jewish myths, and commands of men who reject the truth" (Titus 1:4). In re-
suscitating the rabbinic views of woman, the church fathers not only gave
heed to one of the Jewish myths that Paul warned about, but they even institutionalized that myth.

There is a third irony operative in the ultraconservative position of
keeping women silent and submissive in the church. The Donatist controversy arose in the fourth century of the church's existence and was soon
condemned as a heresy. The Donatists argued that the validity of the
church's activities, such as administering the sacraments and preaching,
was dependent on the spirituality of the person who performed them. Although many sexists in the church today have not explicitly said that the
church's acts—such as preaching and teaching—are only valid when performed by men, they seem to have a Donatist mind-set. To ask them
whether the words and acts of a female pastor (or priest) are valid raises,
for them, an unthinkable question. They cannot bring themselves to say
yes. And therein lies the problem: a belief that the church condemned 1,500
years ago is now, in a slightly altered form, being revived in order to keep
woman out of the pulpit. This set of circumstances brings to mind a theological cliche, namely that there are no new heresies today; they have only
taken new forms.

If one is familiar with Sigmund Freud's theories, a fourth irony becomes visible here. It was Freud who said that biology determined one's
destiny. Thus to argue that a woman's biology bars her from certain socioreligious roles is in effect echoing Freud, a man whose theories have
been anathema to ultraconservatives in the church for years.

Finally, there is a fifth irony in the theology of keeping women si-
lenced. Christ gave his followers the command "Go therefore and make
disciples of nations, baptizing them in the name of the Father and of the
Son and of the Holy Spirit, teaching them to observe all that I have commanded you" (Matt. 28:19-20). Christians have called this the "Great
Commission," and they have taken this command literally and seriously.
Most likely Priscilla was very much aware of this command when she taught
Apollos and was Paul's "fellow worker" in promoting Christianity. As-
suredly Lydia also was moved by Christ's directive. Furthermore, we have
already seen from the scholarly studies of Harnack, Zscharnack, and Ram-

say that the apostolic church grew and flourished in no small measure as a direct result of the active, missionary-minded work of women.

The evidence is strong that during the first century when Christians were persecuted by Nero, for example, that they were persecuted not for being Christians (that came later), but because of what they *did*.[3] And what they did was repulsive to the Romans to no small degree because of the new roles that Christian women performed. For instance, having women involved in missionary activities not only violated the rule against women's speaking in public, but Christianity unintentionally also broke up the Roman family structure that was held together by ancestral religious beliefs and rituals.[4] August Neander notes that "in the first centuries women became zealous Christians, while their husbands remained wholly devoted to paganism."[5] The apostolic Christians, as William Ramsay has argued, were "enemies to civilised man and to the customs and laws which regulated civilised society. . . . They were bent on relaxing the bonds that held society together; they introduced divisions into families, and set children against parents."[6]

Yet, in spite of all the early, active involvement of women in the apostolic age, by the fourth and fifth centuries the church's leaders had for all practical purposes silenced women and barred them from all significant roles in the church. The agrarian culture of the Hebrews, Greeks, and Romans had conquered and reshaped the theology and practices of Jesus and the apostles with regard to women, the Great Commission notwithstanding. The church's leaders and councils were not bothered by the fact that at least one-half of Christendom's population had been silenced and no longer was permitted publicly and formally to speak or teach the gospel message. To this day many ultraconservative churches are not bothered by keeping women silent, even though they make much ado about the Great Commission.

---

[3]William Ramsay, *The Church in the Roman Empire before the Year* A.D. 170 (New York: G. P. Putnam's Sons, 1893) 236.

[4]J. Vogt, "Pagans and Christians in the Family of Constantine the Greek," in A. Momigliano, ed., *The Conflict between Paganism and Christianity in the Fourth Century* (Oxford: Oxford University Press, 1963).

[5]Augustus Neander, *General History of the Christian Religion and the Church*, trans. Joseph Torrey (Boston: Houghton, Mifflin and Company, 1871) 172.

[6]Ramsay, *Church in the Roman Empire*, 236.

What about Tomorrow?

Every scholar and scientist knows that it is dangerous to predict future trends or events. Yet, it seems relatively safe to say that if the present urban-technological elements of the present Western culture continue and expand, as they most likely will, then modern culture will continue to effect still-greater liberation and more equal opportunities for women in society and the church. Certain churches and their male clergy will resist the inevitable trend as long as possible. They will howl and accuse, as they now are, saying that greater freedoms for women are an example of culture's shaping theology. In part they are correct, but they need to recognize that long before the present theological changes began according women equal rights in the church, their theology too was shaped by culture. The difference is that their theology was shaped by the agrarian-patriarchal culture of the past, whereas the present theology of woman's rights is being shaped by an urban-technological culture. The question is not which theology of women is shaped by culture, but which theology is most consistent with the teachings, practices, and mind of Christ, whom the church considers its lord. Had the church fathers, the councils, and synods given more attention to the role and function that Christ and the apostles assigned to women, it would not have been necessary for impersonal forces of the urban-technological culture to return the church to what Christ and the apostles so innovatively practiced almost 2,000 years ago.

In contending that the urban-technological culture has slowly created more freedom and equality for women, I am not saying that this culture has brought—or is bringing—a utopia to women's lives. As Joan Rothschild has shown, there are instances where technology has not always been woman's best friend. While Rothschild's observations are true, I do not accept her proposal that feminists and their allies, in given instances, need to "unthink and rethink the cultural contexts of technology."[7] Such a stance would be helpful primarily where those cultural contexts still contain significant remnants of past agrarian-patriarchal cultures. And, of course, many such remnants do still exist.

Some Christians are fond of saying, "God works in mysterious ways to perform his wonders." When it comes to the present, some might say that God indeed works in mysterious ways, by using urban-technological

---

[7]Joan Rothschild, *Machinea Ex Dea: Feminist Perspectives on Technology* (New York: Pergamon Press, 1983) 161.

culture to bring about sexual equality, in the church and outside of it. To-day when one tells some clergymen or laypersons that the church's theo-logians once used 1 Corinthians 14:34-35 and 1 Timothy 2:12-15 to prevent women from voting in public elections, they stand in disbelief. Perhaps the same will be true fifty years hence with regard to women's teaching and preaching in the church. Maybe people then will also have difficulty be-lieving that those references were once employed to deprive women of the rights and privileges that were announced as theirs by the Old Testament prophet Hosea. He declared, "Your sons and daughters shall prophesy [preach and teach]." Luke, the writer of the Book of Acts, repeated Ho-sea's prediction to the apostolic church; and the apostolic church took the words of Hosea and Luke seriously by implementing them. But, as so often happens, cultural innovations do not fare well when they conflict with deeply entrenched values and practices of the existing culture. So the post-apostolic church went back to defining women relationally to men, rather than seeing them as autonomous and independent beings. This attitude meant, to quote Penny Schine Gold, that the church kept "women in the system but on the periphery, connected to the center, but not at the cen-ter."[8]

It has been said that the way people make their livelihood largely de-termines the content of their culture. The views of Jesus and the apostles regarding women did not mesh with the way people made their living in the agrarian culture of that time. Those agrarian values and practices squelched feminine rights and freedom until the urban-technological cul-ture of the twentieth century forced them to resurface. Thus so long as so-cieties continue to become more urban and technological, women will likely continue to realize their inalienable and God-given rights.

As Western societies continue to institutionalize more urban-techno-logical values into the social fabric of culture, one of which is equal oc-cupational opportunity for women, the resistance to women's becoming pastors or priests will probably diminish and slowly disappear. In time fewer arguments will be heard about women's unfitness to become clergy be-cause Jesus picked only men—the twelve disciples—to carry on his mis-sion. The weakness of this argument, made by many theological chauvinists, will become evident as thinking people realize that if one wants

[8]Penny Schine Gold, *The Lady and the Virgin: Image, Attitude, and Experience in Twelfth Century France* (Chicago: University of Chicago Press, 1985) 101.

to argue in this fashion, then women also should not receive the Lord's Supper because Jesus shared that event only with the disciples. Second, he not only chose twelve men, but they were *Hebrew* men. Not one of them was a fair-haired European descendant. So if one uses this criterion to keep women out of the ministry, then logic also demands that non-Hebrew men are not eligible to become clergy.

Church organization, as Letty M. Russell shows, stems from a paradigm of domination or pyramidical thinking in which males are dominant or on top of the pyramid. She proposes a new model that would value diversity and inclusiveness, one that would welcome the breakup of the old pyramid model in order to realize a rainbow of praise and service.[9] Similarly, Sara Maitland argues that the modern church must adopt the "model of love, justice, and freedom, one that destroys centuries of oppression and exclusiveness that has been directed against women in its midst."[10]

These observations recall Jesus' statement accenting service rather than dominance or power. The church has forgotten his words under the influence of agrarian-patriarchal values. Jesus said: "You know that the rulers of the Gentiles lord it over people, and their great men exercise authority over them. But among you it shall not be so" (Matt. 20:25-26).

One final comment in the form of a question. In August 1986 Pope John Paul II apologized and asked forgiveness for the Christian church relative to its one-time proslavery stand.[11] Now the question: When will the pope and other church leaders ask for forgiveness with regard to the church's longstanding discrimination against women, which is no more defendable than its former stand on slavery?

---

[9]Letty Russell, "Women in Ministry: Problems or Possibility?" in Judith L. Weidman, ed., *Christian Feminism: Visions of a New Humanity* (New York: Harper & Row, 1984) 75-92.

[10]Sara Maitland, *A Map of the New Country: Women and Christianity* (London: Routledge, Kegan Paul, 1983).

[11]Lorrie Lynch, "Pope: 'Forgive Us for Slavery,'" *USA Today,* 14 August 1985, 1.

INDEX